British Cutlery

Best Wishes
Bill Brown.

and Peter Brown

25 June 03.

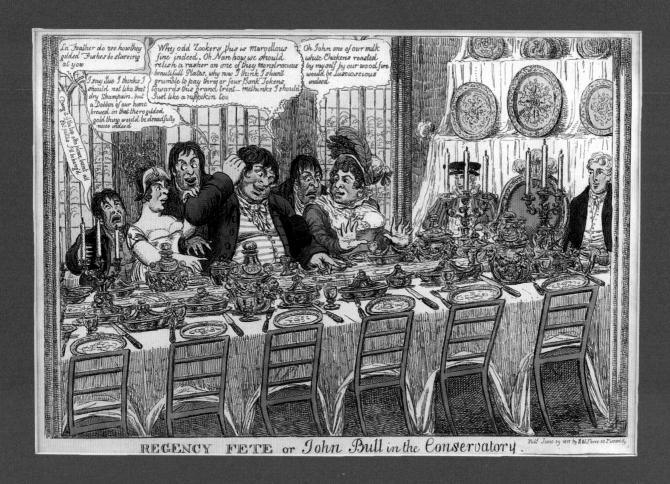

REGENCY FETE or John Bull in the Conservatory.

British Cutlery

An illustrated history of design, evolution and use

EDITED BY PETER BROWN

YORK CIVIC TRUST

PHILIP WILSON PUBLISHERS

The publication of this book accompanies a three-venue touring exhibition:

York – Fairfax House   1 September – 30 December 2001
Sheffield – Millennium Galleries   11 January – 10 March 2002
London – Geffrye Museum   26 March – 2 June 2002

Editor: Peter Brown
Curatorial team: Bill Brown, Peter Brown, Teresa Fazio Gannon, Eleanor John, and Caroline Krzesinska
Essay contributors: Bill Brown, Peter Brown, Ivan Day, and David Mitchell
Captions: Bill Brown, Peter Brown, and Teresa Fazio Gannon
Designer: Peter Ling
Printed and bound in Italy by Società Editoriale Lloyd, Srl, Trieste

First published in 2001 by Philip Wilson Publishers Limited
7 Deane House, 27 Greenwood Place, London NW5 1LB

Distributed in the USA and Canada by
Antique Collectors' Club, 91 Market Street Industrial Park
Wappingers' Falls, New York 12590

All items of cutlery illustrated in this book, with the exception of those on p. 8 and p. 80,
form part of the Bill Brown collection of cutlery.
The collection number, B22, B85 etc is given at the end of each catalogue entry.

The display and documentation has been supported by:

YORKSHIRE MUSEUMS COUNCIL

IDLEWILD TRUST   •   MARC FITCH FUND

FRIENDS OF FAIRFAX HOUSE   •   FRIENDS OF THE GEFFRYE MUSEUM   •   MAXIPRINT

Frontispiece
**Regency Fête or John Bull in
the Conservatory, 1811**
Anon-coloured engraving
Published by S. W. Forrest
Photograph: Jeremy Phillips for Fairfax
House, York
The Prince Regent held a party for
2,000 in the conservatory at
Carlton House on 19 June 1811,
and was lampooned in this print,
published only ten days later.
Judging by the comments, it was
not the lavish 'Grand Service' of
silver-gilt which intrigued the
satirist, but the presence of a
stream running down the centre
of the table with live gold and
silver fish swimming about in the
water. Whether the artist was
actually at the party is always
difficult to determine, but the
silver-gilt on display is a fairly
accurate representation of pieces
in the Royal Collection. Notice
that there is only one knife and
fork for this first course. Fresh
cutlery would be brought on at
the beginning of the next course
and similarly for the dessert.

Contents

Preface and Acknowledgements

THIS book aims to document for the first time a highly important collection of cutlery put together over the last forty-five years by the collector Bill Brown. Serious research into culinary history and presentation of meals at table is quite recent and the evolution of cutlery and the context in which it is used plays an important part in our understanding of this topic.

The publication accompanies a three-venue touring exhibition of Bill Brown's remarkable assembly entitled *Cutting Edge, a History of British Cutlery and Table-Settings*, a collaboration between Sheffield Museums Trust, the trustees of the Geffrye Museum and York Civic Trust. The exhibition has been indemnified by Her Majesty's Government under the National Heritage Act 1980 and arranged through the Museums and Galleries Commission and Department of Culture, Media and Sport.

Bill Brown has been extremely generous and supportive of this project, not only in agreeing to lend his collection for a such a long period of time, but by being unfailingly helpful and willing to share his extensive knowledge and expertise throughout the whole formative process. His collection provides us with a near complete document of the evolution of British cutlery from the Stone Age to the present day, a remarkable achievement brought about by a lifetime's dedication and interest. It has examples from the rich and poor man's table and is particularly strong in the early periods where other collections in national museums like the Victoria and Albert Museum are incomplete. That this collection is of national importance cannot be doubted.

Many have helped to bring our project to fruition, in particular Teresa Fazio Gannon, who worked tirelessly to catalogue the collection in a relatively short period of time. Also the essays from David Mitchell and Ivan Day contribute greatly to our understanding of the early history of this subject and help clear up many of the misunderstandings which have clouded our vision of cutlery and its usage in recent years.

Philip Wilson Publishers have collaborated to produce a superb book which will be a lasting tribute to Bill Brown's vision and passion for the subject. Thanks are also due in no small part to Jeremy Phillips for the photography and to those who have given freely of their time and expertise, to Her Majesty the Queen, His Excellency Mohamed Mahdi Altajir, Broadfield Glass Museum, David Howard, Howard Coutts, Joan Jones, Norwich Castle Museum, Ian Pickford, Quernmore Collection, Barbara Brown, Donald Coverdale, Hugh Murray, Tony Barton, Megumi Iwasa, Charles Kightly, Johnny van Haeften, Marjorie Goodridge, Anthony Dove, Ken Hawley, Anthony North, Joan Unwin, Nigel Wills, Laura Mason, Ivison Wheatley, and to the staff at each venue who worked hard to make this exhibition a success, in particular to Caroline Krzesinska, Christine Lalumia and Richard Turner.

A final vote of thanks must go to the grant-making bodies who made the whole project possible, in particular to the Yorkshire Museums Council for providing a grant from their travelling exhibition fund, also to the Idlewild Trust, the Marc Fitch Find, the Friends of Fairfax House, Friends of the Geffrye Museum, and Maxiprint for their generosity and support.

PETER BROWN
September 2001

An interior with peasants dancing and eating, 1681

Lambert Doomer (1624–1700)
oil on panel, 43 × 60cm
Photograph: courtesy of Johnny Van Haeften

Notice the peasant with the spoon in his hat, a popular method of carrying personal cutlery. Also on the table is a simple carving knife with its wooden handle and metal cap, together with some flat, wooden trenchers. It seems likely to be a faithful representation of the food and utensils, but the artist may have decided to introduce a tablecloth, an extremely expensive purchase at that time, in order to make the items on the table stand out against the background.

Foreword

Left

Regency place setting, c.1810

Photograph: Jeremy Phillips for Fairfax House, York

Reproduced by kind permission of Her Majesty Queen Elizabeth II. In 1811 the Prince Regent commissioned Rundell, Bridge & Rundell to provide a 'Grand Service' for his residence at Carlton House. Comprising over 4,000 pieces, this was sufficient to provide a gilt place setting for 180 guests at both first and second courses.

All the great silversmiths of their day played their part, with plates by Digby Scott, forks and spoons by Paul Storr, verrières and covered dishes by the Smith Brothers and coasters by Phillip Rundell.

The Prince also bought superb linen from Coulsons, the Irish linen weavers at Lisbon and glass from Perrin, Geddes & Co. of Warrington. The wine glasses have a curious and seemingly over-elaborate engraved star-shaped base, which makes little sense when seen standing on a table. The glasses are being cooled in the verrière, and it is clear that the guest is meant to be presented with the base of a wine glass shaped and faceted in the form of a garter star.

Right

A toebackje still life with lemon and knife on a pewter plate, c.1640 (detail)

Pieter Claesz (1597–1660) oil on panel, 32 × 41cm

Photograph: courtesy of Johnny Van Haeften

The knife is probably fitted with an ivory handle inlaid with medallions of amber and ebony. Compare this with a simplified version (see B119, p. 83).

I HAD no intention, all those years ago, of making a collection of knives, or a collection of anything at all! But 'small boy' habits of hoarding bits of shrapnel, spent bullets and all the other miscellany that lay on the ground, seemed to be a passion of mine, formed early on in my life. Consequently, as a result of early years training as a graphic designer, I was drawn to the delights of antique shops in my working locality and, quite by chance, I saw in a shop window a knife and fork of unusual appearance. The handles were of 'half round' section which, when fitted together, looked like a rod. One part was the handle of a knife with tortoiseshell panels in a silver frame, inset with silver animals. The other was a fork, matching the decorative style and having two long, steel tines. I had never seen anything like this before and decided to buy them. They cost ten shillings, which for me, in 1955, was not an inconsequential amount of money.

After a while I found I needed to know more about them. What went before? What came after? I did not appreciate that it would take the rest of my life to find out! Initially I had to find the reason why they 'butted' together. That was not too difficult, for I realised they could be fitted into a sheath and carried around. They were Dutch, c.1720, a travelling set, and this started me looking for more and more information. I visited museums whenever possible (the Victoria and Albert was my favourite haunt) but only for short periods; if I stayed too long I would look at everything and learn nothing.

I trawled the antique markets but to little avail. Most dealers at that time did not recognise what I was asking for – old eating cutlery? Who wants it? Making contact with some of the expensive antique shops and silver dealers proved to be more successful. Some had pre-war stock and spoke of well-known collections, mostly abroad. Others mentioned famous auction sales, whose catalogues were a revelation. Silver dealers would often buy

large, mixed lots of silver which included knives of all dates and they were quite pleased to find somebody who would buy them. I also discovered how knowledgeable and helpful they were, once they recognised a genuine interest.

It soon became apparent, however, that to learn anything about my knives I would have to widen my horizons. I studied the Victoria & Albert collections more closely, getting much assistance from the Keepers and Curators and found books that touched on the subject, notably *The Story of Cutlery* by J. B. Himsworth, himself a Sheffield cutler of distinction and also the Victoria & Albert *Booklet of English Cutlery*, by F. J. Hayward. I managed to visit Sheffield in the 1960s, when it was still producing cutlery, and I was taken aback at their curious lack of interest in their past achievements. They were going through a period of change brought about by foreign competition and this seemed to have knocked the spirit out of the industry. Nevertheless, I found an enormous amount of information was forthcoming about the actual working conditions, sites, items produced, and a general longing for their past pride to return. They were, after all, throughout the nineteenth century the premier producers of cutlery in the world.

My quest took me to the cutlery towns on the Continent; Thiers in France and Solingen in Germany, large centres of industry which, like Sheffield, were originally blessed with abundant water power for their output. Obviously the advances in technology are utilised in all current production, but it is still possible, certainly in Thiers, to see workshops still using these earlier methods. Both these centres have excellent working museums and useful contacts were made.

By now the collection was just an accumulation of cutlery, beautiful and fascinating, but where was it all going? I decided to rationalise it by extracting all unnecessary items, only retaining the British examples, those discovered in Britain and any foreign knives which had a big influence on the design of British cutlery and our eating habits. 'The Collection' then started to take on a life of its own and I could see trends which were not apparent before, such as the way the shape of the blade evolved, and the changes in constructional technique.

This was not the first time that knives had been dated by the shape of their blades. H. Raymond Singleton did this in his admirable booklet *Chronology of Cutlery*, Sheffield City Museum, 1966, which I would recommend to anyone with even a slight interest. However, what also became very obvious was that the evolutionary changes went in 'waves'. They reached a peak now and then with an almost perfect design and would descend into a trough, rising again to another peak; this process is still happening today.

I hope you will be able to reach the same conclusions from this book yourself.

BILL BROWN

CHAPTER 1 *An Introduction to Evolution and Design*

Bill Brown

Knife
Iron blade and bronze handle shaped as a leg with a shoe-clad foot. Continental-Roman, c.50 BC. *B14*
Length: 17cm
Legs were often used as decorative features for knife handles. This particular example is finely modelled with boot straps and a stocking. Notice how the part corresponding to the thigh is recessed on both sides so that it can be fitted with scales.

SINCE man first made tools from stone, he attempted to improve their function and form. At first, convenient fragments of flint were used as a cutting tool, but some chips worked better than others and fitted into the hand more comfortably. These would have been selected with care and, if possible, reshaped. It is here we have the first glimmer of form becoming influenced by aesthetic considerations. By mastering the technique of removing the chips from a core of flint, (even mining large pieces of quality flint) and manipulating shape, the early craftsmen eventually became skilful at producing elegant and sophisticated knives with integral handles (B1, p. 54).

Flint knives proved particularly useful to the hunter/gatherer, enabling him to dissect the carcasses of heavy animals and remove the smaller pieces to a safer place for consumption. It was, however, the discovery and use of copper which brought man into the age of metal knives, but coincident with this early period of metal (5000–3000 BC), the Egyptians still used high-quality stone knives, some with ivory handles and regular 'even ripple' chipped saw edges, probably for ceremonial purposes. Copper knives were inclined to be soft and did not hold an edge well, but were quicker and easier to re-sharpen than a stone knife. Eventually it was discovered that copper could be alloyed with tin, and this combination produced the very successful alloy of bronze. The malleable alloy could be cast in a mould, allowing more scope for the design of knife handles and with its greatly increased strength enabled craftsmen to produce much sharper blades (B4, p. 54).

Further development and specialisation occurred throughout the Middle Eastern and Northern European areas and there exist today some knives with considerable decorative style, probably personal eating knives, but could serve as weapons if required (B6, p. 55). The invading Celtic tribes brought with them improved techniques for casting bronze which, when combined with the introduction of iron for the blade allowed the production of high-quality knives, displaying elements of good design (B11, p. 56).

In Britain, the Roman settlers of the first century arrived with specialised knives designed for a variety of purposes; those for eating, for example, had beautifully figured bronze handles and iron blades (see left). Others of more utilitarian design, like the so-called 'trade knives' (B19 and B20, p. 57) were in frequent use, as were tools made entirely of iron. The Romans also introduced the folding combination knives of iron and bronze, some of which had white metal spoons attached (B24, p. 58), occasionally with a folding spike for extracting snails and shellfish. These utensils were often fitted with decorative bronze handles and probably were intended to be used when travelling or for military campaigns. Also popular at this time were spoons with longer, slender handles and pointed ends (B37, p. 59), which were probably used for extracting snails from their shells.

Throughout the first four centuries of Roman occupation, a large range of knives of bronze and iron was being developed for specialist use, and there seems little doubt that with such a long exposure to Roman culture the indigenous population were adopting these eating habits and customs. The evidence of this civilising effect is rather scarce, however, but one indication is a small, Saxon bronze three-tine fork and spoon (B43, p. 60), probably carried on a chatelaine with other bronze eating implements. This fork may have been used for extracting shellfish.

A further innovation around the time of the Roman withdrawal from Britain was a style of iron knife with Northumbrian monastic connections (the monks in this region were skilled workers in iron and other metals). This knife, called a 'scramasax' (B47, p. 61), is fairly heavy, with a robust blade, thick back and long dropped point; the sides are sometimes inlaid with designs and can have owners' or makers' names inscribed with different coloured metals. These scramasax knives were made in a whole range of sizes from small personal knives to short swords, but all have the same characteristics and all are fitted with a very simple 'bobbin'-type handle. The scramasax was renowned throughout Europe for its great strength and was considered a very valuable possession, of such quality that it could be given as a gift. Some of the medieval knives excavated from the Thames foreshore still manifest this scramasax influence (B55, p. 66).

Medieval illustrations in illuminated manuscripts show tables set with ewers, bowls, a knife or two and occasionally a fork. Most of these early forks are cast in bronze with two short tines (B74, p. 67) and are usually excavated in Europe, particularly Italy. The style did not change very much until the late sixteenth and early seventeenth centuries, when the number of tines sometimes increased from two to four.

The carrying of knives and spoons is well illustrated by the paintings of Bosch and later Dutch artists (p. 6). Their paintings show knives being worn at the belt with or without a sheath, ready to be used for eating or for defence. Spoons are seen tucked precariously into hats and clothing, which might help explain the many spoons excavated at the crossing points of London's ancient ditches. We can assume that if people dropped their spoon in the sewer while jumping over the ditch, they did not bother to retrieve it. It is also possible that cutlery was thrown out with the garbage and washing water – an occurrence that still applies today.

Early medieval knives were rather plain but practical, short, and with simple, bobbin-shaped handles of wood (B55, p. 66). The later medieval knives, however, display considerable innovation in design and construction (see right). The reason for this advancement is not entirely clear but it was probably a combination of location, a broader knowledge of materials, expansion in trade and a quest for novelty. National styles and trends were appearing throughout Europe at this time, though with the expansion of trade and the increasing mobility of people it is not always easy to determine whether a particular style of knife was made in Britain or imported from the Continent.

Very few of the everyday working knives have survived, except in an excavated condition: the condition of those recovered from the Thames foreshore are the result of various factors. Knives were frequently dropped overboard from visiting foreign ships; local inhabitants, who used the river as a highway, were equally careless. The foreshore was also the natural repository for material from demolished buildings. We know that the condition of these river knives depends on the composition of the material in which they were buried. Iron in river mud seems to survive quite well; wood usually rots. Most metals and iron blades will deteriorate in salt water. Some of the Thames finds from the sixteenth and seventeenth centuries also show evidence of having been broken, re-shaped, and used as oyster knives.

Eating knives of the sixteenth century were long, thin and elegant (B71, p. 71), and towards the end of this period the handles were given a more decorative treatment with carved figures of ivory and wood (B101 and B105, p. 77). Jet, ebony and coloured bone were used as inlays in the construction of the handle, as were gilt and precious metals. These ornate knives were popular and accepted as a fashionable part of dress. A pair of identical knives, in one divided sheath of fine needlework (B120, p. 84), made a very acceptable gift for men and women, and indicated both quality and wealth. These pairs of

Knife
Iron, the composite handle of jet scales and silver decorated with engraved panels of roses and leaves on the upper edge and foliate patterns on the underside, with silver shoulders and end cap in the form of a hat, blade mark of a pinnacle. Thames find, c. 1450–1500. B61
Length: 18cm

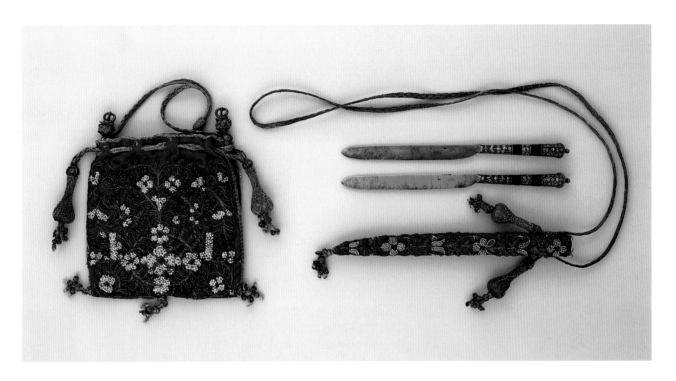

Knives (pair of wedding knives)
With their original case and purse. The iron blades of near parallel shape with centre point tips have solid faceted bolsters decorated with studded silver masks of cherubs amongst pendants of flowers. The handles alternate the same decorative treatment with pairs of jet spacers and terminate in curving caps held in place with ball finials. The blades are marked with a dolphin for HENRY DYKE and a dagger for the Cutlers' Company of London, 1610. *B123*
The matching sheath and purse are of exceptional quality, with embroidered satin decorated in floral patterns with silver-gilt thread and seed pearls.
Exactly how these items were meant to be carried by the owner is illustrated in the print of an English Gentlewoman taken from an early map of London (p. 88) There may be other methods of carrying, however, which are still not clear. Why the sheath and purse slide up and down the cording (but not removed, the tasselled pommels at the end cannot be detached) has not yet been fully explained.
Length of knife: 19cm
Purse: 13cm × 13cm

knives were sometimes given as a wedding gift to the bride by the groom and worn by the wife as a symbol of her status as mistress of her household. A fine example of this style, with sheath, matching purse, and knives by Henry Dyke, London, c.1611 (B123, p. 85), exemplifies a custom which continued until the middle of the seventeenth century.

Many crafts were involved in the making of a quality knife and although a cutler was required by his guild to be able to make a complete knife, in all likelihood the handles of carved ivory, silver, cast bronze or even glass were provided by specialist craftsmen, perhaps even imported from abroad. The sheaths were also fashioned by experts in the field of leather, wood, fabric and beadwork. In Paris, a short, two-tined silver fork had appeared, c.1598, with a bar handle similar to and matching in style with a Puritan spoon (B149). A British version of this is a silver, two-tined, bar-handled fork, bearing the crest of John Manners, Earl of Rutland, dated 1632. It is more basic in design than the French fork but also matches the spoons being produced at this time. There appears to be another Manners fork, which suggests there might have been a 'set'.

The knife of this Puritan period (first half of the seventeenth century) continued to change in size and style. It was becoming shorter with the point removed, presumably because as eating habits changed it was no longer necessary to spike food with the knife. The blade of the knife was sometimes wider at the tip than at the bolster, with a short, cartridge-shaped handle tapering down to a round section of silver or ivory, sometimes decorated with inlaid wire, resulting in an all-purpose 'prime' knife (B141, p. 91). In the evolution of cutlery design there will be examples of a major influence leading to a 'prime' knife of the period – near perfect in respect of time, fashion and balance. From its 'peak' the design deteriorates to a 'trough' of debasement in style and shape, rising again to another fashionable peak. The 'prime' knife of this period (B148, p. 47) matched the basic simple Puritan spoon (B149, p. 47) which had a large plain flattish oval bowl with simple parallel bar handle. The two-tined steel fork that followed copied the style of the knife with a matching handle, whereas the previous silver fork matched the silver spoon.

Early seventeenth-century travellers such as Thomas Coryat brought back from Italy reports of the usage of forks, although not to transfer into the mouth, as is often quoted, but to prevent contamination by holding the meat in place when cutting on the plate. After some ridicule and resistance as an effeminate affectation, this implement was eventually accepted in Britain, but David Mitchell shows in his essay that it was not widely used until at least 1670. Knives that had a matching steel fork (usually with a slightly smaller handle) were often contained in a sheath or case covered with leather, hardwearing ray or dogfish skin. The sheath and its cover were usually attached to the waist for travelling by a leather thong threaded through loopholes. There are examples of one half of a pair of knives being converted into a fork, corroborated by the fact that the handles are the same size. In some cases there are obvious signs of heavier use of the knife than the fork, possibly indicating a reluctance on the part of the owner to use this new-fangled instrument.

A wedding gift to Elizabeth Nordern, c.1647 (B138), comprising a matching knife and fork in a half-round section slotted combination, engraved with her name on the inner steel plate, is a new seventeenth-century variation on the old custom of the groom giving his bride a pair of knives (B129, p. 87). Much of the surviving cutlery from this period appears to be quality pieces, and it is obvious that these have been treasured and preserved as family heirlooms. Most of the everyday cutlery of this period has disappeared, but a good selection of items from Thames excavations survived, probably from household refuse or as fire spoilage. These finds give us a clear picture of the evolution of the design and style of the knife, but in general terms we find that forks do not feature very highly as an excavated item until much later in the century.

With the Restoration of the Monarchy in 1660, the short, rather severe 'prime' Puritan knife was replaced with a longer blade, curved and spatulate at the tip, eventually acquiring a distinct 'sabre' look with a pistol-shaped handle. By the first quarter of the eighteenth century it finally evolved into a classic example of a Baroque-style knife (B186, p. 102). The popular term for this design of knife is 'scimitar' and it can be found in all its evolutionary stages from its rudimentary beginnings to the superb examples of the 1720s. During the latter part of the seventeenth century the traveller still needed companion sets (B170, p. 15) containing knives, spoons and forks, etc. These continued to be used throughout this period and on into the next century, often being brought back by young noblemen returning from their 'Grand Tour'. Most sets consisted of a case containing a knife and fork, and sometimes spoons. Others were more elaborate, perhaps with agate handles, a folding or dismantling knife, fork and spoon and sometimes with a quill knife blade, beaker, corkscrew and other items. It seems likely these companion sets were made to special order and the English craftsmen put a great deal of effort into making the whole unit very compact (B162, p. 95).

Contemporary with this change in style and design was the evolution of a separate dining room with dining tables and chairs and side tables at which some of the wealthier middle class merchants were able to display their fine silver. They could now supply their guests at the table with cutlery from fish skin covered boxes. These early boxes, which were rather utilitarian and naive in construction, had locks and keys and contained scimitar knives, matching forks with steel tines and silver spoons. All this made the carrying of personal cutlery to formal dinner parties less of a necessity.

One of the most prolific suppliers of cutlery at this time and an early entrepreneur of the factory system was the Master Cutler Ephraim How, who together with his son John made cutlery at Southend Mill, Lewisham, Kent, and sold from their shop on Saffron Hill, London. Many of How's knives are still found today, stamped with his mark – the name of HOW and the dagger of the Cutlers' Company of London, of which he became Master in 1706.

Knife and fork
Iron, slotted to fit together as one piece, the knife has a tapering straight blade, round tip and offset scale tang. The shaped ivory scale is decorated with horn, brass pins and coral beads. The exposed face of the knife tang is engraved with the name 'Elizabeth Norden', within a border of punched decoration terminating in stars and pods. The two-tine fork is similarly engraved and constructed, but has a wrythen stem and slotted terminal. The mark on the knife blade is a dolphin for Jonas Melcher and the dagger of the Cutlers' Company of London, c.1622. *B138*
Length of knife: 21cm

Late Stuart place-setting, c.1690
Photograph: Jeremy Phillips for Fairfax House, York

The most significant aspect of this display is the appearance of colour and ornament on the dining-room table. Chinese export dinner plates, in Imari patterns, were available in significant numbers by about 1700, and high-quality travelling cutlery, similar to the set shown from Carlsbad, c.1690 (B170) were imported or brought home by young noblemen on the 'grand tour'.

The spoon, knives and three-tine fork all fold and store in the custom-made compartmentalised leather case, together with an octagonal section blade rest which is also used as a writing implement with screw-in blade and pencil holder.

Each handle is elaborately damascened in typical Carlsbad fashion with gold arabesque patterns of scrolling foliage, flowers, seed pods, squirrels and winged amoretti.

Notice also the robust, baluster stem goblet with mushroom knop, probably made by the Ravenscroft glass factory around this time.

The napkin, woven in Haarlem and folded in the shape of a fan, is decorated with elaborate floral sprays after designs of contemporary botanical prints. These napkins were expensive items often woven with coats of arms, and it is all the more remarkable that this exotic form of folding, which disguises the pattern, should prove so popular.

Around 1720 the scimitar knife reached its optimum shape, but from then on it became debased, with the straightening of the blade and with a 'hump' on the back although still with a spatulated tip, and eventually evolving into the three distinct styles of scimitar blades (B186, p. 102, B195, p. 104 and B239, p. 111) and finally losing its pistol handle.

The first half of the eighteenth century saw the introduction of ceramic handles for cutlery. The earliest handles were probably the tapered, round section handles from China, in 'Imari' and blue-and-white colours, although the pistol-handled shape was soon to follow. These were imitated by factories in Europe: Meissen in Germany and St Cloud in France in particular (B191, p. 103), the latter exporting large quantities to Britain in both straight, tapering and 'pistol' shaped, in blue-and-white patterns. From 1740 Britain's own soft-paste factories such as Bow and Chelsea produced large quantities of knife handles in various patterns and styles (B194, B206, p. 106) but unfortunately, because of the nature of the material and construction techniques, few complete examples have survived.

After the middle of the eighteenth century, an abrupt change occurred in the evolutionary chain of the English knife due to the introduction of the 'French fashion' in furniture and decoration. French-style knives became fashionable (B256, p. 114). Lord Fairfax of Gilling Castle, for example, ordered two dozen 'French blades' in 1754 from the great rococo silversmith Fredrick Kandler. The blades were long and spear shaped with a pointed tip on a central axis, although the handles on the Fairfax knives were still probably pistol shaped with elaborate scrolls and foliate decoration. Other handles being produced at this time were often straight with a round-to-oval section in ivory, green stained or plain shell and ebony (B278, p. 116), some with silver ferrules and caps, whilst Wrythen enamelled handles and pressed horn were also being used (B279, p. 118). The most significant innovation of this period was the use of thin, stamped silver or Sheffield plate for handles with foliate and neoclassical designs, the blades having pointed or oblique ends (B269, p. 115). These stamped silver handles, costing a fraction of their solid equivalents, were 'loaded' with resin to give them strength and weight. Knife boxes continued to be used, but were more stylish, with serpentine fronts and exotic veneers being adopted by cabinet-makers as decorative items in their own right.

By the end of the eighteenth century the French-inspired, spear-shaped blades were no longer fashionable for dinner knives, and whilst British manufacturers made half-hearted attempts to revive the evolution of a 'British' scimitar blade (B281, p. 118), it was the large parallel-sided, round-tip blade which eventually dominated. Handles on knives were being simplified and standardised, although the range of materials used in production was increasing. Simple straight handles of ivory, for example, either green stained or plain, were very popular, as were the stamped and cast silver handles decorated with shells and foliage (B270, p. 115 and B309, p. 126).

It is at about this time, 1800, that boxed dessert sets first appear, with iron blades close-plated with thin silver (B483). These were popular as gifts throughout the nineteenth century and this custom was exploited by the cutlery trade, particularly in Sheffield and Birmingham. The gift trade was further developed by the production of canteens of table cutlery in flat wooden boxes meant for presentation. The potential market was expanded exponentially, however, by the synthesis of silver plating with a base metal of nickel, silver or brass by electrolysis in 1840. This meant that silver cutlery became more accessible, or rather what looked like silver cutlery on the table. It was stamped with what looked like hallmarks and is misunderstood even today.

This is also the period when the retail trade started to use the term 'cutlery' to mean only knives, and 'flatware' to mean spoons and forks. Why this distinction came about is still not clear, but may be related to restrictive trade practices in the cutlery industry. What is clear, however, is that throughout the nineteenth century the market for cutlery (knives) expanded greatly, with services becoming larger and more varied in the number of items. Publicity from trade and European exhibitions such as the Great Exhibition of 1851 at Hyde Park ensured a greater interest with a corresponding extension of requirement.

The parallel-sided blade knife of 1800 was still popular and survived for 100 years with very little change. The silver-plated fish knife (invented in the latter part of the century) could hardly be called a knife at all, being designed for breaking and parting the flesh, not cutting. Handles for cutlery in the nineteenth century were as varied as the market dictated and attempts were made to improve on construction, particularly to counteract the loosening of the handles, for which numerous patents were being taken out.

Many types of natural material were used for handles; bone, ivory, antler horn, wood, shell, etc., and these were commonplace either as 'solid' with metal framing, or as scales, i.e., flat plates rivetted onto a metal plate. By the 1860s, however, demand for natural

Knife and fork
Iron, French-style spear-point blade and three-tine fork of imported style, the composite silver and shell handles decorated with a classical urn motif. Secured with ferrules and scallop-shell caps. Blade mark of London, hand-made, c.1770. *B256*
Length of knife: 26cm
This knife qualifies for the accolade of 'prime' knife for the last quarter of the eighteenth century.

Late Georgian table-setting, c.1790
Photograph: Jeremy Phillips for Fairfax House, York.

By the end of the eighteenth century the English ceramic factories were producing a high standard of porcelain for the dining room table, competing at all levels on quality and price with foreign imports. This superb gilded plate by Chamberlains Worcester, c.1805, has the coat of arms for Thompson of York. Bill Brown's attendant knife and fork (B253) is remarkably up to date in style and shape, although it was made in Sheffield in the 1760s.

Notice also the marvellous 'Beilby' wine glass made for John Thomas, Bishop of Rochester, and the neoclassical silver-gilt candlesticks by John Scofield, 1780.

Manuals of instruction at this time indicate that it was acceptable for a bottle or decanter to be placed on the dining-room table and this example, of mullet shape, is engraved on the body with an uplifting motto: 'Old Brown and Good Company'.

products like ivory had far outstripped supply and a cheaper alternative appeared in the form of 'Celluloid'. This thermoplastic was particularly successful and could be made to look and feel like ivory. It could also be coloured to imitate horn and shell.

The beginning of the twentieth century was not marked by any great improvement in the design of cutlery, although the art-nouveau style had influenced the decoration of commemorative spoons (B417, p. 143 and B418, p. 134) and other table accessories produced by leading designers and sold in exclusive shops.

Knives had hardly changed in concept since 1820, except perhaps for the designs by Christopher Dresser, c.1880, and Charles Rennie Mackintosh's cutlery for Miss Cranston's Tea Rooms in Glasgow, c.1905, but this design has too many echoes of the 'trifid' design of the late seventeenth century to be considered original. His later work, however, with its more austere styling, is much more exciting and probably influenced some art deco and stainless-steel cutlery designers in later years. The social habit of afternoon tea was highlighted with boxed-novelty sets of tea knives and coffee spoons with brightly coloured plastic handles and 'finger point' blades.

In 1914, when stainless steel was first invented in Sheffield by Harry Brearley and commercially produced by Firth Brown, the implications for the cutlery trade were enormous: knife blades would no longer rust and corrode as was the fate of most carbon-steel blades, nor would arduous cleaning be required. The First World War delayed the use of this material for cutlery making until 1920, when it was made available to a number of manufacturers who unfortunately concentrated their efforts on producing an old-fashioned, nineteenth-century design with this distinctly twentieth-century metal. There was, however, one particular style of knife which appeared at the end of the nineteenth century and evolved slowly both in England and Germany. This was the all-metal knife in both iron and steel that had appeared at various times in the past and now reappeared with the introduction of this new material. The one-piece knife is an obvious candidate for a 'prime' knife of the first half of the twentieth century and, with the partnership of stainless-steel spoons and forks, it must have represented the ultimate evolution in cutlery, and it was produced in large quantities. More recently industrial designers have been involved with stainless-steel cutlery both in Britain and the rest of the world, and there has been a proliferation of designs, both good and bad.

We are now well into the age of plastic but have yet to see plastic cutlery that is not just another bright, cheerful, inexpensive throwaway substitute along with ready-to-serve TV dinners on plastic or paper plates. If this trend continues we may all be using tear-off plastic cutlery. Perhaps plastic will take on a completely new dimension in quality and design; however; on the other hand, we may all adopt the American style of eating with the fork alone, especially with the increase of convenience foods. We are certainly seeing examples of the fork redesigned to supersede the knife such as an upgraded pastry fork or a stainless- steel dinner fork with one of the tines sharpened on the outside edge in the manner of an amputees fork of the First World War. Some of these modern implements are also bowl shaped like a spoon but whether these innovations are able to carry out the intended operations satisfactorily is another matter.

Whatever happens, it seems likely that for some time yet we will continue to need implements which transfer food into our mouth in a seemly and agreeable manner. It is to be hoped that designers can rise to the challenge and offer solutions which are not only functional and economic, but also appeal to our tactile and visual senses.

Spoon
Silver and enamel, designed by Archibald Knox, the bowl with *entrelac* motif on a turquoise and green enamelled ground below inscription 'Anno.Coron: ER VII', the tapering pointed stem with pierced symmetrical knot decoration to sides, stamped 'L. & Co.' within three lozenges for Liberty & Co., Birmingham, hallmark for 1901. *B417*
Length: 16cm
This spoon commemorates the Coronation of Edward VII (see also B418, p. 134). Non-enamelled examples of the same design are also known to have been made at the same time.
Cf.: Tilbrook, A. J., *The Designs of Archibald Knox for Liberty*, London, 1976, p.127; *Style Liberty*, Victoria & Albert Museum Publications, London, 1975, D. 81D.

CHAPTER 2 *The Clerk's View*

David Mitchell

T HE principal aim of this essay is to investigate the ownership of cutlery in England
during the sixteenth and seventeenth centuries, using written sources,
particularly probate inventories.[1] A particular concern is the introduction of the
table fork and its impact upon the formal washing of hands at meals with consequent
changes in the holdings of certain types of napery and plate. The study inevitably
concentrates on the holdings of the wealthy, for although many inventories survive from
this period, it is only among a minority from the elite groups of nobles, gentry, rich
merchants and tradesmen that details of cutlery are listed. Objects in base metal are only
occasionally described and both silver and pewter are often inventoried simply in terms of
their total weight: typically the 1661 inventory of the London mercer, Daniel Waldo lists:
plate 328 oz at 5s per oz, £82; fine pewter [220 lb] at 10d per lb, £9 3s 4d.[2] Furthermore,
although silver spoons are listed in the inventories of husbandmen and modest tradesmen,
table knives and forks are rarely found.

The nature of the provision of cutlery together with the napery and plate (or pewter)
that furnished a table depended upon both dining ceremony and cuisine. In turn, these
responded to attitudes towards the purposes of dining which ranged widely and included
the display of largesse and power, the cementing of political or business affinities, and the
enjoyment of the company and conversation of friends. Changes in attitudes occurred
throughout Western Europe but inevitably their pace and detailed nature varied both from
state to state and between social groups within each state. Thus, although the similarities
between dining ceremony in the great houses of France, England and Germany have been

Still life with peacock pie, pheasant, sweetmeats, lemon and knife on folded white tablecloth, 1627
Pieter Claesz (1597–1660), oil on panel, 78 × 129cm
Photograph: courtesy of Johnny Van Haeften
This extraordinary painting, pregnant with detail, is testament to Claesz's masterly skill at still life painting.

The rather plain knife on the table, which has an ivory handle with a slight swell at the end, is housed in a composite leather case with three sliding sections linked together with blue linen cording. The knives apparently lie in opposite directions and in separate compartments, rather than being paired together in the same sheath. It seems probable that the knives are of a different shape, the long, thin, pointed knife still housed in its case, perhaps used eating for oysters.

Lazarus and the rich man's table, 1618
Gasper van der Hoecke
(1585–1648), 47 × 83cm
Photograph: courtesy of Nortmans

A topographic painting of great interest, the table positively groans with food but pride of place on the damask-covered table is given to a majestic peacock pie.

The rich man, Dives, sits in jaded supplication, dressed in archaic robes. He holds a hanap, a tall columnar glass drinking vessel with gilded base. Behind, on the table, is a star-shaped banqueting plate or 'posie' on which some dry sweetmeats are placed. The ebony handled knife with gilded cap sitting precariously on the edge of the table is similar to B61 and on the far side of the table, near to the lattice-work pie, rests a combination spoon/fork which relates quite closely to another example (B156) in Bill Brown's Collection.

rightly noted, at the level of the provision and use of particular types of cutlery or napery, there were distinct differences.

In England, while dining in public or 'in state' at court and in noble households continued throughout the period, its frequency and importance seems to have steadily declined with an increasing desire for privacy. Even Henry VIII frequently dined in the privy chamber served by his personal staff. Sometimes he would eat in greater privacy and informality within the secret lodgings, such as at Hunsdon in 1528 in 'a chamber within a towre where his hignes sometyme useth to suppe aparte'.[3] Around 1600, apart from the desire for privacy, changing conceptions of 'civility' were a catalyst for different visions of hospitality, 'the idea that refinement separates those who possess it from the rest, and justifies them in seeking one another's company'. From this follows the view of the author of *Cyvile and Uncyvile Life* that:

> The great merit of living in London was that one could choose one's own dinner guests, and have friends at your table, 'men of more civilitie, wisedome and worth, than your rude countrey Gentlemen, or rustical Neighboures'.[4]

Conversation had clearly become paramount to William Cornwallis when he insisted in his *Essay* of 1600 that the only reasons for entertaining guests were 'love or business'.[5]

During the sixteenth century knives, forks and spoons were used at table for serving food rather than for eating. In great households, meat was cut by the carver, who used either two knives or a knife and fork, and then presented small pieces to the diner. Carvers were of gentle birth and even with the demise of the gentleman-servant by about 1650 carving remained an art required of the gentleman. Indeed, instruction books for carving meat, poultry and fruit, together with designs for folding napkins into exotic shapes, were published in increasing numbers during the seventeenth century. Among the earliest examples is that of Messibugo, published in Ferrara in 1549, followed by other Italian works by Fusoritto and Giegher.[6] Matthias Giegher was a member of the German community in Padua, and although his book was published in Italian in 1639 it was very influential in later German works by Harsdörffer of 1652 and Glorez of 1699. Similar works were also produced in Holland and France. Indeed, a French work was the basis for Giles Rose's *The Perfect School of Instructions for Officers of the Mouth*, published in London in 1681. The frontispiece to the 1665 edition of Harsdörffer's *Trincir-Buch* is of a gentleman carving a small joint of meat which he holds aloft on a carving fork in his left hand. The lady at the head of the table holds a fork, apparently to transfer the meat to the platter on her right. In earlier periods, the carver presented the meat to the diners with a wide, flat-bladed serving knife of which a number of Italian and German examples survive.[7]

Such *présentoirs* were also used in France, the probate inventory of the Toulouse *marchand-drapier* Guilhem Azema listing *2 grands couteaux et 1 petit coutelas à manche d'ivoire à découper et servir les viandes*.[8] Serving knives were probably included among sets of carving knives in England. Henry VIII's inventory of 1547 contains some twenty carving sets, generally comprised of three but sometimes five knives.

> *Item a case covered with crimson vellat broken with a cover wherin are two great Carving knyves & three small[,] three haftes golde having Lyons vpponther hedees endes.*[9]

As these are the only gold hafts listed, they are probably the 'three carving knives for the Carver and one for the King on his trencher the hafts of fine gold' which were provided at the Garter Feast at Windsor in 1519.[10] The supposition that one of these knives may have been a *présentoir* is supported by the 'servinge kniffe' included in Archbishop Parker's inventory of 1575.[11] Only four of Henry's carving sets included a fork, which suggests that the meat was skewered on a knife with a sturdy blade. Most other sets before 1550 do not include forks such as those belonging to the Earl of Oxford in 1513; 'a pair of kerving knyes wt serpentynes haftes'; and Dame Agnes Hungerford in 1524, 'a sheth of carvying knyfes with every [ivory] haftys'.[12] Possibly carving forks became more popular towards the middle of the century for apart from the royal examples, Lord Sandys in 1540 had 'one stocke of carving knyves with x small knyves and a forke of sylver, with a case of sylver'.[13]

The cases of carving knives belonging to the King often included, like Sandys', ten or twelve small or 'meate' knives. In addition, the Royal Household had separate stocks of small knives giving a total in excess of 600. This profusion suggests that all at court were provided with an individual knife when dining. This was not the case throughout Europe, as Calviac explained in *Civilité* published in 1560:

> *The Italians generally prefer to have a knife for each person. But the Germans place special importance on this, to the extent that they are greatly displeased if one asks for or takes the knife in front of them. The French way is quite different: a whole table full of people will use two or three knives.*[14]

Perhaps this custom persisted, for a study based on some 3,000 Parisian inventories showed that even in the early eighteenth century individual knives were not supplied to diners from the middle sections of society:

> *Knives were even less widely used than spoons and forks, and their rarity raises a question: did each guest bring and use a knife he or she carried about at all times, as was done in the countryside? Or were one or two knives placed on the table to be used by all?*[15]

The majority of the knives in Henry VIII's inventory had silver hafts, some topped by the King's arms and others by heads or flowers.[16] Certain of the hafts were decorated, variously described as 'graven', 'of Damaskin worke' and 'with Morisco worke'.[17] A significant minority had bone hafts in black, white, or green and white, often tipped with silver with two decorated sets, one of 'tourned [turned] bone haftes trymmed with silver' and another of 'white bone of images'.[18] Some knives were housed in the most splendid cases, possibly

Spoon and fork
Silver, the folding four-tine fork with attachable spoon bowl is engraved on the octagonal facetted stem with alternating chevrons. Screwed into the handle is a silver toothpick decorated with the figure of Minerva in repose. A sliding sleeve holds the spoon in the opened position. Engraved with the letters 'SM' on the spoon bowl.
Dutch or Italian, c.1620. *B156*
Length when opened: 17cm

The painting by Gasper Van der Hoecke (fig. 2) seems to illustrate an example of this travelling cutlery.
For similar examples in the Victoria and Albert Museum collection see: Bailey, C.T.P., *Knives and Forks*, The Medici Society, 1927, fig.20.

to give variety to magnificent cupboards of plate such as that illustrated at Binche in 1549 for Philip II of Spain.[19] Henry VIII had cases in the form of a dragon, a greyhound and a woman encrusted with precious stones, (furneshed with knyves having Diamondes at thendes), whereas the Earl of Leicester in 1583 owned 'A George one horsebacke of woode painted and gilte etc withe a case for knyves in the taile of the horse And a case for oyster knyves in the brest of the Dragon'.[20]

Roundel
Probably maple or sycamore, being plain on one side as a receptacle for dry sweetmeats and decorated on the front with a lion in a classical landscape, inscribed with verse: THE LION SNARD THE MOUSE ENTREATS FOR HELP THE MOUSE THE FETTERS FREATES MEANING THE MEN OF DEGREE BY POORER MEN RELEASED MAY BE.
English, c.1600. *B113*
Diameter: 13cm.

Some of these may have been intended for the more intimate surroundings of the banqueting house where great men entertained their principal guests to sweetmeats, fruit and spiced wine, following dinner in the presence chamber. Henry, for example, had three cases of 'silver and parcell gilt of parrys [Paris] worke' which each contained a ginger fork as well as a number of knives.[21] These knives possibly had rounded rather than pointed blades, as in the painting of Lord Cobham and his family enjoying a banquet in about 1570.[22] There are several earlier references to ginger forks with which to eat 'wet suckets', some with attached spoons, such as those belonging to Dame Agnes Hungerford, 'forkes with ther spones, doble gylte, to eete greene gynger withall'.[23] Apart from ginger forks, special roundels or fruit-trenchers were also provided for the banquet (see right). William Puttenham, in *The Art of English Poesie* of 1569, explained that epigrams were 'Put upon banketting dishes of sugar plate, of March paines Etc … We call them poesies, and do paint them upon the back sides of our fruit-trenchers of wood.[24] Martin Bowes, the son of a Lord Mayor of London, owned two sets on his death in 1573, a 'dusson old trenchers painted wt poyses' and an 'old box of frute trenchers'.[25]

Table knives were not only sold in cases but also in pairs, sometimes with decorated sheaths designed to be carried about the person, such as the two 'payre of gyllt knyves and velluet sheaths' owned by Alice Smythe in 1593.[26] A number of the surviving pairs are of very good quality (B120, p. 84), a feature exemplified by the descriptions and valuations in written records. The Earl of Oxford's two knives with gilt hafts decorated with mullets were valued at 26s 8d and a pair belonging to Lady Hedworth at 15s 4d, whereas cases with eight to twelve knives belonging to Sir Thomas Butler, Sir Thomas Ramsay and Alice Smythe were valued at 3s, 2s and 5s respectively.[27] Even the case sold on Archbishop Cranmer's attainder in 1553, 'of Morleies knyves brasell hafted tipped with siluer' fetched only 5s.[28]

Spoon
Cast pewter, with fig-shaped bowl, double baluster stem and wrythen terminal, marked 'H I' on bowl. c.1550. *B94*
Length: 15cm

In addition to carving and table knives, there are occasional references to chipping and voider knives, which were used to clear crumbs from the tablecloth. Chipping knives were used in the pantry for cutting bread, as described in Ivan Day's essay. Presumably, they rarely appeared in public for they were inexpensive, with Sir Henry Guildford's three 'chipping knives for bred' valued at a penny each in 1532.[29] In contrast voider knives had decorated hafts: the Earl of Bedford in 1585 had two 'voider knyves with silver handles' and Sir William Maynard in 1637 a 'steele voyder knife the handle set with mother of perle'.[30]

From the mid-fifteenth century English inventories regularly list spoons, generally of silver with odd entries for pewter.[31] Individual holdings vary greatly, with yeomen, parsons and tradesmen typically having six to twelve silver spoons, but wealthy merchants and noblemen several dozen. In addition, great magnates with 'cabinets of curiosities' had exotic spoons, possibly for use at the banquet, of gold and precious stones, crystal, serpentine, mother of pearl and even 'welke shelles'.[32]

Between 1450 and 1500, the popular patterns seem to have been 'wrethyn knoppes' and 'dyamonde poynts', although finials with acorns and St John's head also occur (B94, right).[33] During the sixteenth century these were upstaged by spoons with finials of the apostles, maiden heads and lions. In 1533 the London linen merchant Alexander Plymley

A kitchen interior with servants, c.1680
Anthonia de Winter (fl.1668–97), oil on canvas, 79 × 102cm
Photograph: courtesy of Johnny Van Haeften.

A well-organised kitchen with custom-made racks for spoons. A useful inventory method for checking in the utensils at the end of each day.

Fork
Bronze, with three tines, figured stem and term finial, Italian, c.1580. *B99*
Length: 15cm

owned six-and-a-half dozen spoons which included all these fashionable designs, whilst appropriately the Bishop of Ely had simply three dozen spoons with the twelve apostles (B98, p. 76).[34] From about 1550 apostle spoons are also listed in sets of thirteen, 'one with Image of God & xii apostles'.[35] The descriptions 'knoppys' (B97, p. 76) and 'slipped ends' also occur quite frequently, but spoons with 'wyld men' and 'of the assumption' are rare.[36] Alderman Austin Hynde ran the full gamut with ninety silver spoons 'with dymonde poynts, with lyons, of the assumption, postells, with maidenheddes and with slyppes'.[37]

Occasionally spoons were personalised with arms, devices or quotations. Dame Agnes Hungerford had a 'gret spone doble gylte with Hungerford Arms' and ironically, in view of her attainder in 1524 for the murder of her husband, a spoon with the inscription 'myne assuryd truth'.[38] Henry VIII had several spoons decorated with the rose or the royal arms including 'a Spone of gold with a wrythen siele having A scripture abowte it the kinges armes crowned in the topp gyven by the lorde Marques of Excetor vppon Neweyeres day'. The King's inventory also lists similar spoons clearly got by attainder, such as 'xvij gilt spones with half knoppes and stafforde knottes at thendes' from Edward Stafford, Duke of Buckingham in 1521, and 'ix spones of silver and gilt with the Lorde Crumwelles armes at ther endes' from Thomas Cromwell in 1540.[39]

Personal table forks seem to have been introduced to Europe from Italy. Although owned by the Medici and other princes during the fifteenth century their use 'was not widely established in Italy until the latter half of the sixteenth century' (for Italian forks, see B95 and B112, p. 73).[40] Fifteenth-century Italian forks were often sumptuously decorated and fashioned with handles of precious materials. In view of their expense they were possibly largely confined to the banqueting rather than the dining table. This seems to have been the case in other European states during the sixteenth century for in an allegorical banquet representing the princes of the House of Hapsburg, painted in 1596, each diner has a gold or silver-gilt fork (of the same form with three tines as B99, left).

Amongst the sweetmeats and fruit set on parcel-gilt trenchers are small octagonal salts.[41] Perhaps the silver-gilt 'confection' belonging to Henry VIII, made in the Hapsburg Netherlands, was intended for such an occasion:

> *One standing Cuppe guilt of Flaunders making garnyshed with perles and enameled in dyuers places … in the foot thereof xij trenchers of siluer parcel guilt standing vpon the sides xij forkes set with three perles the pece … in the cuppe are foure gobletts guilt and three cuppes of Assaye guylt and xij spones guilt and two saltes … in the Toppe a Clocke standing vpon the same a woman …*[42]

If this was ever used the forks did not make a lasting impression, as the English traveller Thomas Coryat, who famously noted in 1611 their use in Italy for eating meat, thought that no 'other nation of Christendome doth use it'. In this he was mistaken, since the sensational tablecloths woven in Haarlem in 1604 by Passchier Lammertijn as diplomatic gifts from the States General to Henri IV of France have fields with 'laid-table' designs comprised of platters of foods, trenchers and both knives and forks .[43] Personal forks were clearly known in France, for in 1560 Calviac wrote that 'the Germans use spoons when eating soup and everything liquid, and the Italians forks. The French use either, as they think fit'.[44] However, they seem to have been little used in France before the seventeenth century when, for example, the Knights of the Order of *Saint-Esprit* were pictured by Abraham Bosse in 1633 eating with simple two-tined forks (above).[45] Several forks of this form survive made by Paris masters as well as that owned by the Earl of Rutland with English hallmarks for 1632. Nevertheless, forks were slow to come into general use despite the assumption by Antoine de Courtin in his influential work *Nouveau traité de civilité* of 1672 that the tables of the refined were always set with forks.[46] Indeed, Annik Pardailhé-Galabrun found that:

> *Forks are mentioned in small quantities in seventeenth-century inventories, as it was frequent practice at the time to eat one's meat with one's fingers. Only in the eighteenth century did the fork come into regular use among the bourgeoisie.*[47]

Knife *(right)*
Iron, with large tapered centre-point blade, solid bolster studded with silver masks and flowers, the ivory handle formed from a tapered round section, marked on blade with a maiden's head and dagger of John Bell. London, c.1632 (Thames find).
Length: 30.5cm. *B133*

The stains on the ivory handle are due to the long immersion in river mud.

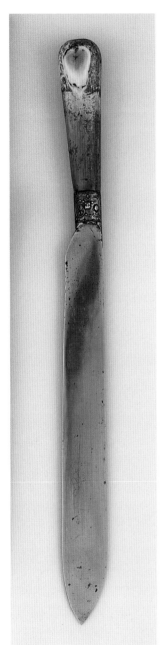

This mirrors the case in England where there are few inventory entries for forks during the first half of the seventeenth century.[48] Surviving forks, which mostly date from about 1630, are generally paired with a knife, often in a personal carrying case (B128, p. 86). In the Goldsmiths' Company records forks begin to appear from 1650 when a number were found to be either 'untouched' or below sterling standard: notably eighteen forks belonging to the Cheapside goldsmith Charles Doe who blamed their maker Thomas Rutter, a silversmith in Foster Lane. Several 'forke spoones' were also found to be 'worse than standard'.[49] These were probably personal implements or similar to French *cuiller-fourchette pliante* or *couvert de voyage* – forks that converted to spoons by sliding the tines into lugs on the back of the separate bowl (B156, p. 21).[50]

From the Restoration, Alderman Backwell, 'the father of English banking' in Lombard Street, sold forks, but in modest numbers: a mere fifty-nine compared with 514 spoons during a twenty-one-month period in 1663–65, a ratio of one to nine. To the west at Temple Bar, the emerging goldsmith-bankers Thomas Fowle and Robert Blanchard both had corresponding ratios of one to six, probably due to the nature of their clientele which consisted of lawyers and gentry with more fashionable tastes than the City merchants who made up the bulk of Backwell's customers. Even amongst the most senior royal servants, attitudes to the fork varied, for although the ambassadorial plate issued to the Earl of Carlisle in 1663 included twelve 'French' forks, that to Sir Richard Fanshaw in the same year had none.[51] ('French' seems to have indicated a trifid end, as in shown on p. 94.)

Lady with mixing bowl, ham, bread and carving knife, c.1650
Abraham De Pape (1620–66), oil on panel, 42 × 35cm
Photograph: courtesy of Johnny Van Haeften
A rare view of someone actually using cutlery. The simple plain stem spoon perhaps mixing meal in the terracotta bowl. Resting on the dish of ham is a carving knife with trowel-like step, similar to that seen on some carving forks, see B289 and B295.

TABLE 1

STOCKS OF KNIVES IN JOHN WATERS' INVENTORY, 1671		
DESCRIPTION	RANGE OF VALUATIONS *PER DOZEN*	PROPORTION OF TOTAL STOCK *BY QUANTITY* %
FRENCH KNIVES	1s 6d	1
SHEFFIELD KNIVES		
Ordinary	1s 6d	
Black hafts	3s	9
BLACK HAFT CASE KNIVES	4s to 5s	3
CASE KNIVES WITHOUT		
DESCRIPTION	7s to 12s	7
BUCKSHORN CASE KNIVES	7s	2
GLASS HAFT KNIVES	7s	1
IVORY HAFT KNIVES		
'Plaine' or 'ordinary'	4s to 8s	
'Threaded'	8s	22
'Tipt with silver'	10s to 20s	
TURNED		
'Turned'	6s to 12s	
'Tipt with silver'	12s to 22s	30
'Shell turning'	19s	
'Double turning'	32s	
FISHSKIN		
'Greene fishskin tipt with silver'	12s to 14s	10
'Fishskin tipt with silver & cases'	20s	
AMBER & SILVER		
Silver and amber haft knives	12s	2
TORTOISESHELL		
'Tipt with silver'	14s	3
AGATE	24s to 36s	8
SILVER		
'Graven Massy silver haft knives'	30s	2
'Massy silver hafted knives'	60s to 70s	
		100

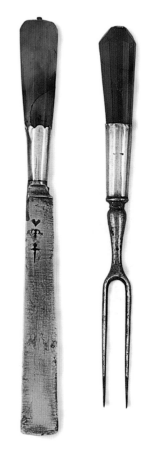

Right
Knife, fork and spoon (not shown)
Iron and silver, the knife with tapered blade, square tip and mean bolster, the two-tine steel fork with baluster stem. An associated spoon, with silver stem and rat-tail bowl, has French marks. The handles are made of faceted and tapered cornelian, with through-tang, faceted silver ferrules, and washered ends (one missing). The knife has the blade mark of EPHRAIM HOW, and the dagger for the Cutlers' Company of London, c.1687. *B165*
Length of knife: 12.5cm

At Court, the royal family probably had personal sets of cutlery that included forks, for in 1671 a case was made for 'ye queenes knife, fork and spoone'.[52] Yet forks were not normally supplied until the late 1670s. For major entertainments cutlery was hired and although spoons and knives were used for the Garter Feast in 1667 and knives for the reception of the Dutch ambassadors in 1673, it was not until the visit of the Prince of Orange in 1677 that forks were first hired.[53]

There are examples of the City elite owning numbers of forks such as the future Lord Mayor, Thomas Bludworth who purchased eighteen forks from Backwell in 1663, and the overseas merchant John Jolliffe, whose inventory of 1680 lists a case of knives and forks,

TABLE 2

STOCKS OF KNIVES AND FORKS IN JOHN WATERS' INVENTORY, 1671		
DESCRIPTION	RANGE OF VALUATIONS *PER DOZEN*	PROPORTION OF TOTAL STOCK *BY QUANTITY* %
SHEFFIELD		
Knives and forks	2s 6d	32
IVORY		
'Ivory haft steele forkes'	7s	
'Plaine ivory pockett knives &		18
forkes tipt with silver'	18s	
TURNED		
'Small turned haft knives with forks'	9s	
'Turned half-knives & forks tipt		19
with silver	18s	
AGATE		
'Agatt haft knives & steele forkes 16 square'	48s	
		31
'Agatt knives with silver forks 16 square'	72s	
		100

Knives and forks
Twelve steel blades and twelve two-tine forks with stamped silver pistol handles. Housed in black fish skin covered standing box with silver ring handles, lockable clasp and pad feet, c.1770. *B477*
Height of box: 33cm (closed)
Length of knife: 27cm

but they are very much the exceptions.[54] More instances are found of personal cutlery with interesting descriptions such as a 'Elletropian [heliotrope or bloodstone] knife and forke' belonging to the scrivener, Sir Martin Noel; two knives and forks with 'agatt' hafts owned by the apothecary Richard Tomlinson; and the 'Agatt hilted sword, knife & forke' carried by the jeweller William Boteler (cf. B165, p. 96).[55] By the early eighteenth century, however, the pattern had changed noticeably, with the middling sort in London often owning a dozen knives and forks and the nobility rather more.[56] By 1730 even larger quantities are found with, for example, the dining room of the linen draper Stephen Aynsworth, graced by a 'shagreen' case containing fifty knives and fifty-five forks.[57] At this time dessert knives and forks begin to appear in inventories.[58]

Knives and forks in silver were principally supplied by goldsmiths but also by the larger cutlers who, in addition, sold a wide range of cutlery with hafts of wood, bone, horn, ivory, fish skin, amber, tortoiseshell and various hardstones, mainly agate, but sometimes cornelian or jasper. The range and relative prices of these goods are shown in the inventory of the substantial London cutler John Waters who died in 1671 (Tables 1 and 2).

Waters had fifty-two dozen forks in stock but six times this number of knives. When combined, these represented a third of the value of his trade goods which totalled £514 and also included swords, surgeons' instruments, scissors, canes, whips and many types of boxes.[59] A contemporary cutler, Edward Knight, whose trade goods totalled a modest £59, stocked a limited range of knives at keener prices, but no forks.[60] Cheap cutlery was more accessible: the spectacle-maker John Clarke had thirty-four dozen knives and forks with an average value of 2s 9d per dozen and the ironmonger Nicholas Roberts had seventeen gross of knives, probably supplied through his warehouse in Birmingham.[61]

Apart from hunting for the table fork in inventories, ledgers and museum cases, its adoption can be tracked through the changing contents of the linen press. During the sixteenth century, in elite circles, hands were washed before going to table by a gentleman-servant pouring perfumed water from a ewer which was then caught in a basin below. The hands were dried on a short towel carried over the shoulder of another servant. After dinner, the tablecloth was replaced by a long towel, normally *en suite* in design and of the same length as the cloth, upon which the basin was set in front of the diner. As both long and short towels are regularly found in inventories until about 1650 it seems that hands continued to be washed in these ways. After the Restoration long towels disappear and towards the end of the century short towels are only found in the inventories of the middle sections of society.[62]

Coincidentally, with the demise of the towel splendid ewers and basins became less fashionable as the formal washing of hands became increasingly confined to great occasions of state.[63] Clearly, once table forks were adopted hands remained relatively clean during dining and it seems likely that the French habit of wiping the hands on a dampened napkin was espoused in England.

Notes and references

1 Cutlery is used in this essay in the general modern sense to include knives, forks and spoons.

2 London, Public Record Office [hereafter PRO], E154/4/34.

3 Brian Tuke to Wolsey, 23 June 1528, London, British Library [hereafter BL].
Cott. MS. Titus B.l. f.306, quoted in Simon Thurley, *The Royal Palaces of Tudor England*, New Haven & London, 1993, p. 138.

4 Felicity Heal, *Hospitality in Early Modern England* (Oxford, 1990), pp. 103–04, including quote from W. C. Hazlitt, *Inedited Tracts Illustrating the Manners of Englishmen*, London, 1868, p. 80.

5 Quoted in Heal, *Hospitality*, p. 101.

6 For discussion of these works, see Stefan Bursche, *Tafelzier des Barock*, Munich, 1974 and David Mitchell, 'Fine table linen in England 1450–1750: the supply, ownership and use of a luxury commodity', unpublished doctoral thesis, University College London, 1998, pp. 79–81.

7 K. Marquardt & U. Haedeke, *Eight Centuries of European Knives, Forks and Spoons*, Stuttgart, 1997, ills 1, 5, 86 & 210A: U. Zischka, H. Ottomeyer & S. Bäumler, *Die Anständige Lust van Esskultur und Tafelsitten*, Munich, 1993, p. 78.

8 *Plaisirs et Manières de Table aux XIVe et XVe siècles*. Ex. Cat. Toulouse, Musée des Augustins, 1992, inv. no. 173, nos. 224 and 225 show two broad bladed knives with ivory handles surmounted by a lion and a dragon assigned to the fifteenth century but without country of origin. They are similar to the Marquardt, *European Knives*, ill. 1, said to be fourteenth century and probably Venetian.

8 David Starkey (ed.), *The Inventory of King Henry VIII*. The Transcript, London, 1998, 1685.

10 B. L. Sloane Ms. 1494, f. 62v.

11 *Archaeologia* 30,1844, p. 24.

12 Earl of Oxford; *Archaeologia* 66, 1915, p. 337.
Dame Agnes Hungerford; *Archaeologia* 38, 1860, p. 367.
Also Lord Lisle; PRO SP1/161, 'three cases with careving knyves'.

13 C. W. Chute, *A History of the Vyne*, London, 1888.

14 Quoted in Norbert Elias, *The History of Manners*, Oxford, 1978, first published as *Über den Prozess der Zivilisation*, vol.1, Basel, 1939, p. 91.

15 Annik Pardailhé-Galabrun, *The Birth of Intimacy*, Cambridge, 1991, p. 99.

16 *Henry VIII Inv.*, 1749, 1755 and 1754.

17 *Henry VIII Inv.*, 1761, 1760 and 11195.

18 *Henry VIII Inv.*, 11051 and 11054. There were also odd cases with hafts of wood, of red glass and 'Christall and Calcedon': 11053, 11100 & 1743.

19 Bob van den Boogert, *Maria van Hongarije*, Zwolle, 1993, no. 214.

20 *Henry VIII Inv.*, 1749, 11196 & 1748, London, Victoria & Albert Museum. Ms 86 cc 35.

21 *Henry VIII Inv.*, 1683 & 1684.

22 Ivan Day (ed.) *Eat, Drink & Be Merry*, London, 2000, fig. 37.

23 *Journal of British Arch. Assn* 33, c.1877, p. 320, Robert Morton Gent, 1488.
PRO SP1/27, from f. 218, Edward Stanley, Lord Monteagle, 1523.
Archaeologia 38, 1860, Dame Agnes Hungerford, 1524.
Henry VIII Inv., 1248, 'Spone with suckett forke at thende of silver and gilte'.

24 Ivan Day, ibid., fig. 41.

25 PRO Prob.2/397, Martin Bowes Esq, 1573.

26 BL Egerton MS 8798. Alice Smythe, 1593 Widow of the Customer of London (one of the senior customs officials).

27 *Archaeologia* 66, 1915, p. 337, Earl of Oxford, 1513.
    Surtees Soc. Series 2 (1835), no. 224, Lady Hedworth (1568).
    Chetham Soc. 51, 1860, Sir Thomas Butler of Bewsey, 1579.
    Archaeologia 40, 1866, Sir Thomas Ramsay, 1590, Lord Mayor
    of London, 2 cases with 16 knives, 4s.
    B. L. Egerton Ms. 8798, Alice Smythe, 1593.
    28PRO E154, 2/41.

29 PRO SP1/70, Guildford had a further 'olde chipping knyfe of Iron' at
    2d. Archbishop Parker's 3 'chippinge knyves' were valued at 8d each
    in 1575. *Archaeologia* 30, 1844.

30 V & A Furniture Archive, typed copy of Bedford inv., 1585.
    Essex Review 61, Jan. 1952, Sir William Maynard, 1637.
    Alice Smythe inv., B. L. Egerton Ms. 8798, 1593, includes a 'knyfe to
    take upp the Table', 2s 6d.

31 Pewter spoons are largely absent as pewter is generally listed by the
    pound weight.

32 *Henry VIII inv.* 112–1155, 1239–47.
    J. O. Halliwell, *Ancient Inventories*, London, 1854, p. 4, Countess of
    Leicester, 1635, 'eleven christal spoones', two forks of christall
    sutable and one guilt spoone'.

33 PRO Prob. 2/16, John Holgrave, 1487, Exchequer official, 12 'sponys
    wt Dyamond poyntes.'
    Jn. Br.Arch.Assn. 33, 1877, Robert Morton, 1488, 2 doz spones with
    wrethyn knoppes' 2½ doz. 'sponys with dyamond poyntes'.
    PRO Prob. 2/28, John Barnys, 1489, London dyer , 12 'sponys wt
    wrethyn knoppes'.
    PRO Prob. 2/4, Lady Lewkener, 1466, 3 'gilt spoones wt acorne lobis
    at ends'.
    PRO Prob. 2/163, John Spristowe, 1499, Northampton Clothier, 12
    'Spones with St Johns Hede'.
    For discussion of design of spoons and illustrations, see G. E. P. & J.
    P. How, *English and Scottish Silver spoons*, 3 vols. (privately printed,
    1952–57).
    Timothy Kent, *London Silver Spoons and their Makers, 1500–1697*,
    London, 1981.
    Timothy Kent, *West Country Silver Spoons and their Makers,
    1550–1750*, London, 1992.

34 PRO Prob. 2/487, Alexander Plymley, 1533.
    PRO Prob. 2/488, Nicholas West, Bishop of Ely, 1534.

35 *Chetham Soc.* 33, 1857, Thomas Tyldisley Est., 1553, Lancashire
    gentleman.
    Sets of 13 also belonged to:
    PRO Prob. 2/252, Stephen Kirton, 1552, Merchant of the Staple;
    BL Add. Ms 5702, Lord La Warre, 1554;
    PRO Prob. 2/321, Thomas Ryce, 1558, gentleman, Isle of Wight.

36 PRO Prob. 2/177, Matthew Ernest, 1505, London tradesman, 17
    'sponys wt knoppys gylt';
    PRO Prob. 2/777, John Wynterhey, 1558, Yeoman, 'A dozyne of
    syluer sponys wt gylte knappys';
    PRO Prob. 2/404A, Wassell Wessells, 1574, London vinegar maker,
    'tenne white spoones with rownde knobbes'. (He also owned 12
    spoons with 'mayden heddes gilte' and 11 pewter spoons.)
    BL Royal Ms. App. 89, Sir Adrian Fortescue (Attainder, 1540), 12'
    maiden hedds', 12 'knopps at the end gilt', 12 'slipped [?] at the end',
    12 'wt spere poynte', 6 'wt woode honords'.
    Surtees Soc. 38 (1860), Marione Chapman, 1583, widow of Mayor of
    Newcastle upon Tyne, 12 'spoones of the wylld men'.

37 PRO Prob. 2/257, Austin Hynde, 1554, London merchant.

38 *Archaeologia* 38, 1860, Dame Agenes Hungerford, 1524.

39 *Henry VIII Inv.*, 114, 1203 and 1238.

40 Susan H. Vincinelli, 'Dining etiquette and Renaissance silverware', in
    Beth L Holman (ed.), *Disegno*, New York, 1997, pp. 66–67 and
    85–90.

41 *Felipe II. La Monarquía Hispanica.* Ex. Cat., El Escorial, 1998, no. 493.
    Alonso Sánchez Coello, 'El Banquete de Los Monarcas', 1596,
    Muzeum Narodowe, Warsaw.

42 Starkey, *Henry VIII inv.*, 631.

43 C. A. Burgers, 'Nogmaals Passchier Lammertijn' in *Oud-Holland*, 80,
    1965, pp. 139–68.
    D. M. Mitchell, 'The linen damask trade in Haarlem. Its products and
    its markets' in A. J. de Graaf, L. Hanssen & J de Roode (eds), *Textiel
    aan het Spaarne*, Haarlem, 1995, pp. 5–33.
    The tablecloths in the sets of linen given to James 1 in 1604 and
    Henry, Prince of Wales in 1606 possibly had the same fields.

44 Quoted in Elias, *Manners*, p. 91.

45 Michèle Bimbenet-Privat, *Les Orfèvres Parisiens de la Renaissance
    1506–1620*, Paris, 1992, no. 79, 1641–42, and no. 80, c.1640: no. 81
    is of similar simple form but with three tines and is marked for
    1653–54.

46 Elias, *Manners*, pp. 92–97.

47 Pardailhé-Galabrun, *Intimacy*, p. 99.

48 Marquis of Salisbury, Hatfield House Box B80 1605. Plate sent to
    Theobalds 16 July 1605 included 7 forks, 11 spoons & 3 table knives.

49 London, Goldsmiths' Company Court Book Y, f. 133v and 142, 12
    April and 3 May 1650: Y f.126v, 27 March 1650: 5 f.218, 19 October
    1668.

50 Michèle Bimbenet-Privat, *L'orfèvrerie parisienne de la Renaissance.
    Trésors dispersés*, Paris, 1995, nos 149 and 150.

51 For more detailed discussion, see David Mitchell, 'To Alderman
    Backwells for the candlsticks for Mr Coventry'. The manufacture and
    sale of plate at The Unicorn, Lombard Street, 1663–72', *Silver Society
    Journal* 12, 2000, pp. 111–24.

52 PRO LS 8/8.

53 PRO LS 8/6, /10, /13 & /17.

54 London, Corporation of London Record Office, Orphans' Court
    inventory (hereafter CLRO) 1630, John Jolliffe Esq.
    Sir John Lewis, Bart., 1671 had 6 silver forks, CLRO 107; Andrew
    Kendrick, 1691, a major linen draper, also had 6 forks, CLRO 2208.

55 CLRO 500, Sir Martin Noel, 1666, Scrivener
    CLRO 1111, Richard Tomlinson, 1676, Apothecary
    CLRO 1634, William Boteler, 1680, Jeweller (Goldsmith's Company).

56 CLRO 2675, James Keay, 1705, Dyer, I doz knives & forks.
    CLRO 2718, Peter Vansittart, 1706, Merchant, 2 doz knives & forks
    CLRO 3010, John Allison, 1716, Draper, 16 forks.
    Bedfordshire Hist. Rec. Soc. 38, 1958, Lord Bruce, c.1726, 11 silver
    forks, 11 walnut hafted forks.

57 CLRO 192, Stephen Aynsworth, 1729, linen draper.

58 CLRO 3330, Thomas Folkingham, 1729, goldsmith.

59 CLRO 1063, John Waters, 11 November 1671, Citizen and Merchant
    Tailor, it is unclear where he lived. He had a lease on a house in
    Whitechapel and on another in Holborn.

60 CLRO 360, Edward Knight, 24 January 1666/7, Citizen and Loriner,
    he probably lived by the gate of St Bartholomew's Hospital. Knives
    without description at 4s 2d to 5s per doz; knives 'threaded' [ivory?]
    at 6s; Buckshorne hafted knives at 6s; and Fishskin hafted knives at
    10s.

61 CLRO 935, John Clarke, 14 May 1674, citizen and spectacle maker of
    Leadenhall Street, 34 dozen of knives and forks, £4.15.0. Most of his
    goods were spectacles.
    CLRO 1221, Nicholas Roberts, 28 September 1676, citizen and
    ironmonger of Gracechurch Street, trade goods valued at £2,926
    include '17 grosse 1½ doz of knives of several sorts, 16 dozen ladles,
    15 dozen bells, 10? lb doore bells, £36.17.9?.

62 For detailed discussion, see Mitchell, 'Table linen in England',
    pp. 56–101.

63 See Mitchell, 'To Alderman Backwells', pp. 114–15.

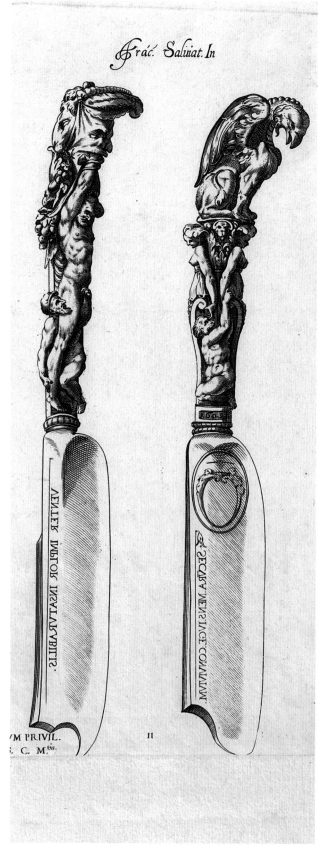

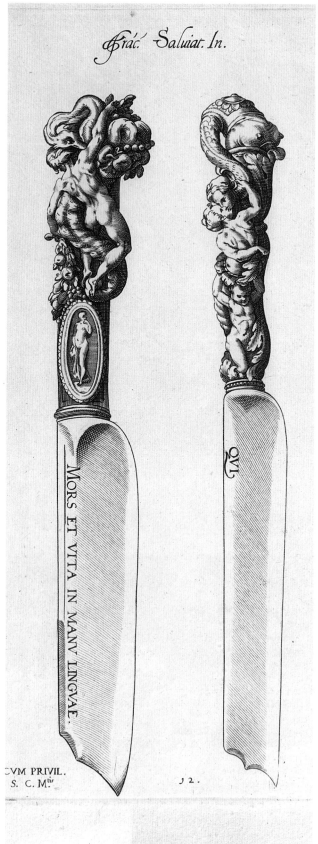

CHAPTER 3 *The Etiquette of Dining*

I N chapters 1 and 2 Bill Brown and David Mitchell present a useful overview of the evolution of cutlery in Britain and add to our understanding of what was available to wealthy clients during the Tudor and Stuart dynasties.

This next section explores the issues of function and context in an attempt to work out the part cutlery played in the developing rituals of behaviour and 'politeness'. The intention is to try and determine exactly what the user would do with these objects, what relationship the cutlery had with other items on the dining-room table and how they were deployed for the convenience of the server and the benefit of the served.

The role of carving, for example, an activity virtually ignored by earlier publications, is covered in detail in Ivan Day's essay. It was a service of paramount importance in the organisation of a well-run meal, the sheer theatre and showmanship involved is a revelation, and this knowledge is fundamental to our understanding of how meals would proceed.

Issues of behaviour at table are also explored; when the Rev. Jonathan Swift published a satire entitled *The Footman's Directory*, 1745, his advice to the servants was culled from a selection of much earlier manners books which attempted a more serious tone. Swift, however, recommended for example that:

> … *While Grace is saying after Meat, do you and your Breathren take the Chairs from behind the Company, so that when they go to sit again, they may fall backwards, which will make them all merry; but be you so discreet as to hold your Laughter till you get to the Kitchen, and then divert your Fellow servants.*

His most thought-provoking suggestion was to the footman:

> … *Never wear Socks when you wait at Meals, on the Account of your own Health, as well as of them who sit at Table; because as most Ladies like the Smell of young Mens Toes, so it is a sovereign Remedy against the Vapours.*

Reading through Swift's fascinating tome, one gets the feeling that many of the tips are based on hard experience.

The final part of the chapter chronicles the evolution of the British place setting, although it is not possible within the scope of this book to provide a comprehensive survey of evolution in style and decoration, more a chronology of turning points which chart the effects of economic pressure, the introduction of new technologies and, perhaps most significantly, the influences of foreign trade.

Set-piece displays often raise more questions than they give answers. We have attempted, for example, to bring together objects which were fashioned at the same time. There are, of course, many other examples to choose from, so the selection is subjective and open to debate. Also explained is the change in the presentation of food on the table, from the medieval style *le grand couvert*, to *service à la françaais* and the more efficient *service à la russe*.

Four knives, c.1640
After Francesco Salviati
(1510–63)
Copy of engravings by Cherubino Alberti (1553–1615)
Photograph: Jeremy Phillips for Fairfax House, York
The blades are sufficiently different to identify their intended use: those with the inward curving hooked tips are for dismembering, whilst the rounded tip blade may be used for serving. The main focus of attention, however, are the extraordinary designs for handles, one carved with a griffin, another depicting the bound satyr marsyas being indecently molested and two scenes of illicit love. The inscriptions on the blades are:
i. SECURA MENS JUGE CONVIVUM (He that is of merry heart hath a continual feast);
ii. VENTER IMPLOR INSATURABLUS (But the belly of the wicked shall want);
iii. MORS ET VITA IN MANU LINGUAE (Life and death is in the hands of the tongue).
From the nature of the inscriptions it seems likely that both knives i and ii were meant to be used together.
See: Holman, Beth, Disegno, *Italian Renaissance Designs for the Decorative Arts*, Cooper-Hewitt, New York, 1997

The Honours of the Table

Ivan Day

Many of us associate medieval feasts with draughty great halls filled with raucous diners tearing apart their food with greasy fingers and throwing their bones to the dogs. We tend to think of these feasts as occasions when poor hygiene and boorish manners ruled supreme. Nothing could be further from the truth. Although the quantity of food consumed was frequently large by modern standards, table manners were refined, cleanliness all-important and the food served with great ceremony and ritual. When the nobleman cleric George Neville (1433–76) was installed as Archbishop of York in 1465, a great feast was given in his honour. The whole affair was a curious blend of high religious ceremonial, pageantry and gastronomic excess. Prepared by sixty-two cooks and served to 2,000 principal guests, including Richard, Duke of Gloucester, this culinary display was perhaps the most extravagant in the entire history of English food. Included among the provisions were 104 oxen, 3,000 geese, 504 deer, 400 herons, eight seals, four porpoises and 6,000 dishes of jelly.[1]

The whole event was organised by the Earl of Warwick, the Archbishop's elder brother, who acted as steward. Other high-ranking noblemen waited on the Archbishop at high table: Lord Hastings was cupbearer, Lord Willowby carver and Sir John Malbury pantler. These 'great offices' required skill and a detailed knowledge of the intricate dining protocol and manners of the period. To be chosen to carve at such an important event Lord Willowby must have been extremely adept at carving each kind of bird and joint in its own prescribed way. As pantler, Malbury would have possessed equal dexterity with a knife, as he was required to neatly trim the Archbishop's bread trenchers and to chip the crust from his loaves.

Principal servants and officers of the late medieval table	
Office	Duties
Steward	Overall responsibility for the running of the feast
Marshall	Ensured guests were seated correctly according to social rank
Usher	Assisted both the marshall and sewer
Cupbearer	The officer who served the lord's wine
Butler	Overall responsibility for the upkeep of the cellar and service of wine
Pantler	Responsible for distribution of bread
Almoner	Led grace and collected up leftovers for distribution to the poor
Ewerer	Supervised the washing of hands
Naperer	Responsible for laying the tablecloth
Sewer	Superintended the arrangement of food on the table and waited directly on his lord
Carver	Cut the bread and carved meat and other foods for his lord

Although they seem like servile duties to us today, expertise in these table crafts was important to all men of high birth. In their own households, yeomen servants performed these roles, but at important ceremonial meals they themselves could be called upon to carve their lord's meat or to top up his cup. In a feudal society, to serve one's superior at table was not only a public display of deference, but also a means of furthering one's own advancement. As a result, acquiring these essential social skills was as crucial to a young fifteenth-century nobleman's education as his ability to ride a horse, hunt with a falcon or handle a sword. Manly pursuits, playing musical instruments, understanding the rules of estate and the ability to carve were actually considered more important at this time than learning Latin and Philosophy.[2] Some young nobles acquired these skills when they served as pages of honour at court during their boyhood and were known as 'henxmen' or henchmen. Three henchmen served in the household of Henry VI, although the number in Edward IV's court at the time of Archbishop Neville's instalment had risen to seven.[3]

Outside the royal palaces, other well-bred youths were lodged in the houses of educated noblemen to acquire the upbringing necessary to steer them through the intricacies of aristocratic life. They often learnt the complex craft of table protocol with their noble lord's sons, serving with them at table on a daily basis. In some directions from the household records of the Earl of Northumberland, entitled 'Persones that shall attende upon my Lorde at his Borde daily' the following are listed:

> *My Lordes Secounde Son to serve as Kerver.*
> *My Lordes Thurde Son as Sewer.*
> *My Lordes first Hauneshman as Cupbearer to my Lorde.*
> *My Lordes second Hanshman to serve as Cupbearer to my Lady.*[4]

These privileged children were encouraged to wait on their parents at a very young age:

> *Of stature then yf thou be able,*
> *It shall become thee to serve the table*
> *In bringynge to it suche meate as shall need*
> *For thy parence upon that time to fede.*[5]

To assist these young men in acquiring a working knowledge of the 'great offices', a professional servant was often employed to teach them service and courtesy. Some of these 'maisters of the hanshmen' passed on their knowledge by writing instruction manuals. With such titles as *The Boke of Nurture, Ffor to Serve a Lord* and *The Boke of Kerving*, they were frequently composed in verse to help the scholars learn the contents by rote. Similar courtesy books were used on the Continent to guide children and servants through the complex rituals of late medieval dining. Apart from a few Latin grammars, *Les Contenances de la Table* (Lyons c.1490), a tiny courtesy book written in rhyming quatrains, was the first printed book to be published specifically for children. Here in England our early pioneers of printing, Caxton and Wynken de Worde, also published manuals of this kind.[6] Some of them continued to be popular well into the seventeenth century.[7]

The most important English *Boke of Nurture* was written in rhyming couplets in the 1440s by John Russell, who was usher and marshal to the humanist scholar Humphrey Duke of Gloucester, the youngest son of Henry IV. This remarkable poem (Harleian Ms. 4011) offers some valuable insights into exactly how a medieval feast unfolded and explains the precise roles of each nobleman 'servitour'. In the prologue of the work Russell meets a despairing young man who is unable to find a master because of his lack of skills. He tells Russell that he wishes to become a 'buttilere / pantere or Chamburlayn' and particularly desires to learn the skills of a carver, 'The connynge of a kervere, specially / of

Carving Meal in a Kitchen, 1570

From Scappi, Bartolomeo, *Opera*, Venice, 1570

Photograph: courtesy of a private collection

This illustration shows exactly how meat was carved *in alto* (in mid air) using a long-tined Italian carving fork. Although no English carving forks from this period survive, those of the seventeenth century have short tines and were only used for holding the meat still on the plate. The spectacle of carving in mid-air, which was at its most fashionable in Europe in the early 1600s, does not seem to have spread to England.

that y wold lerne'. Russell then instructs him in the specialist equipment and skills required by the principal officers of the table – the pantler or butler, the carver and the sewer. He also explains the complex rules of precedence then current in Plantagenet feudal society. As a marshall with responsibility for seating important guests, Russell was a well-qualified tutor. He teaches his pupil that 'The pope hath no pere' and that a cardinal has a higher estate than a prince. We learn that a serving Mayor of London is allowed to dine with the earls, barons and bishops, but one no longer in office has to sit at a much lower table with the Masters of Chancery. Further down the social order, parsons and vicars are seated above merchants.[8] A list of the 'Estates sitting in the Hall' at Archbishop Neville's Feast agrees exactly with Russell's system. At Neville's high table the bishops of London, Ely and Durham sat on his right-hand side and the Duke of Suffolk, and Earls of Oxford and Worcester to his left.

A pantere, pantler or panterer had originally been the household baker, but the term came to mean the officer who controlled the distribution of bread. In some fifteenth-century households the pantler's role was merged with that of the butler, who had responsibility for the upkeep and serving of wine. He also frequently undertook the duties of the naperer and ewerer, who were responsible for covering the table and cupboard with linen and for preparing the équipage and napery used for washing hands. We learn from Russell that a buttery or pantry should be equipped with three sharp knives, one designed to chop or square trencher loaves, one to chip or pare bread crusts and one to trim or smooth the trenchers, the rectangular slices of stale brown bread on which the diners cut their food. The exact forms of the pantler's three knives are not known, but those used at important ceremonial occasions may have been more than just utilitarian in design. An inventory of 1455 listing the contents of Sir John Fastolfe's buttery mentions 'ij. kerving knyves; iij kneves in a schethe, the haftys of every (ivory) with naylys gilt… j. trencher-knyfe'.[9] It is not clear whether a trencher knife was one of the pantry knives used to cut the trenchers, or a broad-bladed knife used by the carver to serve them, a kind of *présentoir*. Whatever its exact form, the bread trenchers seem to have been named after this knife, sometimes itself also just called a trencher (*tranchoir* in Old French).[10]

Trenchers were cut from four-day-old cheate loaves, a kind of wholemeal bread proved with a sour leaven.[11] The chopping knife used to square them must have been of a good size, as cheat loaves were large. After the sliced trenchers had been neatly trimmed to size with the smoothing knife they were put together in sets to be carried on the butler's towel to table. They were used as a kind of bread pad on which the diners cut their food and were not consumed. Placing the covered salt-cellar on the table was also the responsibility of the pantler, who used a pouder, or 'salt-planer', a flat blade of ivory 'two inches broad and three long', to ensure that the surface of the salt was smooth.[12]

The loaves that were actually eaten at high table were the manchets, small six-ounce rolls made from boulted white flour. These were chipped or pared to remove any hard or burnt crust, though pantlers were instructed not to cut too close to the crumb. This was done with a chipping knife, or 'chyppere'. As well as softening the loaves, the chipping process removed any small fragments of charcoal and wood ash which may have adhered to the underside of the loaf from the oven floor. It was essential to remove this dirt, as it would have spoilt the table linen.[13]

The pantler was not allowed to touch the trenchers or manchets with his hands. He had to carry them from the pantry on a linen towel wrapped round his neck and draped along the full length of his left arm.[14] Eight white manchet rolls for eating and four loaves of ready prepared trenchers were carefully balanced on his left arm, over which was also draped his lord's napkin. He used his left hand, also covered with the towel, to carry the

The Palace Kitchen, 1610
From Scappi, *Dell'arte del cucinare*, Rome 1610
Photograph: Jeremy Phillips for Fairfax House, York
The cook roasts meats on a spit whilst a range of steaming pots sit on a bank of stewing stoves to the right. Various utensils can be seen on the tables, but also above the stoves is a suspended wooden tree trunk or block in which most of the knives are impaled for storage. Notice also the fleshing knife with its hooked tip, seen on the cutting bench and the serrated pastry cutter on the left-hand tressle.

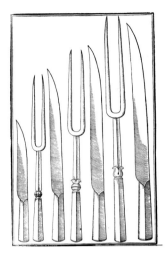

Carving knives and forks, 1593
From Cervio, *Il Trinciante*, Venice, 1593
Photograph: Metropolitan Museum of Art, New York
Instructions in manuals like this volume suggest that the carver had three sets of differing sizes in order to complete his duties satisfactorily.

principal salt-cellar. The end of the towel was held in his right hand, which was used to bear his lord's knife and spoon. The trenchers and manchets were then carefully wrapped in a special towel called a covertour or coverpain and placed on a side table. After the pantler had delivered the bread and trenchers it was the carver's duty to lay and prepare them for his lord. At the beginning of grace the coverpains were removed and the almoner placed an 'almes dysshe' on the table.[15]

After grace the diners washed their hands, the lord first, then those 'such as ben ordeyned to sytte at the sovraynes mess', followed by the rest of the hall. As soon as everyone was seated, the carver placed an offering of a loaf in the alms dish 'to serve god fyrst'.[16] He then picked up four trenchers on his 'table knife' and presented or 'cowched' them before his sovereign, a little to the left of the principal salt. The exact method of cowching could vary. Sometimes two were put down together, the third one on top of these and the fourth situated on its own in front. This last trencher was used for salt, which was removed from the salt-cellar on the tip of the knife. In France, three trenchers were arranged in a triangle with a fourth one on top. Russell instructs one to lay four on the cloth with a fifth on top. Less important diners were given only one. During the course of the sixteenth century, wooden trenchers rapidly started to replace those of bread.[17]

As well as presenting the trenchers, the carver had to 'pare' the manchet loaves into convenient pieces for his lord. The practice of this also seems to have varied. Russell tells us to 'kutt the upper crust for your souerayne'. This portion may have been considered superior because it had not come into contact with the ashes on the oven floor. Other courtesy books instruct the carver to cut the manchet roll into half horizontally and then slice the upper portion into three and the lower into two pieces. The roll was then reassembled and placed beside the lord's trenchers.[18]

The sewer's task was to arrange and serve the various dishes at high table and to this end he worked very closely with the carver. He needed a thorough working knowledge of the order of service and the correct sauce for each dish. Brawn was always served with

Carving in mid-air, 1639
Engraving: in Geigher, Mattia, *Li tre trattati di Messer*, Padua, 1639
Photograph: courtesy of a private collection
Using a long tine fork the carver demonstrates how to carve a duck *in alto*.

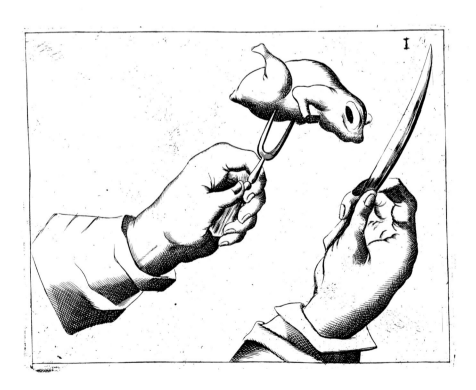

mustard, venison with frumenty, while sparrows and thrushes were dredged with salt and cinnamon. Many more species of bird and fish were consumed at the medieval table than we would consider eating today. At Archbishop Neville's feast 234 cranes, 1,000 egrets and 200 dozen sandpipers were among the delicacies. This taste for unusual wildfowl and game continued well into the sixteenth and seventeenth centuries.[19]

Important meals usually consisted of two to four courses, each containing an assortment of dishes. There were rules for the succession of dishes – web-footed birds were to be served first and of these the largest kinds, such as swan and goose, before duck. Smaller land fowl and baked meats followed.[20] A sculptural centrepiece called a soteltie or device was sometimes displayed during each course. These were usually religious or heraldic in nature and frequently incorporated some scriptural text or verse.[21]

In between courses and at the end of the meal, the table was cleared or 'voided', a process superintended by the sewer and carver. Uneaten food and used trenchers were placed in a voiding basket and the crumbs cleared with the carver's knife, 'Set down a charger or a voyder & gadre vp the fragmentes therin, & wt the voydynge knyfe gadre vp the cromes clene'.[22] The last course, or void, usually consisted of fruit, cheese, wafers, spices and hippocras,

> *Whot appuls & peres with sugr Candy,*
> *With Gyngre columbyne, mynsed mannerly,*
> *Wafurs with ypocras.*
> *Now this feste is fynysced.*[23]

Of all the offices of the table, that of the carver was the most demanding. Every joint, bird and fish had to be carved 'according to art' and a complex specialist terminology was used to describe the various methods. In 1508 Wynken de Worde summarised these in the list opposite.

Generations of young henchmen and yeomen who desired 'the connynge of a kervere' must have learnt this table of 'goodly terms' by heart. It continued to be reprinted in cookery books well into the eighteenth century.[24] Instructions in the nurture books for carrying out these procedures are frequently detailed. However, a great deal of practical experience 'in the fayre handlinge of a knyfe' would have been necessary before a carver became accomplished enough to practise his art at the table of a king or archbishop.

Some carving procedures were highly codified. For instance, to carve venison, or 'break deer', the meat was cut into twelve small dice, each of which was conveyed into the lord's frumenty pottage on the blade of the carving knife. The carver had to avoid serving any 'fumosities' to his lord. These were items considered to be indigestible or dangerous to health, such as fat, undercooked meat, sinews, skin, feathers and bones. Only the best portions found their way on to the lord's trenchers. After cutting and serving each dish, the carver cleaned his knife on his napkin.

The carver held his knife with the two forefingers and thumb of his right hand, the haft securely in his palm. He held the meat he was carving with the two forefingers and thumb of his left hand, which had to be kept scrupulously clean. It was strictly forbidden to touch food with the right hand. There are no references to carving forks in any fifteenth- and sixteenth-century English books of nurture. Nevertheless, they were being used for carving meat in Spain in the early fifteenth century.[25] They were also almost certainly used in Italy at this time, but were not illustrated in detail until the publication of Vicenzo Cervio's *Il Trinciante* in 1581.[26] Italian carving forks had very long tines, which enabled the carver to impale the meat and to carve it in mid-air, or *in alto*. A plate in Bartolomeo Scappi's important cookery book of 1570 shows a carver using a long-tined fork of this

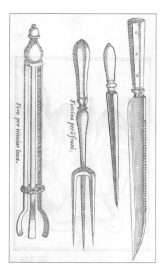

Utensils for the Carver, 1593
From Cervio, *Il Trinciante*, Venice, 1593
Photograph: Metropolitan Museum of Art, New York
This illustration shows a large, serrated knife for meat, a smaller, pointed hone or pairing knife, and a fork for fruit. The special three-pronged utensil is identified as an 'iron to carve the egg'. Cervio and other contemporary cooking books inform us that a favourite dish at this time was *nova de bere*, an 'egg to drink'. Exactly how the carver could clamp the egg, cut off the top, season it and serve without disturbing the contents is still not clear.

Carving set and présentoir, 1639

Engraving in Geigher, Mattia, *Li tre trattati di Messer*, Padua, 1639

Photograph: courtesy of a private collection

A carving set with broad-bladed présentoir. The spatula-like knife was used for serving and could probably help remove bread crumbs and litter from the table cloth. It is possible this is what early English nurture books and inventories refer to as a 'voiding knife' or 'trencher knife'.

Termes of a Kerver

Breke that dere	thye that wodcocke
lesche that brawne	thye all maner of small byrdes
rere that goose	tymbre that fyre
lyft that swanne	tyere that egge
sauce that capon	chyne that samon
spoyle that henne	strynge that lampraye
frusshe that chekyn	splatte that pyke
vnbrace that malarde	sauce that playce
vnlace that cony	sauce that tenche
dysmembre that heron	splaye that breme
dysplaye that crane	syde that haddocke
dysfygure that pecocke	tuske that barbell
vnioynt that bytture	culpon that troute
vntache that curlewe	fynne that cheuen
alaye that fesande	transsene that ele
wynge that partryche	traunche that sturgyon
wynge that quayle	vndertraunche that purpos
mynce that plouer	tayme that crabbe
thye that pegyon	barbe that lobster
border that pasty	[27]

kind to support a fairly large joint *in alto*, which he appears to be rapidly cutting into small slices (see p. 35).[28]

The earliest surviving English carving forks date from the seventeenth century (see opposite). They have short tines and could only have been used for stabilising the meat on the plate while carving. There is no evidence to suggest that carving in mid-air was practised in this country.[29] In fact the English seem to have been very conservative on the whole subject – Russell's instructions to carvers dating from the 1440s were still the last word on the subject in the seventeenth century. A work claiming to be *A New Book of Carving*, published in London in 1631 (fourth edition), was actually Wynken de Worde's précis of Russell's *Boke of Nurture*, with very little effort being made to modernise the original author's archaic English. However, it was a popular book, running into at least seven editions (seventh 1650). A translation of the much more up-to-date French carving book *L'Ecuyer-Tranchant* (1662) was eventually published in London in 1682.[30] Its detailed 'dissection' illustrations and directions for Italian-style carving are heavily dependent on the works of Cervio and Geigher, but it was not successful and only one edition was ever printed.[31] Continental carving methods do not appear to have caught on with the British. As late as 1783 directions for lifting swans, displaying cranes and dismembering herons in true medieval English style were still being given by John Farley, the principal cook of the London Tavern.[32]

The sentiments of the medieval English courtesy and carving books are also still strongly evident in John Trusler's *Honours of the Table*, a small work on table manners and carving 'for the use of young people', published in 1788. On the title page, the author quotes from Lord Chesterfield's *Letters*, 'To do the honours of the table gracefully, is one of the outlines of a well-bred man; and to carve well, little as it may seem, is useful twice

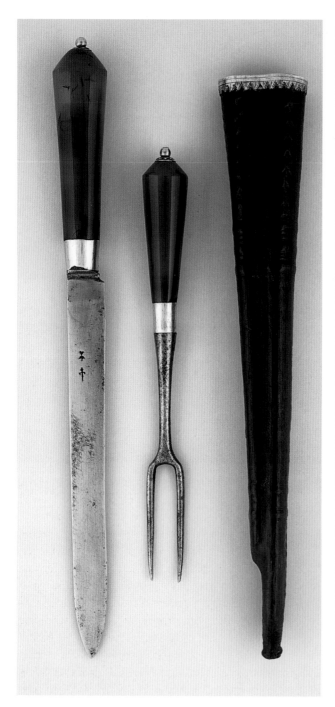

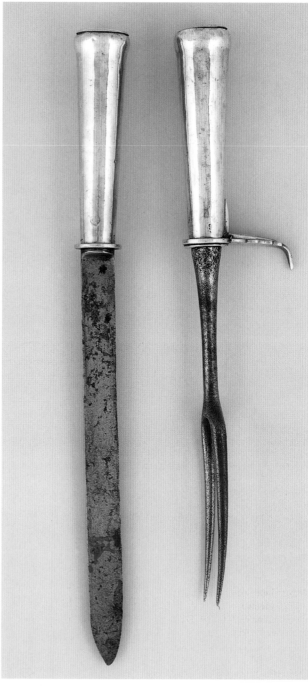

Above

Carving knife and fork
Iron, the knife with parallel-sided blade, centre point tip and mean bolster. The fork with tapered stem and two steel tines of round section. The tapering ,round agate handles are secured to the through-tang with silver ferrules, silver knobs and washered ends. The knife marked on blade with heart and dart for John Wharrey and the dagger of the Cutlers' Company of London, c.1667. *B147*
Length of knife: 35.5cm
The original leather slip case is decorated with panels of thistles and banded in imitation of stave construction. At the rim is a silver ferrule which provides reinforcement.

Above

Carving knife and fork
Iron, the knife with parallel blade, centre point tip and mean bolster. The tapered, iron stem fork has two tines of round section. Both are fitted with plain silver cartridge handles and the 'seal top' engraved with the arms of the Ingram family of Temple Newsam, Leeds. Both have small, round silver guards, the fork with extended shaped catch plate. Marked on knife blade with letter 'K' over 'Y', probably the mark of William Boswell and the dagger for the Cutlers' Company of London, c.1668. *B152*
Length: 30cm

every day, and the doing of which ill is not only troublesome to ourselves, but renders us disagreeable and ridiculous to others'. Later in the book, Trusler expands on Chesterfield's observations that, 'We are always in pain for a man, who, instead of cutting up a fowl genteelly, is hacking for half an hour across a bone, greasing himself and bespattering the company with the sauce'.[33]

Trusler's thoughts on bad table manners also have strong echoes of the early courtesy books, 'it is exceedingly rude, to scratch any part of your body, to spit, or blow your nose (if you can't avoid it turn your head), to act greedily, to lean your elbows on the table, to sit too far from it, to pick your teeth before the dishes are removed'. Compare this to the following lines from John Rhodes' *Boke of Nurture* (c.1550):

> *Scratch not thy head with thy fingers*
> *When thou arte at thy meate;*
> *Nor spytte you over the table boorde:*
> *See thou doest not this forget.*
> *Pick not thy teeth with thy Knyfe*
> *Nor with thy fingers ende, …*
> *Blow not your nose on the napkin*
> *Where you would wipe your hande.*[34]

A hundred years before Rhodes composed these lines, Russell warned his protégé in a much more graphic style about unacceptable behaviour at high table,

> *Good son, thy tethe be not pikyng, grisynge, ne gnastyng;*
> *Ne stynkinge of brethe on youre soveragne casting;*
> *With puffynge ne blowynge, nowther fulle ne fastynge;*
> *And all wey be ware of thy hyndur part from gunnes blastynge.*[35]

At medieval feasts, women of royal birth could join their male family relatives at their mess, but those of lower rank were segregated to their own tables. This practice continued well into the early modern period and at some court functions women were only allowed to watch the proceedings from a gallery. However, when Trusler wrote his book in the late eighteenth century, it was becoming acceptable in England for the sexes to be mixed much more freely, a new fashion he called 'promiscuous seating'. Men and women might be seated alternately round the table, but the servants still had to serve them according to rank. Trusler has some interesting observations on the demeanour of female diners, 'As eating a great deal is deemed indelicate in a lady (for her character should be rather divine than sensual), it will be ill-manners to help her to a large slice of meat at once, or fill her plate too full'. It was also common at this time for the mistress of the household to help her husband with the carving. Smaller carving knives and forks were designed with ladies in mind. The master would carve the large joints at one end of the table, while his wife would tackle those dishes before her at the opposite end.

Rolls of estate continued to be vital to servants responsible for seating guests well into the nineteenth century and are still used at court today. In *The Footman's Directory* of 1823 Thomas Cosnett published two, one for gentlemen and one for ladies. By this time footmen needed to know where to seat military officers and up-and-coming professionals such as physicians, as well as the aristocrats and high-ranking clerics whose estates had remained more or less unaltered since the fourteenth century. Cosnett tells us that naval officers had to be given a more honourable place than army officers. Married sisters had to be seated above widows, but widows had priority over their unmarried sisters. Sorting out 'who was who' must have been a nightmare.

Dessert being served at a party, c. 1725 (detail)
Marcellus Laroon II (1679–1772), oil on canvas, 36 × 34 in

Photograph: by gracious permission of Her Majesty the Queen

The host, a knight of the garter, displays his skills with an osier-covered bottle probably containing the sweet red 'mountain' wine of Malaga. A young page attends with a large-footed salver which he will use to distribute the drinks among the assembly.

It is an informal gathering and the guests are seated in the 'promiscuous manner'. On the left the hostess distributes sugar 'comfits' from her gold casket.

Notes and references

1 Anon., *The Great Feast, at the Inthronization of the Reverend Father in God, George Neavill Arch-Bishop of Yorke, Chancellour of England, in the sixt yere of Edward the fourth. Wherein is manifested the great pride in vaine glory of that prelate. The copy of this feast was found inrolled in the Tower of London, and was taken out by Mr. Noy*, London; printed for Edward Husbands, 1645. In addition to the 2,000 principal guests, 4,000 were fed outside the hall. See also h.b., *The Accomplished Ladies Delight* (seventh edition), London, 1696 and King, Richard John, *Handbook to the Cathedrals of England: Southern Division*, London, 1903.

2 Furnival, F. J. (editor), *Early English Meals and Manners*, Early English Text Society, O.U.P., 1868, iv. See also Furnival, F. J. (ed.), *John Russell, The Boke of Nurture*, Roxburghe Club, Bungay, 1867.

3 In 1565, much to the surprise of her courtiers, Queen Elizabeth did away with these 'chyldrene of honor', 'Her highnes hath of late, whereat some doo moche marvel, dissolved the auncient office of the henchemen'. Alen, F., *Letter to Earl Shrewsbury*, 11 December 1565, in Lodge, Edmund, *Illustrations of British History, Biography and Manners in the reigns of Henry VIII, Edward VI, Mary, Elizabeth, and James I*, London, 1791 I. 358.

4 *The Regulations and Establishment of the Household of Henry Algernon Percy 1512.* New edition, London, 1905.

5 Seager, F., *The School of Vertue, and booke of good Nourture for children and youth to learne their duty by*, London, 1557.

6 Furnival, F.J., *Caxton's Boke of Curtesye*, Early English Text Society, O.U.P., 1868. *Boke of Kervinge*, Wynken de Worde (printer), London, 1508.

7 Murrell, John, *Murrells Two books of Cookerie and Carving*, London, 1638 (fifth edition). This is really a reprint of Wynken de Worde's *Boke of Kervinge*, itself a précis of Russell's book. It was probably first published in 1630. May, Robert, *The Accomplisht Cook*, London, 1660: this seminal work also contains a shortened version of Wynken de Worde's text and table of carving terms.

8 In Wynken de Worde's *Boke of Kervinge* there is a similar roll of estate, almost certainly plagiarised from Russell's work. In the Cambridge University Library's copy of the book, an unknown reader defaced this list during the Reformation. The line 'A pope hath no pere' has been inked out and a marginal annotation tells us that he should be placed 'lower down' together with his cardinals and bishops!

9 Turner, Thomas Hudson, *Some Account of Domestic Architecture in England, from the Conquest to the end of the Thirteenth Century*, Oxford, 1851–59, vol. 3, pp. 157–58.
   The earliest mention of a trencher knife seems to be in an inventory written by the Earl of Derby's treasurer in 1392, 'Clerico panetrie per manus eiusdem, pro j trenchurknyff per ipsum empto'. Smith, Lucy T. (editor), *Expeditions to Prussia and the Holy Land made by Henry Earl of Derby, afterwards King Henry IV, in the years 1390-1 and 1392-3. Being the accounts kept by his Treasurer during two years*, Camden Society, London, 1894, p.195.

10 The word trencher could also signify the blade of a knife, 'My baselard hath a trencher kene, Fayr as rasour scharp and schene', c.1400. In *Song's Costume*, Percy Society, 1849, p. 50. A baselard was a kind of dagger or knife worn at the girdle. If the trencher knife was that used to present or 'cowche' trenchers, it may have been synonymous with the carver's table or 'boorde' knife (mensal knife, *mensalis*) used to remove crumbs from the tablecloth. Hugh Rhodes, in his *Boke of Nurture*, London, c.1550 instructs the carver to remove crumbs, 'Then with your Trenchour knife take off such fragmentes, and put them in your Voyder'. Also known as voiding knives, these seem to have been broad-bladed spatulas rather than orthodox knives. One is illustrated in Mattia Geigher's *Li tre trattati*, Padova, 1639.

11 Markham, Gervase, *The English Housewife*, London, 1615. Markham gives detailed instructions for making both cheat bread and manchets.

12 Russell, John, *Boke of Nurture*, p. 4, in *Early English Meals and Manners*, edited by F .J. Furnival, Early English Text Society, O.U.P., 1868.

13 The coarse 'Chippings of Trencher-Brede' were used in the Duke of Northumberland's household for the fedyinge of my lords houndis', *Percy Household Book* p. 353. However, in the royal palaces, all bread chippings were given to the pantlers as a perk of the office: 'The yeomen [of the Pantry] have for their fees, all the chippings of breade…for the which they find chipping knives', *Queen Elizabeth's Household. Book* (1601). In *A Collection of Ordinances and Regulations for the Government of the Royal Household, made in divers reigns, from King Edward III. to King William and Queen Mary*. London, 1790, p. 294. The curious practice of rasping bread or 'chipping' continued into the eighteenth and nineteenth centuries. However, by this time, a file-like tool called a bread rasper had replaced the medieval chipping knife.

14 These towels varied in length. In a list of 'the household stuff occupied at the Lord Mayor's Feast' in 1505, we are told that the 'butlers towellis' were an ell and a half long and a quarter broad. Since the English ell at this time was about 45 inches, this would have made them just less than two yards long and slightly over 11 inches wide. At the same occasion, the towels used by the sewers and carvers were the same length, but twice as wide. Those used at court were even longer. Balliol *Ms*. 354, ffl C iii.

15 Grace, led by the almoner, was recited in Latin and varied in content and length according to the time of year. The graces recited on feast days were not the same as those used on fish days, while the graces before and after dinner differed from those at supper.

16 Furnival, ibid., p. 202.

17 Sometimes wooden trenchers were placed on plates of precious metal to protect the surface from knife damage. Brears, Peter, *All the King's Cooks*, Souvenir Press, London, 1999, p. 175.

18 Russell, John, *Boke of Nurture*, Furnival, 1868, p. 23.

19 The following extract from a poem by Edward Hake, describes some of the dishes enjoyed at a London livery company feast in 1579:
   Both Capon, Swan and Hernshoe good, fat Bitturne, Larke, and Quayle:
   Right Plover, Snype, and Woodcock fine, with Curlew, Wype and Rayle;
   Stonetivets, Teale, and Peeteales good, with Busterd fat and plum,
   Fat Pheasaunt Powt, and Plover base for them that after come.
   Stent, Stockard, Stampine, Tanterveale, and wigeon of the best;
   Puyt, Partrich, Blackbirds and fat Shoveler with the rest.
   From E. Hake, *Newes out of Powles Churchyard*, London, 1579.

20 Morris, Richard (editor), *Liber cure cocorum*, (Sloane Ms., 1986) Berlin, 1862, p. 55.

21 In a bill of fare for a late fifteenth-century bridal feast, the soteltie accompanying the first course was a sculpture of a lamb with the text, 'I meekly unto you, sovrayne, am sente, to dwell with you, and ever be present'. That of the second course was 'an antelope sayng on a sele that saith with scriptour, beith all glad & mery that sitteth at this messe and pray for the king and all his'. An angel with the verse 'thanke all, god, of this feste' featured in the third course. The soteltie of the fourth and final course was appropriately 'a wif lying in childe-bed, with a scriptour'. Very rarely, the subject matter contained references to themes from classical antiquity. The first course soteltie at the wedding feast (after 1414) of Hugh Courtenay, Duke of Devonshire (1389–1422) was a sculpture of Ceres, one of the earliest recorded uses of a pagan deity in English art. Made from food materials and wax, brightly painted and gilded, these edible

sculptures probably resembled the polychrome sculpture of the period. Harleian Ms. 279. See Austin, Thomas, *Two Fifteenth-Century Cookery-Books*, Early English Text Society, O.U.P, 1888.

Another detailed description of a soteltie is given by Robert Fabyan, in his account of the coronation feast of Henry VI. He describes a representation of the Virgin and Child, with St George and St Denis kneeling on either side, presenting the Queen with a small figure of Henry. The king holds a scroll on which are written the following verses:

'O blessyd Lady, Cristes moder dere,
And thou, seynt George! that called art her knyght;
Holy seynt Denys, 0 marter most entere,
The sixt Henry here present in your syght,
Shedyth, of your grace, on him your heuenly lyght:
His tender youth with vertue doth auaunce,
Borne by discent, and by tytle of ryght,
Iustly to reygne in Englande and in Fraunce.'

In Fabyan, Robe*rt, The Chronicles of Fabyan*, R. Pynson, London, 1516.

22 Whittington, Robert, *Uulgaria Roberti whitintoni Lichfeldiensis, et de institutione grammaticulorum Opusculum: libello suo de concinnitate grammatices accomodatu: & i quatuor partes Lodon.: impres. apud wynadum de worde*, 1527, 42b.

23 Russell, *Boke of Nurture*, Furnival, F. J., 1868, p. 52. Fruit was also served before a meal to whet the appetite. Russell tells us that plums, damsons and grapes were all suitable for this purpose. Furnival, F. J., 1868, p. 6.

24 Anon, *The Whole Duty of a Woman*, London, 1701, Nott, John, *The Cooks and Confectioner's Dictionary*, London, 1723. Both these works give instructions for carving based on Wynken de Worde's list of terms and directions.

25 Carving forks are illustrated in the *Arte Cisoria* of Enriques de Aragón (1423), the earliest surviving treatise on carving. They appear among drawings of various other carving tools, some of which resemble Arab surgical instruments. Enrique de Aragón, Marqués de Villena, *Arte cisoria, ò del tratado del arte del cortar del cuchillo*, Madrid, 1766.

26 Cervio, Vincenzo, *Il Trinciante*, Venezia, 1581.

27 Wynken de Worde, *The Boke of Kervinge*, London, 1508.

28 Scappi, Bartolomeo, *Opera*, Venezia, 1570.

29 Perhaps the earliest description in English of using a fork for carving is in Wooley, Hannah, *The Queen-like Closet*, London, 1670. The authoress tells us that the carver, equipped a with knife and fork probably identical to that illustrated in plate 00, should 'take the dish he should carve from the Table till he hath made it ready for his Superiours to eat and handsomely to carve it, not touching of it so near as he can with his fingers…the neatest Carvers never touch any Meat but with the Knife and Fork: he must be very nimble lest the Meat cool too much, and when he hath done, return to the Table again, putting away his Carving Napkin, and take a clean one to wait withal: he must be very Gentile and Gallant in his Habit, lest he be deemed unfit to attend such Persons'.

30 The translation of *L'Ecuyer-Tranchant* (first published Paris, 1662) is the chapter called *A Master Carver* in Rose, Giles, *A Perfect School of Instructions for the Officers of the Mouth: shewing the whole art of a master of the household, a master carver, a master butler, a master confectioner, a master cook, a pastryman…adorned with pictures curiously ingraven, displaying the whole arts; by Giles Rose, one of the master cooks in His Majesties kitchen*, London, 1682.

31 The most influential carving book of the early seventeenth century was *Li tre trattati di Messer. Mattia Giegher bavaro di Mosburg*, Padova, 1639. Geigher was a member of the German community in Padua. Illustrated with detailed etchings, it was much plagiarised by other authors of carving books. Georg Harsdörfer's *Vollständiges Trincer-Büchlein* (Nuremburg c.1640), the most important German carving book of the period was heavily dependent on it. It also influenced carving books published in Holland (Anon., *De Cierlyke Voorsnydinge aller Tafel-Gerechten,*.Amsterdam, c.1668) and Sweden (Anon., *En Myket Nyttig Och Förbettrad Trenchier-bok*, Vesterås, 1696). Remarkably, copies of Geigher's illustrations were still being reproduced in French carving books nearly a decade after the Revolution (Anon., *L'Art de découper les alouettes*. Paris, 1796).

32 Farley, John, *The London Art of Cookey*, London, 1783.

33 Trusler, John, *The Honours of the Table*, London, 1788. Carving books similar to Trusler's little work continued to be published in the nineteenth century. The most important was *The Hand-book of Carving: with hints on the etiquette of the dinner table*, London, 1848. The anonymous author's sentiments echo those of Trusler and Lord Chesterfield, 'Nothing can be more disagreeable to one of a sensitive disposition, than to behold a person at the head of a well-furnished board, hacking the finest joints, and giving them the appearance of having been gnawed by the dogs'.

34 Rhodes, Hugh, *Boke of Nurture*, London, c.1550

35 Russell, John, *Boke of Nurture*, Furnival, 1868, p. 20.

Late Elizabethan place-setting, c.1600

Photograph: Jeremy Phillips for Fairfax House, York

Two types of wooden trencher from the Norwich Castle Museum are in use, the rectangular version, some 15 × 10cm in size, depicts the apocryphal story of Lazarus and the rich man's table, whilst the roundel decorated with some knotwork patterns and uplifting spiritual text displays a selection of dry sweetmeats of the period.

The pair of knives with agate handles is part of a set of five, c.1600 in a free-standing travelling case (not shown).

In attendance is a silver spice box, 1610, from the Bowes Museum, Barnard Castle, a Norwich wine cup of c.1605, a small slip top spoon of the same period. To the left a folded napkin, c.1595, woven in Flanders, tells the story of Abraham and Isaac.

Dining by Design

Peter Brown

Knife

Iron, with through-tang and solid
bolster, terminating in a copper-
alloy finial. The shaped horn
handle is inscribed with the
motto: BETTER IT IS A POORE HOUSE
TO HOLD THAN TO LY IN PRISON IN
FETTERS OF GOULD. The blade, of
earlier medieval shape, bears the
mark of a tree.

Housed in the original leather
sheath, stamped with medallions
of roses and floral pendants over
a pattern of vertical lines and
banding in imitation of staves.
Both sheath and cover are pierced
with loop-holes which allow
both pieces to be kept together
without loss.
English, c.1550. *B85*
Length of case: 21.5cm
Length of knife: 20.5cm

Although we are certainly much less concerned about hierachy and sensibility at supper
parties today, entertaining guests at home around a well laid out dining-room table has
experienced a renaissance in recent years. A proliferation of cookery programmes, from
Naked Chef to *Two Fat Ladies* has rekindled our interest in the delights of food and helped
to focus attention on the pleasures of dining at a table where all the senses are being
brought into play.

Large superstores make the realisation of this all too easy for us; we obligingly shuffle
past a series of well lit fantasy dining rooms arranged with matching cutlery, crockery and
glass, then stroll painlessly into the warehouse to purchase all the items on display at
heavily discounted prices. The economic advantages of mass production and bulk buying
are obvious, but it has also meant that patterns of behaviour which were the prerogative of
a privileged middle and upper class are now being enjoyed by the great majority of the
population.

Ivan Day, in his essay, has shown that a great deal of attention was paid to the question
of how to behave in company at table, a situation where people found themselves put
closely together, in a position to watch and be watched by others. From medieval times the
tables of the wealthy were being structured to maintain the position and importance of the
guests. Prints like the German banquet of Nuremberg (page 68) help us understand the
hierachy when we observe the limited number of objects available on the secondary tables.
The lord, however, has a grand standing salt, a popular status symbol on dining-room
tables even into the seventeenth century (p. 46). Central to each place-setting was the
bread trencher and the personal cutlery associated with this period, usually placed to the
right of the main trencher and comprising a knife and spoon (B70 and B71, p. 71) are good
examples of cutlery in use in England during this period). Forks were being used in
Southern European countries at this time; Lorenzo de' Medici, for example, possessed
eighteen silver forks and matching spoons in 1491,[1] but as David Mitchell has shown,
nearly two centuries were to pass before we see them in common usage in Britain.

The *Book of Nurture*[2] provides us with an early description of a complete table setting
for a lord. In this, the author notes that on spreading the tablecloth a salt cellar should be
placed at your lord's right hand, to the left of it one or two trenchers, then a knife, then
white rolls, then a spoon resting on a folded napkin. The trencher, knife and spoon were
then to be protected with an elaborate coverpane (a decorated cloth used to keep the place-
setting clean). These coverpanes were not usually available for ordinary guests in the
fifteenth century and given the paucity of knives in early inventories, it seems likely only
spoons were being provided. The visitors could, of course, bring their own cutlery with
them, but evidence of knives designed for travelling, i.e., housed in their own case, is rare
before 1550 (see B85, left, for a superb example from this period).

Napery played an important role in the arrangement of the dining table. Damask
napkins and tablecloths were expensive items to be treasured and prized, and this
reverence may help explain why it is rare at formal dinners to discover references to glasses
or cups being placed or left on the table in the manner that is common today. To reduce
the risk of staining the cloth, the vessels for wine or beer were usually filled at the

sideboard, away from the table. The base of the glass was then thoroughly dried and brought on a waiter or salver to the person requesting it. The footman waited for the drink to be consumed and afterwards took the glass or beaker back to the sideboard where he would rinse, dry and place it back on display. Such a system can only function, of course, if there are sufficient servants to attend the dinner guests and in England the development of a country-house system where large numbers of dependencies were associated with the estate meant there was usually a plentiful supply of servants who could fulfil these functions.

By the end of the sixteenth century the most significant development taking place on the dining-room table was the replacement of the bread trencher with one made of wood or metal. A 1594 inventory for Sir William Fairfax at Gilling Castle lists amongst the contents:

Pantrye

Item v dozin Trenchers xs
Item one dozin rounde Trenchers ijs

White Plate

Item one dossen of silver plates cont Vxx xj ounces
Item ij dossen of silver sponnes cont XLiX ounces
Item one spice box with a sponne cont XV ounces[3]

The Gilling trenchers were made of maple[4] and a clear distinction is noted in the 'pantrye' between the normal rectangular shape and the round examples probably used for the sweet banquet course. These 'roundels', 'trencher plates' or 'poesies', as they were often referred to, were charmingly decorated on one side with flowers, animals and improving texts. A fine example in Bill Brown's collection (B113, p. 82) is inscribed with the verse:

The lion snard the mouse entreats for help – the mouse the fetters freates.
Meaning – the men of high degree by poorer men released may be.

Sizes vary in diameter from 12cm to 18cm but they are still quite small, being only intended as receptacles for prepared food. The silver plates in the Gilling inventory weigh some 42ozs each and were probably intended as chargers or servers. Poesies could also be made from sugar and a rare shaped and decorated example is illustrated on page 20.

Netherlandish paintings are our best source of European table settings for the early part of the seventeenth century. That they depict real objects must be beyond doubt, the only remaining question being whether the artist rearranged everything for his or her convenience. One painter who seems more reliable than others is Clara Peeters, working in Flanders from c.1615 to c.1640.[5] Her settings are extraordinary compilations of food and objects meticulously recorded in marvellous detail. Her tables of the wealthy are shown laden with produce from home and abroad, leaving little space for the participant to fit his plate on to the table. Other artists show the table arranged in this way and it is perhaps one reason why the napkin has moved away from the left-hand side of the plate

Lazarus and the rich man's table, c.1605
Frans Franken II (1581–1642)
oil on panel, 76 × 107cm
Photograph: courtesy of the German Bread Museum, Ulm
Illustrating the parable of Dives and Lazarus (Luke 16, 19–34), this image offers an interesting combination of still life and figurative painting and provides a sophisticated interpretation of a popular religious theme. The meal, and indeed the metaphor, is being concluded with the arrival of the desert course. To the right a servant enters with a large fruit pie decorated with the word EPILOG, whilst on top is the stem of a lily coated in sugar. White lilies are often used to symbolise purity, charity or goodness, but the artist gives this example a black trumpet to represent the evil and greed of the uncaring rich man.

In the centre of the table is a raised pie, probably still warm, with stamped and cut-work decoration. Notice how part of the upper-crust has been carefully removed and placed on top to allow access to the warm meat. The spoons, the rosemary toothpicks, and silver-handled knife stand ready to play their part in the consumption of the meal.

If one assumes the artist is being faithful in his representation, it is interesting to note that the guests have a wine glass each, but there are only two spoons, two toothpicks and one knife to share amongst this august company.

and starts to appear on the plate, often folded to enclose a bread roll. It may also be a valiant attempt to keep the bread warm, but whatever the reason, Peeters is utterly convincing and achieves what she set out to do, to appeal to our sensory and culinary appetites.

There were several artists who made a speciality of these table-settings,[6] and a study of their works shows the spoon moving away from the side of the plate and taking up position next to the pie. One such detail is seen below where the pie case is used as a form of tureen like container and the spoons stand guard at the entrance to the 'temple'. Notice also the toothpicks deployed about the table. These were often made from rosemary,[7] presumably because the scent would help to freshen the breath.

Personal hygiene was becoming increasingly important at both individual and group level throughout the seventeenth century and this had a fundamental effect on the evolution of dining practices. Compared to the Middle Ages, the standards of delicacy required in any given social situation had increased dramatically. 'It is very impolite', wrote Antoine Courtin in 1672, 'to touch anything greasy, a sauce or syrup etc, with your fingers, apart from the fact that it obliges you to commit two or three more improper acts. One is

to wipe your hand frequently on your serviette and to soil it like a kitchen cloth, so that those who see you wipe your mouth will feel nauseated. Another is to wipe your fingers on your bread, which again is very improper. The third is to lick them, which is the height of impropriety.'[8]

The German philosopher Norbert Elias argues that it was this gradual refinement in manners and civilised behaviour which gave rise to the common usage of the fork.[9] Such a movement would certainly have been a significant factor, but there were other events which must have played their part: the return of Charles II to the throne, for example, bringing with him a long exposure to European dining practices, the dramatic rise in wealth and consumerism; increasing trade with the Far East and a resurgence in manuals of instruction, are just a few of the other contributing factors. What they were all doing, of course, was to help ritualise and refine our so-called 'principles of politeness' and flesh out new codified behaviour patterns.

In 1682 Giles Rose, one-time master cook in Charles II's kitchen, published his translation of the anonymous 1661 French tome *L'Ecole parfait des officers de bouche*.[10] He included the duties of senior members of the household and there are some curious divisions of labour. The butler, for example, was responsible for the carving of fruit into fanciful shapes, but primarily, he carried out the duties we have come to expect of this post.

Rose's description for the presentation of a seventeenth-century dining room has not been published in recent times and is worthy of repetition:

> *The hour of Dinner or Supper being now come [presumably around 3.00 pm], he and his helper or servant, takes the basket into the hall or chambers where they are to eat; not forgetting the pepper-box, and cruet of vinegar both furnished, the one carrying one, the other with them into the room.*
>
> *And so soon as you are come into the room set down the basket, and so begin to cover the side-table first, with a clean cloth, and then set on your plate; first your bason and ewer; and your flagons ranged against the Tapestry-hanging, mingled one amongst the other; then underneath compose another range of essay (sic) cups, sugar-castars, and glasses with the feet downward, and upon each of them put an Essay Cup, or cover over them.*
>
> *This done, the Butler begins to cover the table thus, first the table cloth, then the salts, and the riders for plates, or enter-mese, then the plates with the coat of arms towards the middle of the table, so many as are necessary, but let them not touch the edge of the table by three or four fingers. At the right hand of each plate place a knife, with the edge towards the plate, then the spoons, the brim or edge of the spoon downwards, with forks; but be sure not to cross or lay them one on the other, then the Bread upon the plate, and the napkin upon the bread, and so much for covering a table.*[11]

The concentration of all cutlery on the right-hand side of the plate (with spoon and fork face down) is a typical French trait.[12] The left hand was used to hold the napkin up to the throat whilst the right hand selects the required item of cutlery to cut or transfer food from plate to mouth. It would be interesting to determine just how much influence Rose's publication had on English presentation at table and whether this manual proved a further impetus for the large-scale production of English forks. Rose also recommends that the number of plates should far exceed the number of persons present and spare plates be formed in piles along the side table with napkins on top folded in *baston rompu* or broken staff, 'and over this another or more, if need so require, unfolded, which serves to wipe the hands when washed'.

Folding napery into fanciful designs was a further innovation for Rose's publication

The Reade Salt, silver-gilt, 1568
William Cobbold, Norwich,
Photograph: Jeremy Phillips for Fairfax House, York
Reproduced by courtesy of Norwich City Council
A drum-shaped body decorated with engraved shield between masks and garlands. The warrior finial holds a shield bearing the arms of the City of Norwich.
Height: 42cm

Puritan place-setting, c.1670

Photograph: Jeremy Phillips for Fairfax House, York

With England recovering from a long period of austere puritanism, and the crown reclaimed by a monarch used to extravagance and ornament, it still took time for luxury to manifest itself again on the dining-room table.

The one exotic item in this particular assembly is the napkin, woven in Flanders with patterns of flowers, but folded in the shape of a fish, after instructions in Giles Rose's manual.

The knife and two-tine fork by Abraham Brock and spoon by Jacob Isaac could not be simpler, although there is some decoration on the Façon de Venise goblet.

It is the monumental silver candlesticks by Jacob Bodendick, 1677, which stand out, however, resting on their spreading square base and cushion-shaped knop. Notice also how the baluster stem terminates in a square candle socket.

and his instructions were supposed to help the reader create shapes like 'cockleshells, double melons, pheasants and a dog with a choker about its neck'. This section of the book takes its inspiration from an earlier Italian text of 1639, published by Mathias Giegher,[13,] but Rose did not include the original drawings showing what these creations should look like. The results and instructions are not that easy to follow and it seems doubtful, therefore, that this form of conceit was popular at the table of the late seventeenth-century English aristocrat.

Rose also alludes to the early use of porcelain: 'After the Butler has thus covered his table,' he notes, 'let him now begin to dish up his fruit either in Plate or Cheyney, or such as he finds in the house ... and to make use of a three-pointed fork to present them with.'[14] Finding Chinese plates in country-house stores at this time, in sufficient quantities to serve a large meal, would be rare. Imports to Britain and elsewhere had been sporadic in the last quarter of the seventeenth century and it was not until the safe arrival of the *Dorothy* in 1696 that regular supplies of porcelain plate were made available to the public at large. These brightly coloured imports caused a sensation and stimulated great demand with the Chinese potters able to include the family crest at only a modest extra charge. Plain unadorned silver plates were now being relegated to the buffet for display during the first quarter of the eighteenth century, whilst Chinese porcelain dinner plates took pride of place at the rich man's table.

Another significant transformation at this time was the development of flint glass by George Ravenscroft during the 1670s. This heavy 'metal' replaced the imports of rather fragile soda glass with a more robust and inexpensive product and proved the start of English domination of world glass markets which lasted for the next 150 years. There were large quantities of glass produced and purchased for the country house estate[15] throughout the eighteenth century, but wine and beer glasses still do not seem to have claimed their permanent place on the table at formal dinner parties.

Medieval service, with its buffet-like courses of many dishes followed by a void at the close of the meal formed the basis of court dining protocol throughout Europe until the middle of the nineteenth century. More strictly defined rules for this kind of arrangement were imposed at the court of Louis XIV, leading to a modified form of medieval-style service known as *le grand couvert*. The pre-eminence of French cuisine during the seventeenth and eighteenth centuries led to the adoption of this *modus operandi* at every other European court and it became internationally known as *service à la française*. A meal of this kind consisted of two courses served from the kitchen and a third course from the 'office' (pantry or confectionery), called *le fruit* or *le dessert*, rather than *la voidée*. Each course usually consisted of the same number of dishes arranged in perfect symmetry, though there was room for variation. A typical first course of an important meal *à la française* might start with a choice of four different soups (*grosses entrées*), accompanied by four *hors-d'oeuvre*, two fish dishes, four main meat dishes (*relevés* or *grosses pièces*), twelve side dishes (*entrées*) and four cold dishes (*pièces froides*). The second course would consist of a variety of roasts (*rotis*) and *entremets* (light dishes, both sweet and savoury). The third course or dessert was frequently laid out on a different table in a separate room and consisted of seasonal fruit, cheese, ices and confectionery.

Although *service à la française* was visually a sumptuous way of dining, it was wasteful and impractical and gradually started to be replaced in France during the early nineteenth century by *service à la russe*. This much simpler approach, in which the dishes arrived at table one after the other, rather than in two large mixed buffet-like courses, ensured that the diners could enjoy the hot dishes at the correct temperature and afforded plenty of room in the middle of the table for decorations. This custom was apparently introduced into France by Prince Kourakine, the ambassador of Tsar Alexander I, but did not become widespread until the Second Empire, when it was popularised by Urbain Dubois and Émile Bernard, chefs to William and Augusta of Prussia. Their remarkable illustrated book of recipes *La Cuisine Classique* (Paris, 1864) was the first work to fully explain service *à la russe*. Dubois was also responsible for its adoption at the English court through his *Artistic Cookery* (London, 1870), another lavishly illustrated work with sample dinners *à la russe* for royal occasions and ball suppers of up to 5,000 covers. Dubois also discusses *service à l'anglaise*, an English arrangement in which there were two separate courses served on the main table, with removes such as roasts and ham on a side table.

The dessert course, c. 1760

Photograph: Jim Kershaw for
Fairfax House, York

In April of 1763, Viscount Fairfax paid a French confectioner working in York the sum of 15 guineas for a dessert course comprising pyramids of wet and dry sweetmeats. This is an accurate recreation, not only of the type of confection available at this time, but also using silver, porcelain and glass similar in design and date to pieces in Lord Fairfax's collection. The central epergne by William Roberston, 1756 is filled with *Manus Christi*,

small spheres of sugar candy coated in gold, also quince paste rolled into lovers knots, some leaping carp, "Queens Chocolata" marbled pastels and other such novelties. Even the oval dishes used to house the sugar strawberries are edible and can be consumed when empty.

The so-called "wet"-sweetmeats comprised fruit pyramids of Jargonelle pear, Ribston Pippin apple, Grosse Mignonne peach and Brussells apricot whilst the bowls have figs, morello cherries steeped in

brandy and prunellos. Notice also on the silver salver a group of glasses filled with wine-flavoured calfs-foot jelly. At each place setting is a blue and white 'Nankin' porcelain plate c. 1751, flanked with Hanovarian pattern cutlery. The forks and spoons are displayed, as was the fashion, face down which allowed the engraved family crests to be clearly seen. Standing next to these are various wine glasses and also engraved fingerbowls used to rinse the fingers between delicacies. Fairfax paid 1s. 2d. each for

these "flowered water glasses" whereas those for wine and beer cost only 6d.

The main meal of the day usually started around 3 pm but because of the inefficient mode of service it was not until around 6 pm that the dessert course appeared. This was the time to light the candles and the pair of four-branch candelabra by Paul Delamerie, 1735 would be deemed sufficient, as Isaac Ware noted in *A Complete Body of Architecture*, 1756, to light a dining room of this size.

Temperance enjoying a frugal meal
James Gillray (1757–815), 1792
Photograph: Courtesy of Donald Coverdale

The miserliness of King George III and his Queen was a favourite subject of caricature. The King sits in an armchair in profile to the left, bending forward to eat a boiled egg, holding the egg cup in his left hand. Opposite him, and partly concealed by the left margin, sits the Queen avidly stuffing salad into her mouth with a two-tine fork. On the small round table is a bowl of salad with large salad servers, the fork clearly a three-tine variety, and next to the fluted bowl are crossed rat-tail spoons and a trowel-like cake server, although no cakes can be seen.

Everything in the room denotes miserliness: the King has tucked the end of the table cloth into his collar to protect his clothing; his breeches are patched; his chair is swathed in protective coverings; his feet rest on a mat which protects the carpet. A richly chased flagon decorated with the royal arms which stands on the ground beside him is inscribed AQUA REGIS. The handle of the bell-pull is covered by a bag and behind the King's back, and on the extreme right is a fire-place; in the grate is a vase containing snowdrops, holly and mistletoe, to show that although it is winter, there is no fire.

By the second quarter of the eighteenth century, it is recorded that cutlery in England was now being presented on either side of the plate, the fork to the left, with knife and spoon on the right. Fresh cutlery (spoons and forks still presented face down) were brought on at each change of course, but exactly how this arrangement came about is still not entirely clear.

A French visitor to England in 1784, François Rochefoucauld offers a useful contrast between French and English practices:

> *I do not like to prick my mouth or my tongue with these little sharp steel tridents which are generally used in England … I know that this kind of fork is only intended for serving and fixing the pieces of meat while they are cut, and that the English knives being very large and rounded at the point, serve the same purpose to which forks in France are applied, that is, to carry food to the mouth … The fork seizes, the knife cuts, and the pieces may be carried to the mouth with either. The motion is quick and precise … In France … when meat is cut to pieces, the knife is laid down idle on the right side of the plate, while the fork passes from left to right.*[16]

Napkins now started the meal on the left hand side of the setting again, presumably to allow the new-fashioned porcelain plates to be shown off to advantage.

A further innovation at this time was the introduction of specific plates for soup. Lord Fairfax at Gilling paid £88 for '12 Soop Plates' from the great rococo silversmith Fredrick Kandler.[17] John Trusler explains how these would be presented:

> *If there is a soup for dinner … to lay each person a flat plate, and a soup-plate over it, a napkin, knife, fork and spoon.*[18]

Spoons used for soup did not have a round bowl as we know them today (this was an American invention of the 1860s), but normal tablespoons were employed for this purpose. Also, the presentation of the soup plate in this way was only for show. Each plate would, of course, be taken away to be filled and brought back to the table by the footman.

At the beginning of the nineteenth century these fundamental changes in service had dramatic effects on how a table was laid out. Many of the dishes were now being presented on sideboards, leaving more space available on the main table for plateaus or centrepieces. Also the concept of self-sufficiency had become a more acceptable mode of behaviour even at formal dinners and this resulted in more and more of the equipage needed to complete the meal being on hand for individual convenience. Thomas Cosnett's *Footman's Directory*, first published in 1823,[19] explains that one wine glass, a glass cooler and decanters can be placed directly onto the dinner table and that 'for convenience', he says:

> let the soup plates be all put at the bottom of the table, a little to the left of the person who helps it, and close to the tureen.

Cosnett was still recommending, however, that cutlery be changed at each course and it was not until the end of the nineteenth century that Mrs Beeton and others[20] were illustrating complete sets of cutlery ranging outwards on either side of the plate, sufficient for some six or seven courses and with upwards of five or six different types of wine and water glass waiting close by to be used throughout the meal.

Most of us will recognise elements of this presentation in the 'self-service' dinner parties of today and it will be interesting to observe how we as a society respond to changes in culinary and sociological behaviour throughout the twenty-first century and how this will manifest itself in the presentation of the British dining room.

Notes and references

1   Marchese, P. *L'Invenzione della Forchetta*, Rome, 1989, pp. 80–81, 84.
2   Furnival, F. J., ed., *The Babees Book*, EETC, no. 32, London, 868. This includes the John Russell, *Book of Nurture*, pp. 130–31, II 197–228.
3   Peacock, E., 'Inventories made for Sir William and Sir Thomas Fairfax. Knights of Walton and Gilling Castle', *Archaeologia*, 1884, pp. 124–131.
4   Ibid, p. 137, inventory at Walton, 1624.
    'In the lithe Chamber at the Great Chamber end'
    'in that p[r] esse 12 dozen of maple trenchers never yet used, 2 dozen of trencher plates'.
5   Decoteau, P., *Clara Peeters*, Lingen, 1992.
6   Pieter Claesz (1597–1661), Lambert Doomer (1624–1700), Jacob Foppens Van Es (c.1596–1660), Frans Francken the younger (1578–1628,) Dirk Hals (1591–1656), Gerrit Willemsz Heda (fl.1642–1700), Hieronymous Janssens (c.1624–93), Roelof Koets (c.1592–1655), Sumon Luttiehuys (c.1610–67), Jan Olis (c.1610–72), Abraham de Pape (1620–66), Peter Gerritsz van Roestraten (1627–98), Juriaen van Streeck (c.1632–87), Jan Jansz Treck (c.1606–52), Jan Jansz den Uyl (1595–1640), Jan Jansz van de Velde (fl.1619–64).
7   *The Goodman of Paris*, trans, E. Power, New York, 1928, p. 299. In Renaissance Italy, toothpicks were frequently perfumed (stechi profumati), Scappi, B. *Opera*, Venezia, 1570.
8   Courtin, A. de, *Nouveau traite de la civilité*, Paris, 1672.
9   Elias, Norbert, *The Civilising Process*, published posthumously in English in 1996. I am grateful to Richard Wendorf for drawing this to my attention.
10 Rose, G., *A Perfect School of Instructions for the Offices of the Mouth*, London, 1682.
11 Ibid, pp. 90–1.
12 Brown, P., Day, I., *Pleasures of the Table*, York, 1997.
13 Giegher, M., *Li tre trattati*, Padova, 1639.
14 *A perfect school etc.*, pp. 86, 93.
15 Brown, P. and Schwartz, M., *Come Drink the Bowl Dry*, York, 1996, pp. 69–70, 92–102.
16 Rochefoucauld, F. De La, *A Frenchman in England*, 1784, ed. Marchand, J. (1933).
17 Northallerton Records Office (Newburgh papers) ZDF, HC4BO..E of Fredrick Kandler, Goldsmith against St. James's Church, Jermain Street

	oz	s d	£ s d
To 12 Soop Plates	244: 15	@7 : 2	87 14 0
Engra crests & corots			0 12 0
			London, 8 January, 1754

18 Trusler, Rev. J., *The Honours of the Table*, London, 1788.
19 Cosnett, T., *The Footmans Directory*, London, 1st edition, 1823, revised and enlarged 1825.
20 Beeton, I. M., *The Book of Household Management*, London, 1861 and revisions to 1901. Also Murray, A., *The Domestic Oracle*, London, c.1850.

The Catalogue

3000 BC – 1000 AD

This first section, spanning some 4,000 years, covers a period when evolution and progress is slow, but from the artefacts which survive we can see that the knives not only reflect an understanding of design, but were also produced with a specific purpose in mind. Stone knives from the late Neolithic period, for example, display an appreciation of beauty in their form and some evident fashioning of the handle.

When the process of smelting malachite to extract copper was first discovered and used to make knives, the material did not replace stone immediately as the metal was too soft and could not hold a sharp edge. The early Egyptians, who already had skilfully executed flint knives, started making copper knives which were small and leaf-shaped in design. Both stone and copper were being used in tandem for some considerable time and it seems likely that the similar shapes which evolved for both materials were a result of this long-standing association.

At least 2,000 years were to pass before the discovery of bronze, an alloy of copper with tin, which is a much stronger material, is easier to cast and can be hardened by hammering. It was a technology that eventually spread throughout the civilised world and successive invasions of Celtic tribes brought not only bronze casting, but iron working into Britain. Interestingly, a number of knife blades made during the Bronze Age, a technological development which occured at different times and in different places throughout the civilised world, still have the same elegant curve to the line of the blade whether they were made in Siberia, China, Mycenae, Hallstat or Syria.

The Romans arrived with their Bronze and Iron Age culture, and produced knives that tend to be short and straight, perhaps more practical than ornate. The Romans also left a wonderful legacy of spoons made in silver and other metals – some made in matching sets – and innovations like folding knives, spoons that hook on the side of vessels, strainers and specialised cooking implements. Their folding combination tool for eating whilst travelling was an ingenious creation, especially with the inclusion of a spike of fork.

The Roman withdrawal from Britain in the fifth century allowed the Anglo-Saxon population to develop their own artistic customs and rituals. Northumbrian monks, for example, were forging a style of knife blade known as the scramasax, which became popular throughout Europe. One of the design characteristics of this knife was the broadness of the blade and the dramatic 'dropped point', whether it be for a small knife or a full-length blade of a sword. Sometimes the blade was inlaid with contrasting metal designs and occasionally the owner's or maker's mark. When the Viking invaders arrived in 789, they brought with them their long knives and elaborate wooden spoons.

Exactly when the fork first arrived in Britain is still not clear, but the existence of the tenth-century, three-tine fork in the collection and a similar fork on the multi-function eating implement in the Fitzwilliam Museum, Cambridge, must surely suggest an earlier date than has been previously accepted.

A Voluptuary under the horrors of Digestion
James Gillray (1757–1815), 1792
Photograph: Courtesy of Donald Coverdale Esq

The Prince of Wales, languid with repletion, leans back in an armchair, holding a fork to his mouth. His waistcoat is held together by a single button across his distended stomach which supports a watch fob in the shape of a corkscrew.

On his right is a circular table covered with the remains of a meal, with decanters of Port and Brandy (the 'B' is deliberately obscured to reveal only the word 'randy'), and a castor of Chian, a pepper noted for its contribution to corpulence. Gillray shows the Prince's coat of arms, top right, as a crossed scimitar-bladed knife and three-tine fork mounted on a dinner plate. The Prince's motto *Ich Dien* (I SERVE), written on the ribbon above, seems entirely appropriate for this armorial display.

On the shelf below is a triple stand of jelly glasses, amongst which stands a small pot: *For the Piles*, and a bottle: *Drops for a Stinking Breath*. Beside it are a box of *leakers Pills*, and a bottle of *Velmos Vegetable Syrup*. On the wall above the Prince's head is the portrait of an old man drinking from a glass inscribed *Aqua*. This is Luigi Cornaro of Padua, whose discourse *Discorri della vita Scobria*, c. 1560, extolled the virtues of the 'ascetic diet' and its conbribution to long life.

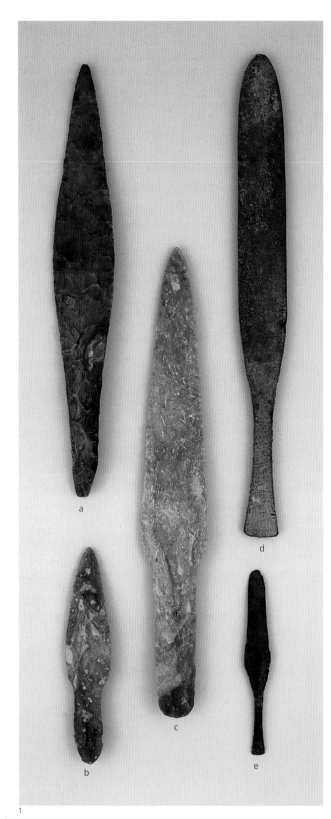

1

1 (Left)

a, b, c Knives

Flint. Denmark, Neolithic period, c.3000 BC. *B1*

Length: 12.5–27.5cm

The tapering form of these Neolithic stone knives shows how men could improve the shape of their multi-purpose implements for better comfort and easy use. Knives like these would be fashioned to the form required by hammering out the sides of a flint stone. The stone would be polished and given a smooth finish by rubbing against sandstone with water and/or sand.

Their two-sided configuration represents a step forward in the making of such an implement. A haft made of hardened animal skin, wood or bone would often be attached along the back of the blade to facilitate the grip.

These examples were probably intended for common use, whilst others which survive were more likely to be for ceremonial purposes. The Pitt-Rivers knife (c.3100 BC), for example, in the British Museum, has an ivory haft finely carved in relief with rows of wild animals.

Cf.: Similar knives from Denmark are illustrated in Oakley, K., *Man the Toolmaker*, British Museum Natural History, 1967, pp. 17–18.

d, e Knives

Copper. Egypt, pre-Bronze Age, c.3000 BC. *B2*

Length: 11–28.5cm

A further development in the making of cutting implements was achieved with the discovery and use of metal (c.3000 BC). Metal-blade knives were first made from copper and later bronze, a much harder alloy that could be also cast in moulds. A bone or wooden haft was often attached to the tang and a binding used to fix the blade and the haft together.

Because of their simple construction, this particular type of knife is known as a 'scale-tang'. The scale is sometimes a double band of material fastened to the haft by means of rivets. One particular characteristic of knives in this period is the gently curved blade.

2 (Right)

a Knife

Bronze, with stylised wound handle and ring terminal. Siberian-Chinese, Karasuk culture, c.1000 BC. *B4*

Length: 21cm

The stylised design of the handle would suggest that its modelling is based on earlier knives which had wrapped handles. The design on the reverse differs from the front, having a diamond cross-hatching pattern reminiscent of leg bindings.

In China, in the fourth and third centuries BC, the practice of using knives of similar style as barter was well established. 'Knife money', as it became known, originated among the nomadic population of fishermen and hunters in the northern and eastern provinces of China. The scraper-knife (flint knife) would have been its direct source.

Cf.: Phillips, E. D., *The Royal Hordes*, Thames & Hudson, 1965, p.44; Thierry, F., 'The origins and development of Chinese coins' in O. Boperachchi and D. P. M. Weerakkody (eds), *Origin, Evolution and Circulation of Foreign Coins in the Indian Ocean* (Manohar, Sri Lanka), 1998, pp. 15–62; William, J. (ed.). *Money: a history*, London, BMP, 1997; *World of Money* CD-ROM, British Museum Multimedia, 1998.

b Knife

Bronze, handle decorated with ibex head and hieroglyphic inscription. Siberian-Shang, c.1000 BC. *B5*

Length: 30cm

Cf. Watson, W., *Ancient China*, BBC, 1974, illus. 25.

c Knife

Bronze, with scale tang (scales missing); possibly Mycenaean, c.1200 BC. *B3*

Length: 23cm

This knife has the characteristic curve found in many knives of the Bronze Age. This example has ribbed decoration on the blade which converges to the tip. The handle has holes and rivets for scales of bone or wood.

3

3 *(Above)*

a **Knife**
Bronze, the spine of the blade decorated with bars and chevrons along its length, the handle missing. European, Bronze Age, c.1000 BC. *B6*
Length: 18.5cm

b **Knife blade**
Bronze, folding, the spine of the blade decorated with sets of bars, crosses and chevrons.

Continental, c.1000 BC, ex-Bateman Collection. *B8*
Length: 12cm

c **Knife**
Bronze, of socket type, round-section tang missing. The ribbed and hatched triangular decoration repeated on the outer spine of the blade. Austria, Central European, Bronze Age, c.1000 BC. *B7*
Length: 26cm

2

4

4 *(Above)*

Knives
Bronze, the handles fashioned to take inset scales which are missing. Luristan, Western Iran, c.700 BC. *B9*
Length: 17.5–27.5cm

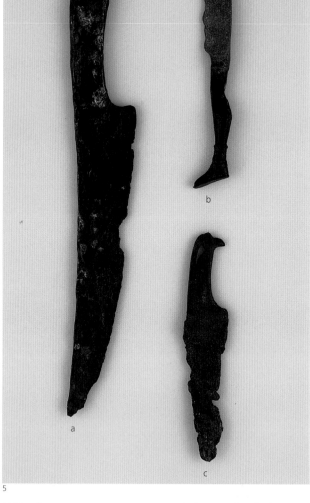

5

5 *(Above)*

a **Knife**
Iron, of robust construction, with integral looped handle, the blade retaining the characteristic curved shape of earlier Bronze Age knives. Iron Age, Austrian, c.500 BC. *B10*
Length: 29cm

b **Knife**
With iron blade and bronze handle shaped as a leg, with a shoe-clad foot. Continental-Roman, c.50 BC. *B14*
Length: 17cm

Legs were often used as decorative features in knife handles. This particular example is finely modelled with boot straps and a stocking. Notice how the part corresponding to the thigh is recessed on both sides in order to be fitted with scales.

c **Knife**
With iron blade and bronze handle shaped as a bird, the mark of a crescent (half moon) engraved on the handle. European Celtic, c.250–150 BC. *B11*
Length: 13.5cm

This would probably have been a personal knife, perhaps carried in a sheath.

6

6 (*Above*)

Spoon
Bone. Etruscan, c.50 BC. *B13*
Length: 7cm

Cf.: Donald, J., *European Spoons Before 1700*, J. Emary Pub., Scotland, 1976, p.43.

He illustrates a similar example in The British Museum, London.

7 (*Right*)

a Knife handle
Part of a folding implement, bronze, modelled as a standing panther. British find, Roman, c.50 AD. *B12*
Length: 7cm

The design for this handle is based on a contemporary 'trapezophoron' leg, which often incorporated features representing animals. The panther was the animal favoured by Bacchus.

b Knife handles (2)
Bronze, one moulded as a ram's head with faceted stem decorated with bands of hieroglyphic symbols, the other with a panther's head terminal and decorated with cross-hatched strapping in imitation of binding, Roman, c.20 AD. *B15*
Length: 6cm

c Knife handle
Bronze, with turned knop. East Anglia find, Roman, c.100 AD. *B21*
Length: 5cm

d Knife handles (2)
Bronze, folding. Romano-British, c.50 AD. *B16*
Length: 6cm

This type of handle is a common find. They would have been part of a folding knife, probably carried on the person.

e Knife
Iron, formed of one piece, with naïve stamped decoration on the handle and terminating with a punched hole. London find, Romano-British, c.100 AD. *B19*
Length: 18.5cm

f Knife
Bronze, with iron blade, the handle modelled as a ram's head, Oxford find. Roman, c.100 AD. *B17*
Length: 11cm

This small personal knife would perhaps be carried in a sheath. In Roman times the ram's head was a popular symbol of power and often used on the prow of a ship.

g Knife
With iron blade and hollow iron socket handle, probably used for food preparation. Romano-British, c.100 AD. *B18*
Length: 15.5cm

h Knife
Iron, formed of one piece and terminating with a ring terminal. London find, Romano-British, c.100 AD. *B20*
Length: 13cm

Used around the house for personal domestic purposes, this knife would be attached to a cord around the body and carried all the time during the day. Knives similar to this one can be seen at the Museum of London.

7

The Romans were not the first to invent folding cutlery but they certainly exploited the concept to their advantage. These small works of art, usually cast in bronze, displayed considerable skill and inventiveness. The human form was a popular subject, often shown in erotic positions and with a concentration on male genitalia. Other representations of a zoomorphic nature such as lions, panthers, or birds were favoured, as were elements of contemporary furniture (above 7a). An exceptional survival of some early folding cutlery, now in the Fitzwilliam Museum, Cambridge, is a silver combination tool with six attachments: the blade is of iron, the spoon terminates in a trident-like fork and there are three other small implements of unknown use. Other less sophisticated examples in bronze with white metal spoon and spike for snails (B24, p. 58) reveal how inventive the Cutlers were at this time.

Interest for this type of cutlery waned in Britain during the Anglo-Saxon and early medieval periods. It was not until the sixteenth century that a genuine revival occurred in the form of folding forks with detachable spoon bowls and a screw-in terminal (B156, p. 93).

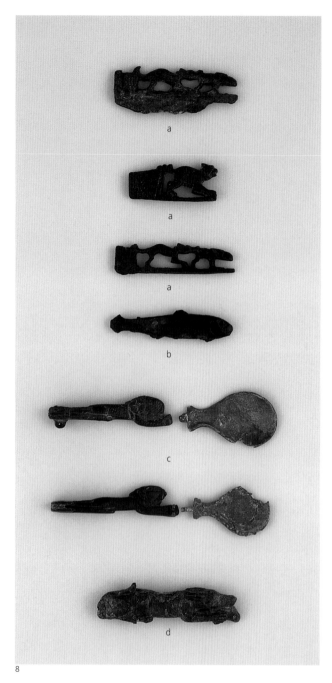

8

9

8 *(Above left)*

a **Knife handles** (3)
Bronze, the remains of folding knives. Two examples are modelled as dogs chasing hares, one with the remnants of the original iron blade. The third shows a cat escaping from its kennel. Romano-British, c.100–200 AD. *B22*
Length: 5–7cm

This commonly found type of handle is usually excavated without the blade, possibly discarded when too worn or broken.

b **Knife handle**
Bronze, part of a folding knife, modelled as a fish. South Kent find, Romano-British, c.100 AD. *B23*
Length: 7cm

c **Knife handles and spoons** (2+2)
Bronze and white metal, part of folding implements, modelled as lions with slightly different profile, the two spoon bowls of white metal unattached herewith. Roman, c.100 AD. *B24*
Length: 12cm (extended)

These handles have provision for the addition of other implements, possibly a hinged spike for eating snails. Unfortunately these have not survived.

Cf.: Sherlock, D., 'Roman Folding Spoons' in *Transaction of the London and Middlesex Archaeological Society*, 27, 1976, pp.250–55.
Greek and Roman Art, Fitzwilliam Museum Handbooks, Cambridge, 1998.

d **Knife handle**
Bronze, modelled as a hunting dog with prey issuing out of a flower-like ferrule. Roman, c.100 AD. *B25*
Length: 8cm

Hunting with dogs was a popular subject for knife handles at this time, representing the Roman countryman's love of the chase. Other variations from those shown include a hound wearing a mask and a dog emerging from a lily.

9 (Left)

a Knife handle
Hollow bronze with remnants of the iron tang inside. From Wroxeter, Roman, c.200 AD. *B28*
Length: 10cm

b Knife handle
Bronze, part of a folding knife, representing a female caryatid standing on a console bracket. Roman, c.300 AD. *B35*
Length: 9cm

c Knife handle
Bronze, part of a folding knife, modelled as a chair leg. Roman, c.100 AD. *B26*
Length: 6.5cm
A sinuous and slim handle, its popular design taken from fashionable cabriole leg furniture.

d Knife handle
Bronze, part of a folding knife, modelled as a falcon on a perch. Roman, c.100 AD. *B27*
Length: 9cm
Birds of prey were favoured decorative motifs on Roman artefacts.

e Knife handle
Bronze, with banded and foliate decoration terminating in the head of a wrestler. Roman, c.300 AD. *B33*
Length: 7.5cm
Wrestlers appear frequently on Roman knife handles.

f Knife blade
Iron, part of a folding knife. Roman, c.200 AD. *B30*
Length: 9cm

g Knife handle
Bronze. Roman, c.300 AD. *B32*
Length: 8cm

h Knife handle
Bronze, in the shape of a Roman candelabrum with banding on the column and a bowl above. Late Roman, c.300 *B31*
Length: 7cm

i Knife handle
Bronze, Roman, c.200 AD. *B29*
Length: 5cm

j Knife handle
Bronze, with bird terminal. Late Roman, c.300 AD. *B34*
Length: 4.5cm

Spoons were the common eating implement for use at the table during the first century AD. The two basic types which are well represented in the collection are firstly the little round-bowled spoon (10b), or 'cochleare', intended for eating eggs and shellfish. This was confirmed by the excavations at Hildesheim and from descriptions in one of Valerie Martial's poems published in the *Epigrammist* AD 80, around the time of the opening of the Colosseum. The larger examples with pear-shaped bowl (10a) are dessert spoons or *ligula*, used for eating cereal foods. These spoons have a handle linked to the bowl with a downward curving arm set at an angle, which can sometimes continue in the form of a rat-tail down the back of the spoon.

The handles can be of circular section, or faceted or fluted, and terminate in a variety of finials. D. E. Strong, in *Greek and Roman Gold and Silver Plate*, British Museum, 1966, mentions knops, cloven hooves and caps.

By the second and third centuries a new type of spoon appears in the form of a fiddle-shaped bowl (10d) offset from the handle as in earlier examples, but sometimes the junction is adapted into an openwork scroll or disc.

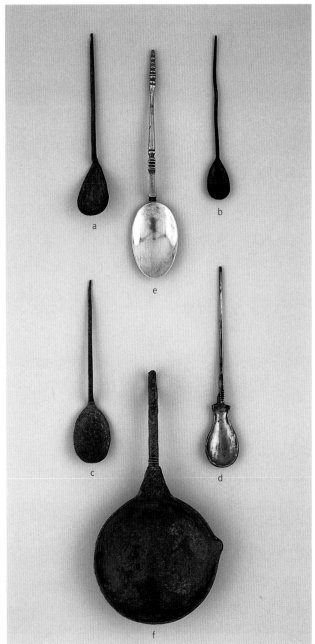

10

10 (Right)

a–d Spoons (4)
Bronze, of different shapes, one showing signs of tinning, all with more or less pointed ends to assist in the eating of shellfish. A flat handle is attached to the bowl of the smallest spoon, the others have the characteristic stepped or dropped handle. Romano-British, c.300 AD. *B37*
Length: 11.5–14cm

Many theories have been put forward to explain the stepped constructional technique used to join the handle with the bowl. One explanation may be that the shape derived from an unfinished folding spoon (B24) being attached to a handle in a permanently open position.

e Spoon
Silver (bowl restored), British find, Roman, c.300 AD. *B36*
Length: 16cm

f Ladle
Bronze, the round-shaped handle decorated in the form of a swan's head, creates a loop for hanging the ladle to the side of a vessel. The flat profile also allows the bowl to rest level on the table. British find, Roman, c.300 AD. *B38*
Length: 17cm

This type of paterae if often described as a wine-holder and used in religious ceremonies. In classical legend the swan was said to sing just before its own death and as such can be said to represent Apollo, Erato and Clio.

11

11 (Left)

a Spoon
Wood possibly sandalwood. Coptic Egypt, c.500 AD. *B40*
The handle decorated with a cartouche set with a cabochon of ebony.
Length: 16.5cm

b–e Spoons
Bronze (two showing coating of tin), of different size and construction. British finds, Roman, c.400 AD.

b Of robust construction, with tapering rectangular handle attached to the pear-shaped bowl on the inside rather than on the outside edge.
Length: 17cm

c Constructed in the usual manner with stepped rectangular handle fixed to the edge of the bowl and carrying down the underside in the form of a rat-tail. The orientation of the bowl is unusual in that the narrow point of the pear-shaped bowl is to the front.
Length: 15cm

d Long spoon with large disc connection between bowl and handle. The square-section stem is forged round at the end and tapers to a point. The bowl has a pronounced rat-tail running along the majority of the underside.
Length: 24cm

e Of similar construction to 11c but having a connecting plate decorated with piercing. Also traces of simple decoration on the tapering handle.
Length: 18cm

12 (Right)

a Knife
With iron blade, scale-tang and engraved wooden scales. British find, possibly Saxon, c.900 AD. *B45*
Length: 12.5cm

b Hone
Stone, with pewter animal head and ring as terminal. East Anglia find, Saxon, c.900 AD. *B42*
Length: 7.5cm

c Fork
Bronze, with twisted column handle terminating in a horse's head finial. The tines of the fork have Helenistic acanthus and leaf decoration at the base of each prong. Byzantine, c.500 AD. *B41*
Length: 28.5cm
cf: a matching silver spoon and fork in the Dumbarton Oaks Collection, Washington.

d Spoon and fork
Bronze, the spoon with ring-and-dot decoration at the join between bowl and handle, the fork with three tines. Probably a metal detector find in Yorkshire, Saxon, c.900 AD. *B43*
Length: 12cm (knife) 7.5cm (fork)

These implements were apparently recovered together. Markings and laminations on the ends of the handles suggest these may have had loops or rings and perhaps have been carried on a chatelaine with other implements.

The existence of a three-tine fork of this age, of such sophisticated profile and being discovered in a British location, invariably raises many more questions than answers. Forks for personal use, as opposed to aids in carving, are virtually unknown in Britain before the seventeenth century.

The Italian nobility owned silver forks in the fifteenth century, but the British were slow to accept forks as eating implements.

The main variations in spoon shape dating from the fourth and fifth centuries are well covered in the selection illustrated. The bowl was usually pear shaped and joined to the handle at its pointed end by means of a round disc or pierced scroll attachment. The bowls are sometimes canted at an angle to the handles, which are usually square sectioned at the start and then taper to a point.
This basic shape had certainly appeared in earlier times but later spoons are generally larger.

Another innovation were the handles of spoons or ladles (B38) formed into the shape of a swan's head, a favoured animal in Roman iconography. Both Venus and Apollo deemed it a sacred animal; symbolising the bird of life and the dawn of day. In Celtic mythology the swan possesses the therapeutic powers of the sun and water, which depict benevolence, love, purity and harmony.

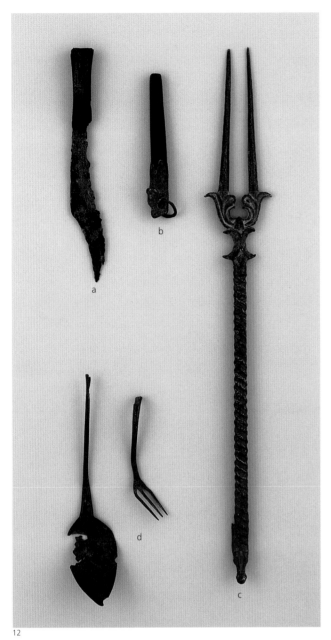

12

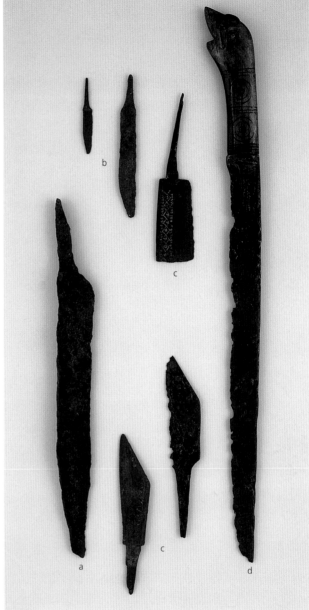

13

13 *(Above right)*

a Knife
Iron, showing scramasax influence. British find, Saxon, c.900 AD. *B44*
Length: 25cm

This robust knife would have been used for general purposes, including heavy duties. Probably fitted with a 'bobbin'-type handle burnt onto the tang.

b Knives (2)
Iron, of small size, perhaps intended for a woman or child, showing scramasax influence. Kent find, Saxon, c.900 AD. *B46*
Length: 5.5cm and 10cm

c Knife blades (3)
Iron, of small size, two with blades nearly in intact, one decorated with twisted white metal inlay in pendant design, the third example with broken blade and damascened with a band of gilt metal inlay near the top. All blades show a scramasax influence. City of London finds, Saxon, c.900 AD. *B47*
Length: 11–12.5cm

These knives probably had 'bobbin'-type handles and would have been carried in a sheath. The blades were sometimes inlaid with inscriptions and the owner's name, but are occasionally discovered inscribed with the text of graces to be said at meals.

d Knife
Iron, long, with through tang, ring-and-dot decoration on bone 'Sea Serpent' handle. Netherlands find, Viking, c.950 AD. *B48*
Length: 38cm

1000 – 1400

At the time of the Norman invasion in 1066, Britain was already a multi-racial country with communities of Celts, Anglo-Saxons, and Norwegian and Danish Vikings, although they were distinct tribal populations, each with their own national culture and life styles. Eventually these cultures became integrated and the process of assimilation manifests itself in the gradual sophistication of cutlery produced during this period. The simple type of knife, for example, with 'bobbin' handles of earlier times, still with scramasax features, gave way to another type which had a scale-tang fitted with plain wooden scales and, finally, the sophisticated French-style knife with bone scales, a copper-alloy bolster and strap ends.

The Normans brought with them fine table manners, rich tableware and implements which are well illustrated in contemporary manuscripts and tapestries. One scene in the *Bayeux Tapestry* illustrates food taken from a pot with a long-handled 'fleshing' fork, similar to B49 on page 64. Paintings of this period reveal tables laid with napkins, ewers and bowls, and only one or two knives (insufficient for the number of diners present), which suggests that anyone who hoped to eat well needed to carry their own personal knife and spoon. Clearly this was not the case for the serfs and the people on the land, who had a fairly meagre diet, and required only a wooden bowl and spoon, with a simple knife in their belt.

During this time spoons evolved from the Anglo-Saxon version of the Roman metal spoon from a period of perhaps bone or wood to the long French metal style of B54 shown on page 65.

Another sophistication in the early medieval period was the elaborate decoration on the leather sheath or scabbard, although a form of incised linear pattern is known on knife scabbards from Neolithic times. The designs were usually engraved or stamped on the early eleventh-century examples and embossed on later pieces. This embossing of leather had its origins in Spain and involved the modelling of animals, leaves and flowers within bands of interlacing vine. Usually drawing upon architectural detail and marginal illustration of manuscripts, the designs reflect the motifs and patterns popularised by an earlier Celtic tradition.

By the end of the fourteenth century there were fundamental changes taking place in the construction of knives. Instead of having solid handles fixed onto a spike 'whittle' tang, many knives were fitted with composite handles consisting of plates, riveted to a flat 'scale' tang. These might be decorated with patterns of alloy rivets as is the case with B58, p. 66, or shaped and carved to make them more comfortable to hold. Other materials besides wood were being used to fashion the handles and Museum of London excavations have unearthed examples made in copper, brass, tin, horn and bone which date from this period.

Surviving bone handles are often carved in the form of a falconer (B52, p. 65), which suggests perhaps that they were meant to be used whilst hunting.

The use of a maker's mark on the blade became increasingly popular at this time, spurred on, no doubt, by Edward III's decree in 1365 that: 'makers of swords and knives and other arms in the City of London shall put their true marks upon all their work…and the work of everyone shall be known by his mark'.

The cook from the prologue of Chaucer's *CanterburyTales*
Ellesmere Chaucer
(private collection)
Photograph: Bridgeman Picture Library

Flesh forks were used to lift joints and other large pieces of boiled meat from cooking cauldrons. Their large, hooked tines were designed to grip heavy portions of meat securely in order to remove them from the boiling water in a safe and efficient way. Bill Brown's flesh fork (B49, p. 64) is unusual in that it required a wooden handle. They were more usually forged in one continuous piece with an iron handle, as in a sixteenth-century example excavated from the cellar of a house in Pottergate, Norwich. The one illustrated in a marginal illumination in the *Ellesmere Chaucer* is also of this type. In common with the Norwich fork it has a ring at the end of the handle for hanging it up in the kitchen.

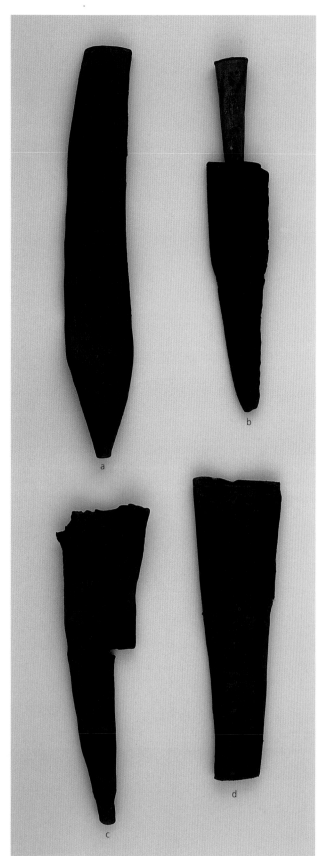

14

15

14 *(left)*

Knife sheaths (4)
Leather: two sheaths have stamped and embossed guilloche decoration containing motifs of animals and plants. The two smaller examples (one with its original knife) have slots through which the thong passes in order to fix the implement to the waist and are decorated with punched matted patterns and gothic tracery. Thames finds, London, c.1200. *B50*
Length: 15–18cm
Cf.: Cowgill, J., M. de Neergard and N. Griffiths, *Knives and Scabbards*, HMSO/ Museum of London, 1987 (many similar examples illustrated).

15 *(Above right)*

Fork
Fleshing, iron, minus long wooden handle for hooking meat from cooking pot. Thames find, c.1100. *B49*
Length: 15cm
Its function is illustrated in the *Bayeux Tapestry*, the eleventh-century French tableau which charts the life of William the Conqueror. One kitchen scene shows a cook lifting food from an oven.

This small selection of medieval scabbards exemplifies a tradition of working on leather which has its origins in ancient times. The most common method of decoration involved the use of line engravings, but stamped dots in the form of leaves, circles, quatrefoils, lozenges or fleur-de-lys as infill were also popular. Other more sophisticated designs appear in the thirteenth and fourteenth centuries, usually based on interlacing patterns, a form of decoration seen on contemporary Celtic architecture or in the margins of medieval illuminated manuscripts.

The two large scabbards illustrated (14a and 14d) are good examples of this later period, with their intertwining tendrils of foliage, simplified to represent oval panels and containing zoomorphic representations of animals. The beasts are recognisable as chasing dogs, hares, boars and cats, and it seems likely that the scabbards were meant to hold hunting knives.

Another group of thirteenth-century scabbards not illustrated, but excavated in numbers at various London sites, features long-bodied crested birds with tail feathers which are seen extending into a three-feathered curl. The designs have stamped ring and dot backgrounds creating a high relief that gives a sculptural quality to the whole concept. Similar 'birds of paradise' are included in the borders of contemporary manuscripts or appear to be coiling themselves within the decorative capitals of buildings.

A further variety of decorated scabbard that does not fully appear until the fourteenth century are those with heraldic decoration.

33

33 (Above)

Knife handle
Carved morse ivory in the form of a lute player. European, c.1400. *B57*
Length: 9cm

16

16 (Above)

Knife handle
Carved bone, in the form of a falconer, Northern Europe, c.1400. *B52*
Length: 9cm

About thirty similar handles have been found in Northern Europe, and from Oxford in the West to St Petersburg in the East.

17 (Right)

a **Spoon**
Latten (an alloy of copper, zinc, lead and tin), the diamond-shaped faceted handle with a pine cone terminal. A partly rubbed mark on the reverse is probably an orb. French, c.1300. *B53*
Length: 17cm
This type of spoon is frequently excavated in various locations throughout Britain.

b **Spoon**
Silver, with diamond-point terminal, the stem shaped as a stylised, rudimentary animal head grasping the bowl. British find, probably French, c.1200. *B51*
Length: 16cm
Cf.: Smith, E .J. G., 'The English Silver Spoon', in *Antique Dealer & Collectors' Guide*, March, April, May and July, 1973, parts I–IV; Smith, E. J. G., 'The Early English Silver Spoon', in *Antique Dealer & Collectors' Guide*, February 1996, pp. 14–19.

c **Spoon**
Latten, the diamond-shaped faceted handle with tower steeple terminal, the back of the bowl with a diamond ring mark, showing traces of tinning. British find, probably French, c.1300. *B54*
Length: 17.5cm

d **Spoon**
Pewter, the fig-shaped bowl set below the level of the faceted stem, the handle with acorn terminal, natural gilding, no mark. Thames find, c.1500. *B73*
Length: 16cm

e **Spoon**
Latten, with fig-shaped bowl, flat based stem and Apostle terminal, (possibly St Jude) European, c.1500. *B76*
Length: 14cm
In relation to items B53–54–73 see: Homer, R. F., *Five centuries of Base Metal Spoons*, privately printed, distributed by The Pewterers Company, London, 1975.
Recommended reading on this subject: Price, F. G. H., *Old Base Metal Spoons*, Batsford, 1908.

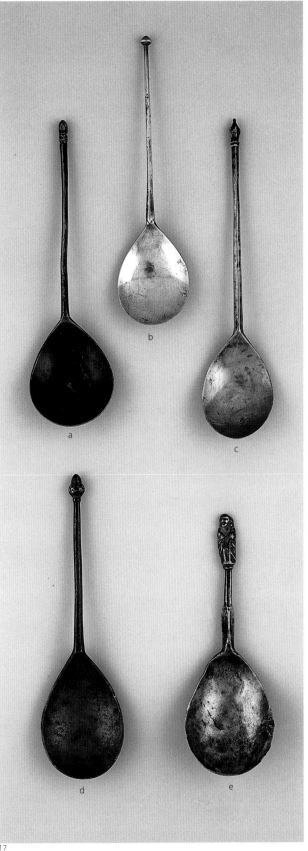

17

18

18 (Left)

a **Knife**
With wooden handle, through-tang and 'candle' end (the end of the tang is simply folded over with no attempt at any degree of finish. It resembles the wick of a candle, hence the common name). The iron blade is marked with a stylised cross. The shape still retains the dropped point of the scramasax blade. Thames find, London, c.1300. *B55*
Length: 16cm

Cf.: Cowgill, J., M. de Neergard and N. Griffiths, *Knives and Scabbards*, HMSO/ Museum of London, 1987.

b **Knives** *(2)*
One cook's knife with wooden handle, marked on blade with a hammer, the other smaller example a belt knife with wood handle, marked on blade with a ragged staff. Thames finds, London, c.1300. *B56*
Length: 23–26cm

Cf.: Cowgill, J., M. de Neergard and N. Griffiths, *Knives and Scabbards*, HMSO/ Museum of London, 1987.

19 (Below)

Knife
Iron, with broken blade and scale-tang. The mud-stained scale decorated with white metal pins and the legend BE MERIE. The reverse side (missing) is probably inscribed with DRINK AND. A blade mark of a hammer and a horseshoe still retains some of its white metal inlay. British find, London, c.1300. *B58*
Length: 11cm

Cf.: Cowgill, J., M. de Neergard and N. Griffiths, *Knives and Scabbards*, HMSO/ Museum of London, 1987.

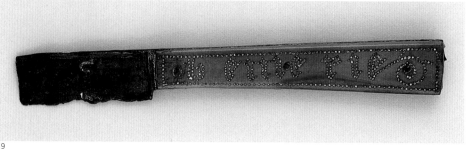

19

20 (Right)

a Knife (2 of 3)
Iron, all with wooden handles, one with a through-tang and iron ferrule. Thames finds, London, c.1300. *B59*
Length: 19–24cm

b Knife (1 of 3)
Iron, with copper alloy shoulders, the scale tang with scales of wood and bone; one knife with copper-alloy ring end cap. Obscure blade marks. Thames finds, London, c.1400. *B65*
Length: 20cm

c Fork (1 of 2)
One of iron, the other of copper alloy, South European, c.1500. *B74*
Length: 12.5cm

In the sixteenth century forks were not yet a companion to the knife. This early example was usually laid on the table to assist with the eating of sticky or slippery foods, performing the same function as that of a pickle fork today.

The earliest pictorial indication that forks were used to bring food to the mouth is recorded in a book dated 1023. In an illustration from Hrabanus Maurus's *Glossiaria* two men are shown eating melon with a large two-prong fork.

d Knife (1 of 4)
Iron, one piece, with solid bolster and end, inset scales of bone and wood, with copper inlaid blade mark. Thames finds, c.1550. *B77*
Length: 21.5cm

This knife illustrates a new style of construction, where blade, tang and end are all forged in one piece. The copper inlaid blade mark is a rarity, since this is often lost in excavated pieces.

e Knife (1 of 3)
Iron, with a scale-tang, wood scales and copper-alloy shoulders, with copper-alloy pin end. Thames finds, London, c.1350. *B60*
Length: 24.5cm

f Knife (1 of 3)
Small iron knife with copper-alloy shoulders and scale-tangs, the scales of bone and leather, strap ends and thong hole. Thames finds, London, c.1400. *B63*
Length: 15.8–17.8cm

1400 – 1600

The later medieval period was a time of great change and innovation, and this diversity manifests itself in the cutlery being fashioned in Britain and elsewhere. National styles were starting to appear, although with a rise in international trade and mobility of people it is not always easy to determine where a particular knife was made, especially if the maker had imported some of the parts. Many of the excavated knives found in Britain, for example, have strong affinities with those discovered in Holland. These are usually constructed with narrow, elegant blades and have decorative alloy caps and bolsters. It is still not clear whether they were made in the Flanders region or by Flemish craftsmen working in Britain, but other knives recovered from the Thames foreshore or found by metal detectors are very plain and simple in construction and likely to be indigenous of the British cutler. The two main centres of production, London and Sheffield, however, were known to be supplying sophisticated decoration. The Hallamshire records (of which district Sheffield was the centre) of 1565 make references to 'damasking, inlaying and studding'.

At around the time when Henry VIII became King of England in 1509, the construction of the eating knife changed. The bolster, which was previously a copper alloy component soldered or riveted on to the blade, was replaced with an integral forged iron bolster. Later on in the century the scale-tang gave way to a pin-tang (a long, slender spike emanating from the bolster). Towards the end of the Tudor dynasty the decorative focus of the knife was no longer in its construction but on the handle itself, where a variety of materials such as carved ivory, amber, agate, cast bronze, silver and gold inlay were being used. Decorative sheathed knives were now worn as an article of fashion; most travellers and guests still needed to carry their own eating utensils and these were designed as outward manifestations of wealth and status.

Spoons of this late medieval period progress from the long-handled, small bowl spoon that were imports from France, made of copper alloy or silver with small acorn, tower or diamond point finials, to the so-called 'fist' spoon from Holland with a terminal figure of a saint. Some of these spoons have part-spiral or baluster stems and at the end of the sixteenth century we see the introduction of a straight, plain stem in silver with a small 'seal top'.

Forks of this period were usually either silver or bronze with two tines, found mostly in Southern Europe, especially in Italy, but rarely in Britain. They were used on the table as a serving accessory and the form changed little until the late sixteenth century, when the number of tines increased to three or even four.

The rise of the Tudor dynasty also coincided with the introduction of books on etiquette. Correct behaviour in the dining room was crucial for the advancement of a young man joining the court of a wealthy nobleman. How to use your cutlery at the table was carefully set down in a series of publications that also provided instructions on what not to do with your knife. Actions not permitted, for example, included the paring of fingernails, picking teeth and transferring chunks of meat to the mouth which, before the advent of the fork, had to be done with the fingers.

Treasures of the Table, 1491
Engraving from *Shatzbehalter*, Nuremberg, 1491
Photograph: Walters Art Gallery, Baltimore

A marvellous evocation of a rich man's banquet. The carver uses his 'presentoir' to supply the cut bread trenchers to his Lord's table. Notice on the right a footman holding aloft a stack of dishes wrapped in a long towel which he uses to prevent spillage and to protect his hands. The dishes may look like tureens, but are in fact upturned plates placed on top of each other in a valiant attempt to keep the food warm.

The hierarchy of the assembly is well documented when we consider the range of equipment available for the rest of the guests. Each place setting on the back tables has a round trencher plate, but there are no knives and only a few spoons are available on the adult table to the right.

a

d

e

b

f

g

c

h

21

21 (Left)

a Knife
Iron, the composite handle of jet scales and silver decorated with engraved panels of roses and leaves on the upper edge and foliate patterns on the underside, with silver shoulders and end cap in the form of a hat, blade mark of a pinnacle. Thames find, c.1450–1500. *B61*
Length: 18cm

b, d, g Knives (3)
Iron, all with solid bolsters, scale-tangs with wooden scales, two with copper-alloy caps, one with iron horse-hoof shaped cap, two with copper inlay blade marks of a crown and a rosette, the other of a cross. Thames finds, c.1500. *B71*
Length: 19–27.5cm

c, e, f Knives (3)
Iron, all with small solid bolsters, scale-tangs with wooden scales and iron end caps. The blade marks include a copper inlay of an animal, the letter 'S' and what seems to be a phoenix rising form the sea. Thames finds, c.1500. *B72*
Length: 13.5–25cm

h Knife
Folding, with iron blade, the bronze cast handle decorated with stylised vine branches in relief. Thames find, c.1500. *B75*
Length: 13.5cm (open)

21a Above

(detail)
The upper edge of the handle showing the sophisticated foliate engraving.

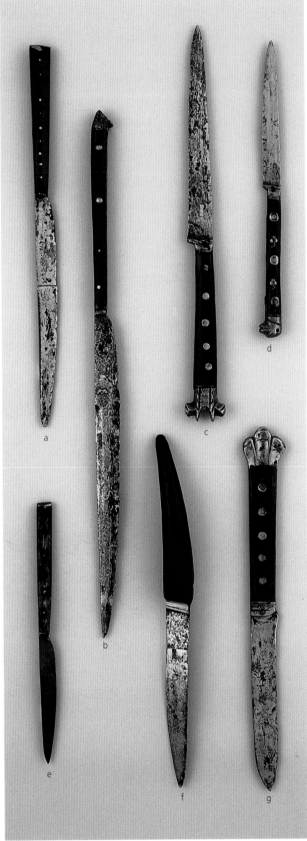

22 *(Left)*

a, b Knives (2 of 3)
Iron, both with solid bolsters, scale-tangs and wooden scales, one with copper alloy cap, the other with iron horse-hoof shaped cap. Both have copper inlay marks. Thames finds, c.1500. *B71*
Length: 19cm–27.5cm

c, d Knives (2 of 4)
Iron, with scale tangs and wooden scales, one knife with copper-alloy decorative pins, clover leaf insets and monkey's head terminal, marked on blade with a copper inlaid fish. The other, with baluster-shaped copper marks, has saddle-pommel end cap. Thames find, c.1500. *B70*
Length: 15.5cm–20.5cm

e Knives (1 of 3)
Iron, with small solid bolster, a scale tang with wooden scales and iron end cap. Thames find, c.1500. *B72*
Length: 13.5cm

f Knife
Iron, the horn tip handle with copper-alloy shoulders, half tang. Thames find, London, c.1450. *B66*
Length: 18.5cm

g Knife (1 of 3)
Iron, with scale tang and wooden scales, having a white metal shoulder and rivets, terminating in an iron finial shaped in the form of a trefoil. Thames find, c.1450. *B68*
Length: 19cm

23

23 *(Above)*

Knife
Folding, iron blade, bronze handle, cast vine decoration. Thames find, c.1500. *B75*
Length: 13.5cm (open)

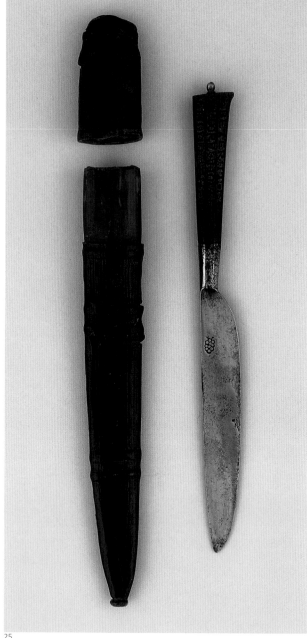

24

25

---

24 (Above)

a Spoon
Latten, with round bowl and flat cast, short bisectional stem with Madonna-style terminal, European, c.1550. *B78*
Length: 12cm

b Spoon
Iron, with corroded fig-shaped bowl, thin flat stem and trefoil terminal. Thames find, probably Dutch, c.1550. *B90*
Length: 11cm

c Spoon
Latten, with round oval bowl and rectangular-section stem terminating in a mitre terminal. Southern Europe, c.1580. *B82*
Length: 13cm

d Spoon
Latten, with round oval bowl and diamond section faceted stem terminating in baluster finial, Southern Europe, c.1580. *B80*
Length: 13cm.

25 (Above)

Knife
Iron, with through-tang and solid bolster, terminating in a copper alloy finial. The shaped horn handle is inscribed with the motto: BETTER IT IS A POORE HOUSE TO HOLD THAN TO LY IN PRISON IN FETTERS OF GOULD. The blade, of earlier medieval shape, bears the mark of a tree.

Housed in the original leather sheath, stamped with medallions of roses and floral pendants over a pattern of vertical lines and banding in imitation of staves. Both sheath and cover are pierced with loop-holes which allow both pieces to be kept together without loss.
English, c.1550. *B85*
Length of case: 21.5cm
Length of knife: 20.5cm

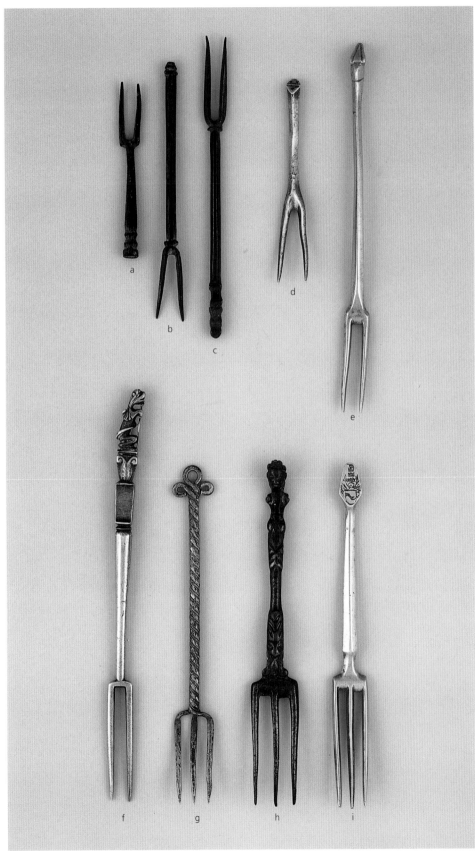

26 *(Left)*

a,b,c **Forks** (3)
Copper alloy or latten, with two tines, South-eastern Europe, c.1550. *B79*
Length: 7.5–13cm
These would have been brightly polished and used on the table in the manner of a pickle fork or during the 'banquet' or dessert for fruit and wet sweetmeats. The word 'banquet' was used in Elizabethan England to denote the food presented at the end of the meal.
Cf.: Day, I. (ed.), *Eat, Drink and Be Merry*, Philip Wilson Publishers, London, 2000.

d **Fork**
Silver, with a crest of three stars engraved on a slanted minimal terminal, the letters 'F G' engraved on the reverse. Italian, c.1550. *B81*
Length: 9cm

e **Fork**
Silver, with two tines and stylised hoof terminal, Italian, c.1550. *B96*
Length: 16cm

f **Fork**
Silver, with two tines, the tapering stem surmounted by a lion rampant. Probably Italian, c.1550. *B95*
Length: 18cm

g **Fork**
Tinned copper alloy, formed of three twisted and compressed wires separating to form three prongs, the other end of the stem fashioned to form a trefoil finial. Thames find, possibly Dutch, c.1550. *B91*
Length: 14.5cm

h **Fork**
Bronze, with three tines, figured stem and term finial. Italian, c.1580. *B99*
Length: 15cm

i **Fork**
Silver, with diamond section stem and stylised hoof terminal giving a flat surface for an engraved crest, Italian, c.1600. *B112*
Length: 15cm
The style of this fork is typical of the period, although probably derives from a Roman form.

27

27 *(Left)*

a, b, c, d, f **Knives** (5)
Iron, of different construction,
Thames finds, c.1550. *B86*

a Short solid bolster with
scaletang which turns through 90°
halfway up the stem, fitted with
four wooden scales and
terminating in a copper alloy
wrythen finial. (Blade has
been shortened.)
Length: 14.5cm
There seems no obvious reason
for constructing the tang in this
way other than to provide extra
decoration.

b With solid bolster and through-
tang fitted with wood and metal
washered handle, probably yew,
ebony and copper, terminating
in a copper ball finial. (Blade has
been restored.)
Length: 19.5cm

c With solid bolster, scale-tang
and wooden scales decorated with
copper rivets, terminating
in cap and ball finial.
Length: 17cm

d Long blade with solid bolster,
and transverse scale-tang fitted
with shaped tapering wooden
scales.
Length: 21.5cm

f With long solid bolster, short
through tang, metal and wooden
handle fixed with small copper
alloy terminal. (Blade has
been repaired.)
Length: 21cm

e **Knife**
Iron, with solid bolster, scale-
tang, stag scales and iron end
plate. The blade has been repaired
at some time and bears the mark
of the letter 'G' inlaid with a
copper alloy. Thames find,
c.1550. *B84*
Length: 22cm

There is a long-held tradition
of finding treasure by
searching through other
people's discards, and if it
occurs on a river foreshore
this foraging is usually
termed 'mud-larking'.

Amongst the many items
recovered from the Thames
over the years are knives,
forks and spoons, dating from
Roman times up to the
eighteenth century.

There are several reasons
why they should appear on
the banks of a large river.
The foreshores were often the
repository for fire-damaged
buildings used as in-fill
behind revetments. These
eventually collapsed, or were
demolished as part of a later
re-development, which
caused the deposits to be
released out into the river and
exposed to the sifting and
scouring of tidal waters.

Rivers have also been, until
fairly recent times, our main
means of transport and many
knives and spoons have been
dropped overboard by people
attempting to board or alight
from ferries or ships tied up
at the wharfs.

It also seems likely that
significant quantities were
literally thrown out with the
dishwater, a problem which
modern caterers will still
wrestle with today in an effort
to maintain their meagre
profit margins.

Another factor that
required an act of
deliberation rather than
carelessness is evidenced by
the presence of several knives
illustrated in this section with
restored blades.

Whatever the reason for
being there, these Thames
finds are especially interesting
and useful indicators of the
cosmopolitan nature of
cutlery being used in Britain
over a long period of time.
They are, of course, rather
difficult to date precisely, but
archaeological excavations
undertaken by the Museum
of London and other bodies
provide us with opportunities
to compare and contrast.

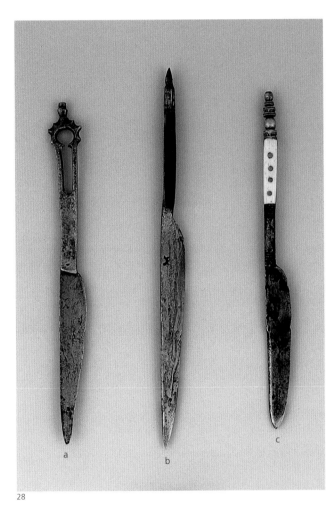

28

29

28 (*Above*)

a Knife
Iron, short tang into copper alloy flat handle with aperture and integral finial. Thames find although similar to knives found in Netherlands, c.1550. *B88*
Length: 15cm

b Knife
Iron, small one-piece, inlaid with wooden scales, integral terminal. Thames find, c.1550. *B87*
Length: 17cm

Evidence of striations on the blade suggests that the knife has been given a steel edge. Imports of low carbon iron (steel) from Sweden, Russia and Spain were expensive and the material was used sparingly at this time. Cutlers would forge the steel onto the iron in the minimum quantities necessary to create a sharp cutting edge.

It was also common, certainly in later years, to have a cheaper iron tang and bolster forged onto a steel blade.

c Knife
Iron, small, with scale-tang, inset ivory scales, long solid bolster, copper-alloy baluster terminal. Thames find, c.1550. *B89*
Length: 15cm

29 (*Above*)

Knives (5)
Iron, all formed from one piece, with tapering stem, three with baluster-shaped finials, one with faceted stem and ribbed decoration, the other with wrythen shaped terminal.

Thames finds, c.1500–1600. *B93*
Length: 19–24.5cm
These knives, of a distinct style, show evidence of black enamel and could possibly be *memento mori* gifts bequeathed to mourners.

30

a Spoon
Cast pewter, with fig-shaped bowl, double baluster stem and wrythen terminal, marked 'H I' on bowl, c.1550. *B94*
Length: 15cm

b Nutpick
Copper alloy, with *Apostle St James the Less* as terminal. The stem is heavier in section and length than a spoon handle, although possibly made by a spoon maker. English, c.1590. *B98*
Length: 13cm

c Spoon
Silver, with fig-shaped bowl and small seal top, silver mark of R P ROBERT PLANCKNEY and leopard's head for London struck on bowl. Thames find, London, 1577. *B97*
Length: 15cm

d Spoon
Tinned latten, with decorated seal top finial. The spoon is very light and has a particularly thin section to the bowl. English c.1600. *B118*
Length. 17cm

e Spoon
Tinned latten, Puritan style, maker's mark comprises a notched circle containing the letter 'RS' on either side of the spoon. English, c.1640. *B137*
Length: 18.5cm

30 (Above)

Spoon
Copper alloy, wrythen handle. Perhaps Dutch, c.1600. *B100*
Length: 30cm

Cf.: a similar spoon is illustrated in *A kitchen interior with servants*, oil on canvas, by the artist Anthonia de Winter on p. 23

a

b

c

d

e

31

Apostle spoons can be identified by the following attributes:

1. St James the less – with a fuller's bat.
2. St Bartholomew – with a butcher's knife.
3. St Peter – with a key or sometimes a fish.
4. St Jude – with a cross, club or carpenter's square.
5. St James the Greater – with pilgrim's staff and a gourd.
6. St Philip – with a long staff usually incorporating a cross.
7. The Saviour, or 'Master' – with orb and cross.
8. St John – with a cup (the cup of sorrow).
9. St Thomas – with a spear or sometimes a builder's rule.
10. St Matthew – with axe or halberd.
11. St Simon Zelotes – with a long saw.
12. St Andrew – with a saltire cross.

32 (Right)

a Knife
Iron, with solid bolster and 'knock-on' ivory handle carved with a figure of a youth wearing a ruff. The ivory is now stained brown through prolonged burial in the mud. Thames find, c.1550. *B101*
Length: 18cm

b Fork
Silver, with three tines, and twisted wrythen stem, the silver wire wound ferrule bearing the initials 'W L' on the reverse, fitted with a finely carved wooden handle carved with a figure of Justice. Possibly English or French, c.1590. *B105*
Length: 17.5cm

c Knife
Iron, with solid bolster and ivory handle carved with a figure of a pilgrim, English, c.1550. *B102*
Length: 20cm

The cult of the pilgrim was powerful in sixteenth-century Europe. *The Pilgrim's*, published around this time, extolled the virtues of following a direct and purposeful path. The journey is difficult, but in time the true pilgrim will regain paradise and find his spiritual fulfilment.

d Knife
Iron blade with the mark of a bunch of grapes, with solid bolster and short tang, the stained ivory handle carved with a woman's head wearing an Elizabethan ruff as a finial. Thames find, c.1580. *B104*
Length: 19cm

e Knife
Iron blade with the mark of a crown fitted with brass-alloy handle in the form of a mannerist female term or column. Possibly Continental, c.1550. *B103*
Length: 18.3cm

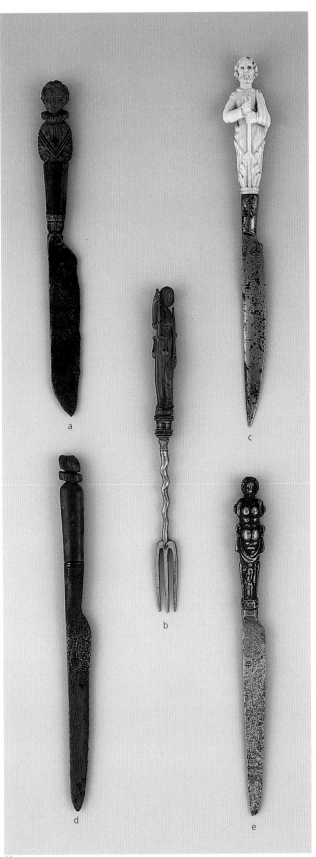

32

35

35 (Above)

Fork
Silver, with wrythen stem, wire wound ferrule surmounted by a carved wooden handle with the figure of Justice. Possibly English, c.1590. *B105* (detail)
Length: 17.5cm

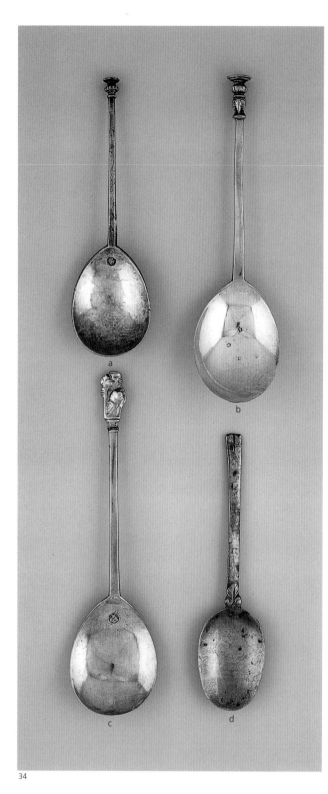

34

34 *(Left)*

a **Spoon**
Silver, with fig-shaped bowl and small seal top. A mark 'R P' on the back of the handle for ROBERT PLANCKNEY. Thames find, London, 1577. *B97*
Length: 15cm

b **Spoon**
Tinned latten, of light weight and section with fig-shaped bowl and elaborate seal top. English, c.1600. *B118*
Length. 17.5cm

c **Spoon**
Silver and parcel-gilt, Apostle style with gilt figure of St Jude on the finial and assay marks for ROBERT DAVYE. Exeter, c.1665. *B154*
Length: 18.5cm

d **Spoon**
Latten, small Puritan style, with leaf motif at the end of the stem and short rat-tail below. River find, English or Dutch, c.1650. *B142*
Length: 15cm

Spoons played an important part at mealtimes in the days before the introduction of forks, and everyone was striving to possess one, preferably one made of silver. Examples fashioned in wood, pewter or latten were no bad substitutes, however, and there were many advantages to owning less expensive spoons: the likelihood of having them stolen was greatly reduced, food tasted just as good, and no costs were incurred in keeping them clean.

The shapes of the bowl, the stem and the end of the 'knop' varied significantly throughout the early and later medieval periods, although this process of change was extremely gradual. Spoons of the thirteenth century, for example, usually had a fig-like bowl with tapering stem ending in some form of knop (p. 65). Any variations were confined to the shape at the end and designs might include a pine cone, a wyrthen twist, a diamond point or even an animal head.

By about 1400 the so-called 'maidenhead' spoons were being introduced. Sometimes the woman's hair is shown braided, a convention restricted to those with married status at the time, which may well suggest that these spoons formed part of a wedding trousseau. Other variations found in the fifteenth century included a 'lion sejant', and also a 'wodewose' – a ferocious barbarian wielding a club – and an 'Apostle' spoon, which is specifically mentioned in a York Will of 1494, but examples are known with earlier hallmarks. A full set of these Apostle spoons would comprise thirteen in number, each Apostle carrying his own emblem with Christ holding an orb. The saints are usually portrayed wearing a halo, although this is not always the case and provincial peices like the Exeter spoon (B154) display a considerable freedom of interpretation.

Another significant variation at this time is the so-called 'seal-top', a descriptive term which is not used in contemporary accounts. Known then as 'flat knoppes', these spoons have a circular end resting on a baluster, which is decorated to a greater or lesser degree with gadrooning and acanthus leaves (see left).

a
b
c
d

36

36 (Left)

a Knife
Iron, with solid bolster and through-tang fitted with crudely engraved bone handle, marked on blade with an orb, (cap missing). English, c.1590. *B107*
Length: 23cm

b Knife
Iron, with solid bolster and through-tang. The bone handle is engraved with panels of scrolls and floral decoration, and terminates in a turned ball finial inter-spaced with an amber washer. Marked on blade with an acorn. English, c.1590. *B109*
Length: 22cm

c Knife
Iron, with solid bolster and through-tang, the bone handle engraved with dot and circular decoration, secured with a flat brass cap and elongated ball finial. Marked on blade with a crown and the dagger for the Cutlers' Company of London, c.1590. *B108*
Length: 21.5cm

d Knife
Iron, with solid bolster, the iron handle inlaid with scrolling foliate designs using silver and gold wire and having faceted ivory spacers. Marked on blade with a heart and the dagger, for the Cutlers' Company of London, c.1590. *B110*
Length: 23cm
This elegant knife would easily qualify as a 'prime' knife for the end of the sixteenth century.

Although each blade has a distinctive mark, it is still difficult to positively identify the manufacturer of a late sixteenth-century knife. Marks could change hands within a matter of months or years, although there were some makers who kept their original marks throughout their working life.

Designs for blade marks were many and varied, an early table of which had been drawn up by Thomas Jadwyn, clerk to the Cutlers Court in 1602. This started a process of regulation which the London Cutlers' Company formalised in 1606.

1600 – 1700

For such a politically disturbed period, the seventeenth-century craftsmen in England were producing some remarkable cutlery. The contrast in decoration between those pieces fashioned during the reign of the Stuart kings and the plain simple styles of the Commonwealth is dramatic, but both Royalist and Puritan cutlers were working to the very highest standards of quality and design.

In 1606 the Cutlers' Company of London required every foreign cutler working in London to strike their mark on the blade and to include a London dagger mark above their own. The Freemen Cutlers of London had been obliged to do this for some time, but the registration of all makers helped to improve standards and gave the company a measure of control.

Eating knives of the sixteenth century had been thin and elegant whereas the seventeenth-century blades were shorter and with a rounded tip. Handles were becoming much more decorative, having composite examples in carved ivory, jet, ebony, amber, agate and precious metals.

The custom of producing pairs of knives in a decorated sheath became popular at this time, often given as a wedding gift from the husband to his spouse and personalised to commemorate the betrothal.

The use of the fork gained slow acceptance in England during this period. An often misquoted reference by the traveller Thomas Coryat (1585–1632), which was first published by Samuel Purchas in *Purchas his Pilgrims*, 1625, records that forks were being used to hold meat on to the plate during the cutting process, but only as an aid to hygiene and cleanliness; it prevented each diner from using the left hand to hold down the meat and thus reduced the risk of cross-contamination. There was no suggestion that the fork was being used to transfer food into the mouth.

The earliest surviving English silver fork, 1632, made for the Earl of Rutland, had two tines and a straight bar stem, but it was not until the restoration of the monarchy in 1660 that we see sets of matching knife, fork and spoons. By the end of the century cased sets of cutlery were produced in numbers, not only in England but at centres like Carlsbad in former Czechoslovakia. They were essential for the traveller, who could not guarantee to be offered an acceptable range of cutlery when visiting in the country or staying at inns and taverns on his journey.

Significant changes in the shape of knife handles and blades are also evident at this time. The blades were becoming slightly curved with a simple bolster, eventually evolving into a scimitar-like shape with distinctive 'flying' bolster, so called because the blade appears to 'fly' away from the handle. The handles themselves were being fashioned in a whole range of exotic materials and starting to take on a pistol-grip shape, a design which the English cutlers adopted as their own distinctive style. Makers like Ephraim How of Saffron Hill, London, capitalised on these developments, introducing a factory system at his workshop and become the most prolific of the British cutlers working at the turn of the century.

Dessert Setting, c.1670

Photograph: Jeremy Phillips for Fairfax House, York

Improvements in table layout at this time included the idea of raising some of the food onto stands. This gave the opportunity to place extra dishes on the table and created a more sumptuous and three-dimensional concept of presentation. Large footed salvers of this type were often embossed on the broad rim with repoussé decoration of fruit and flowers. The *Glossographia* (1661) explains their early use "in giving beer or other liquid thing to save the carpit or cloathes from drips", but they were soon put to other uses as stands for fruits, sweetmeats or even for glass crewetts. They were often fashioned by re-working old plate and it seems to be the case for this elaborate stand from Norwich Castle Museum.

Another innovation was the so-called 'sucket fork' a spoon and fork combination for use with 'wet' or 'dry' sweetmeats. This set of five by John Smith, London, c. 1680 is a rare survival, as are the superb candlesticks by Jacob Bodendick, 1677. It was at the end of the meal that the candles were lit for the dessert course and whilst table candlesticks from the Restoration period survive in numbers, none are more majestic and innovative with their square fluted sockets, gadrooned square bases and cushion-shaped knops on baluster stems.

37

37 (*Above*)

Roundel
Probably maple or sycamore,
being plain on one side as a
receptacle for dry sweetmeats and
decorated on the front with a lion
in a classical landscape, inscribed
with verse: THE LION SNARD THE
MOUSE ENTREATS FOR HELP THE
MOUSE THE FETTERS FREATES
MEANING THE MEN OF DEGREE BY
POORER MEN RELEASED MAY BE.
English, c.1600. *B113*
Diameter: 13cm

38 (*Right*)

a Knife
Iron, with near-parallel blade and
square point tip. Probably a
memento mori knife, with ribbed
ivory handle and carved skull
terminal, blade mark of man's
head and the dagger mark of the
Cutlers' Company of London,
Thames find, c.1600. *B115*
Length: 21cm.

b Knife
Iron, with near-parallel blade,
square point tip and mean bolster,
the ivory handle carved with
lozenges containing amber and jet
insets, blade mark 'V' for Arnold
Cornelius, below the dagger mark
of the Cutlers' Company of
London, c.1629. *B125*
Length: 21cm

a   b

38

a **Knife**
The iron blade of earlier sixteenth-century shape with spear point, solid bolster, through-tang and shaped ivory handle now stained through burial in mud and fitted with ball end finial. The blade marked with a copper inlaid figure of a dog. Thames find, English c.1600. *B117*
Length: 18.5cm

b **Knife**
The iron blade with short, gilded baluster-shaped bolster, fitted with a hollow cast silver handle decorated with flowers, scrolls and panels of arabesques. Blade mark is a thistle. English, c.1600. *B114*
Length: 17.5cm

c **Knife**
Iron, all in one piece of half-round section, decorated on the handle with stylised acanthus and punchwork. This knife was made to fit into a case with another of the same section. English, c.1580. *B92*
Length: 21.5cm

d **Knife**
The iron blade of earlier 16th-century shape with spear point and solid bolster. The facet-shaped ivory handle has amber inserts to all sides, all set within engraved panels of arabesques. Marked on blade with cross on hill and the dagger mark of the Cutlers' Company of London. Possibly Thomas Almond, London c.1600. *B119*
Length: 21cm

e **Knife**
Iron, with solid bolster and through-tang, fitted with a 'chip' carved ivory handle, obscure inlaid mark on blade. English, c.1590. *B106*
Length: 23cm
This type of knife is often illustrated in Dutch still-life paintings.

40

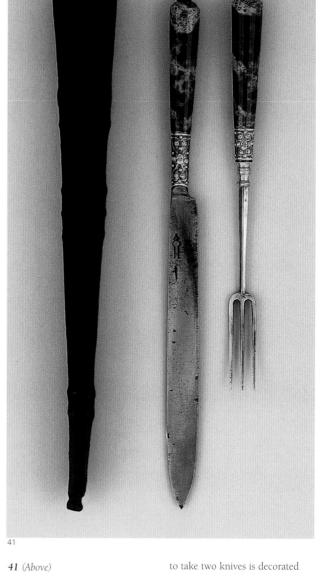

41

40 *(Above)*

Knives (pair of)
Iron, octagonal bolsters engraved and turned on each facet with panels of flowers and foliage. The flowered engraving spills out onto the blade and the whole is damascened in gold. A short half handle of faceted rock crystal is secured in place between a gilded ferrule and a pierced 'pomander' finial made of looped and twisted wire. The blades are marked with the letter 'T' for Henry Stanus and the dagger of the Cutlers' Company of London, c.1606.

The pair of knives are housed in their original sheath of stumpwork decorated with interlacing loops of seed pearls and trailing floral pendants made of gilded wire and silk embroidery. *B120*
Length: 20cm

Rock crystal, a natural quartz, was a commodity highly prized by most cultures from ancient times. It was held to have magical properties and used on objects of veneration or dedication. It was a difficult material to carve and consequently very expensive. The leading source of rock crystal at this time was Freiburg im Breisgau, in Germany.

Pairs of knives in their own exotic sheath are often referred to as 'wedding knives'. This may be the case with these knives, but for a set to qualify for this accolade, there should be some extra clue, like an inscribed dedication (see B138, p. 89) or a motto like this interlacing knot of seed pearls, a pattern which symbolises love (see B129, p.87).
Cf.: Hughes, B., 'Wedding Knives', in *Country Life*, 25 March, 1949, p. 666.

41 *(Above)*

Knife and fork
The knife with an earlier sixteenth-century style blade and spear point tip, has a solid bolster, studded with silver masks and flowers. The faceted agate handle secured in place on the through-tang with a silver ball finial. The later silver fork similarly constructed, with three tines and stem in the sixteenth-century style, the whole being converted from the original companion knife. The blade mark is of a pair of tongs for John Arnold and the dagger mark for the Cutlers' Company of London, c.1606. The original leather sheath made

to take two knives is decorated with patterns of ribbing and stylised fruit. *B121*
Length of knife: 20.5cm

The handles of 'moss' agate, a form of calcedomy with iron oxides and petrifactions of vegetable forms, were probably manufactured at Oberstein or Idar in Germany. Supplies of agate, a quartz stone occurring in rounded nodules, were imported from as far afield as India, Brazil, Iceland and the Faroe Islands. In its natural state, the colours of the different types are rather muted or 'muddy', and these can be intensified or heightened by soaking in honey and heating in the presence of sulphuric acid.

42

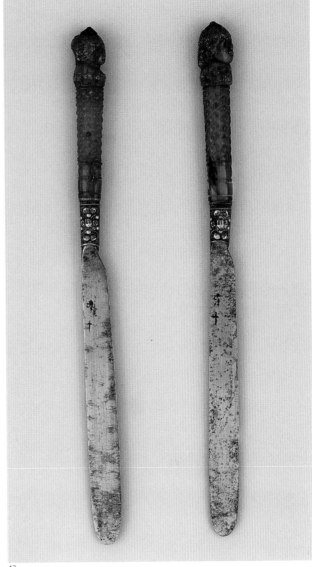

43

42 (Above)

Knives (pair of wedding knives)
With their original case and
purse. The iron blades of near-
parallel shape with centre-point
tips have solid faceted bolsters
decorated with studded silver
masks of cherubs amongst
pendants of flowers. The handles
alternate the same decorative
treatment with pairs of jet spacers
and terminate in curving caps
held in place with ball finials.
The blades are marked with a
dolphin for Henry Dyke and a
dagger for the Cutlers' Company
of London, 1610. *B123*
Length of knife: 19cm
Purse: 13 × 13cm

The matching sheath and purse
are of exceptional quality, with
embroidered satin decorated in
floral patterns with silver-gilt
thread and seed pearls. The
pattern of flowers also seems
to include the initials K.L. on
one side of the purse and I.I.
on the other.

The print of an English
gentlewoman taken from an early
map of London (see p. 88)
illustrates how these items were
meant to be carried, although
there may have been other
methods of carrying. It is not yet
apparent why the sheath and
purse slide up and down the
cording (but remain attached as
the tasselled pommels at the end
remain fixed).

43 (Above)

Knives (pair of)
Iron, with near parallel blades
having round tips and solid
bolsters studded with silver masks
and scrolling seed pods in
grotesque fashion. The design of
these bolsters is similar to that
seen on B121. The blades bear the
mark of a fleur-de-lys for John
Wood or John Wessell and the
dagger for the Cutlers' Company
of London, c.1635. *B122*
Length: 18cm

The amber handles are carved
with the heads of a man and a
woman wearing a type of
decorative collar which did not
appear in English costume until
c.1630. Known as the lace-edged
falling band, it appears in
numerous portraits by artists
like Van Dyck.

It is rare to see amber being
used for the whole section of the
handles. The fossil resin is quite
soft, often with irregularities and
inclusions, and can be easily
damaged, especially when
subjected to fine carving. Most of
the amber coming to England at
this time was either yellow or
orange, and was found on the
Baltic coast near Kaliningrad and
in Lithuania. There were other
varieties, however, found in Sicily,
which had a distinct red colour
and this may be the origin of
these elegant examples.

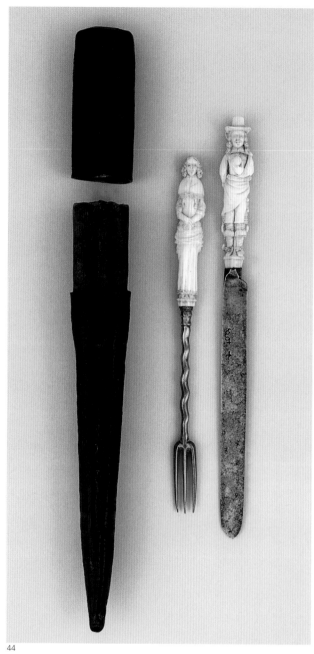

44

45

44 (Above)

Knife and fork
The iron knife has a parallel-sided blade and square point with small faceted bolster. The unmarked silver fork with three tines has an elegant wrythen stem and faceted bolster. Fitted to the knife and fork are a pair of ivory handles of exceptional quality, showing a couple wearing costume popular during the period 1650–60.
The blade mark, however, seems to be a bunch of grapes for Lambert Williamson, c.1610–40,

and a dagger for the Cutlers' Company of London. The accompanying leather slip case indicates that these examples were meant to be carried on a cord which is attached to a belt. Both the case and cover have thong holes at front and back, to prevent the cover from being lost and the punched decoration comprises banding and fish-scale imbrication. *B124*
Length of knife: 18.5cm
Length of case: 21cm

45 (Above)

Knife and fork
Iron, the knife with near-parallel blade, round tip and no blade mark. The fork with two steel tines. Both the knife and fork have solid bolsters decorated with well-rubbed masks and scrolling pods, a feature seen on many knives and forks during this period. The jet handles are shaped as inverted balusters and fixed with delicate filigree ball finials.

The black leather slipcase is decorated with panels of ring and flower. It is clearly moulded to fit the knife and the smaller fork. English, c.1630. *B128*
Length of knife: 22.5cm

The medical virtues of jet, a black fossilized wood, have been well known since Roman times. Said to be an excellent cure for toothache and an antidote to poison, this may well explain the use of this material for cutlery objects.

(detail)
A solid bolster with grotesque mask at the centre of scrolling seedpods. *B129*

(detail)
This type of bolster decoration was popular on the high quality knives of the early 17th century. *B121*

46

46 (Left)

Knives (pair of)
Iron, with near-parallel blades, square point tips and solid bolsters studded with silver masks and scrolling seed pods in 'grotesque' manner. The lathe-turned ivory handles with interlaced panels and raised knops are held in place with filigree end caps. One knife marked on blade with fleur-de-lys for John Wessell, the other marked with a bunch of grapes for William Balls. Both are marked with the dagger of the Cutlers' Company of London, c.1630. *B129*
Length of knife: 23cm

The accompanying sheath, although in poor condition, reveals a lavish design of scrolls and roses finely executed with silver and coloured thread. At the top, amongst the foliage and formed on both sides, is what appears to be an armorial crest showing a standing swan, stork or wild goose surmounted upon a coloured twisted ribbon torse.

If the sheath was meant to house a pair of wedding knives, and this may well be the case, the inclusion of a stork in the decoration would be used to represent the theme of constancy. What is missing from this sheath is the attendant cord and tassels, to complete what was generally known as the 'cauld and string'. The cords were often elaborately plaited and the tassels or pendant drops jewelled or studded with pearls (see B123, p. 85). An English needlework pattern book dated 1620 illustrates twenty examples of cords, laces and strings suitable for wedding knives.

Using ivory, bone, horn or antler for fine carving has its antecedents in ancient history. The material earns its place in cutlery production as one of the most favoured of all substances by its combination of special qualities. Ivory carving became popular in northern Europe during the early middle ages and by the sixteenth century the carvers at Augsburg, Nuremberg, Antwep, Vienna, Dieppe and to a lesser degree London, had become renowned for their domestic production. In the late seventeenth century, however, it was the Russian workshops at Archangel, Kholmongory and latterly, St Petersburg, who were probably supplying a significant proportion of handles to the European cutlery trade at this time. The trade fluctuated dramatically and it was the emerging middle classes of the eighteenth century, however, which helped re-establish ivory as an important medium for cutlery production.

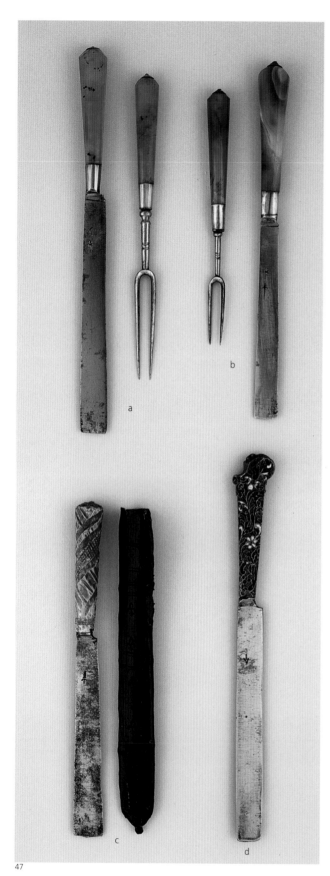

47

47 *(Left)*

a **Knife and fork**
Iron, the knife with near-parallel blade, square tip and mean bolster. The fork with two tines and turned stem terminating in a baluster knop. The multi-faceted agate handles are secured with matching silver ferrules and silver washered ends. The blade with copper inlaid 'Y' marked with the dagger of the Cutlers' Company of London, 1631. *B131*
Length: 20cm

b **Knife and fork**
Iron, the knife with near-parallel blade, square tip, mean bolster and through-tang. An agate handle of tapered ovoid section is secured by a silver ferrule and a silver-washered end. The associated contemporary two-tine fork similarly constructed. Blade mark a dagger of the Cutlers' Company of London and Peter Spitzer, c.1621. *B130*
Length: 18.5m

c **Knife**
Iron, with tapered blade and near-square tip ground to a shallow point. A mean bolster, and through tang is fitted with a turned green stained bone handle decorated in imitation of twisted ribbon. The blade engraved with
IF YOU DO USE ME DO NOT ABUSE ME.
Probably Sheffield, c.1650. *B139*
Length: 17.5cm

The black leather slipcase, decorated with banding and fleur-de-lys patterns, is probably contemporary.

d **Knife**
Iron, with parallel blade and square tip. The cast-copper alloy handle has cloisonné flower and plant decoration with some of the original blue-and-white enamel inlay still surviving. The terminal of the handle is in the form of a grotesque mask. Dutch, c.1650. *B144*
Length: 20cm

This type of imported handle, modelled after designs by the German artist Michael Le Bon (ft.? 1605) is frequently excavated in England.

Right
J. Speed, A Map of Europe, 1631 (detail).
Notice how the caul and string hangs low from the girdle.

48 *(Right)*

Knife and fork
Iron, the knife with near-parallel blade, square point tip, a mean bolster and through-tang. The tapering, faceted agate handles are secured with faceted silver ferrules and silver-washered ends. The fork is similarly constructed with turned stem and spoon-shaped tines, marked on blade with the dagger of the Cutlers' Company of London and the fleur-de-lys for Jeremy Knowles, c.1637. *B134*

The original leather slip case, decorated with delicate panels of banding, feathers and fish-scale imbrication, shows the early introduction of a divided case, where the space for the fork is shorter than that for the knife.
Length: 21.5cm

What is particularly noticeable about these early British forks is a distinctive haunch curve where the fork joins the stem. The tines themselves can be of oval section, as in this case, or of near triangular form (see B130 and 131) and must draw their inspiration from Italian cutlery of the period.

The publication of Vincenzo Cervio's *Il Trinciante*, first printed in 1593, included numerous illustrations of cutlery and these drawings were presumably very useful for the British cutlers.

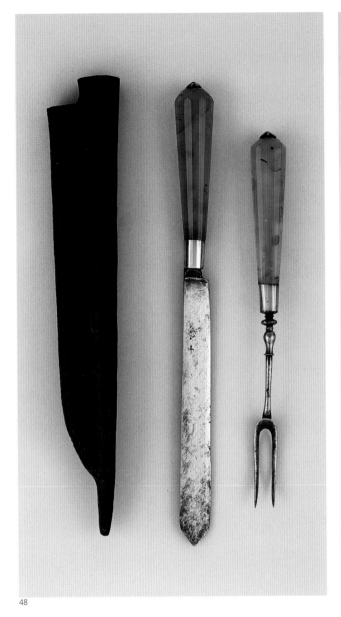

48

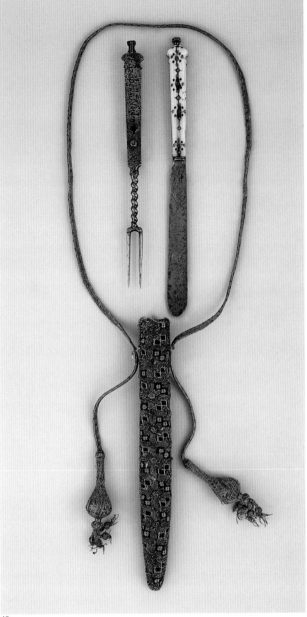

49

It was customary for a pair of knives, and later on, a matching knife and fork, to be given as part of the bridal trousseau, and the London Marriage Licences 1521–1800 records a marriage of a certain Elizabeth Skinner to a Mr John Norden in 1647, so B138 could have been a wedding gift from him, following the custom of the day.

The practice of giving knives first started in Britain during the reign of Henry VIII (1509–47), but the custom has longer traditions on the Continent. Marriage contracts in the mid-fourteenth century record the 'attestation of knife', a practice derived from the convention of presenting a purchaser with a knife when conveying property.

However, the gift of a pair of knives in an exotic embroidered sheath was not restricted to weddings. The Cutlers' Company of London, for example, have records from Elizabethan times of gifts to the wives of men who helped the Company in some practical way.

49 (Above)

Knife and fork

Iron, slotted to fit together as one piece, the knife has a tapering straight blade, round tip and offset scale-tang. The shaped ivory scale is decorated with horn, brass pins and coral beads. The exposed face of the knife tang is engraved with the name 'Elizabeth Norden', within a border of punched decoration terminating in stars and pods. The two-tine fork is similarly engraved and constructed, but has a wrythen stem and slotted terminal. The mark on the knife blade is a

dolphin for Jonas Melcher and the dagger of the Cutlers' Company of London, c.1622. *B138*
Length of knife: 21cm

The accompanying sheath of petit-point stitching in a pattern of squares, is overlaid with stars and floral motifs made from silver-gilt thread.

The long cord, which allowed the 'cauld and string' to be attached to the girdle of the owner, (*see opposite*), is woven with silver-gilt thread and terminates in pendant drops and gathered tassels.

50 (Left)

Fork
Iron with two thin tines and turned stem. The tapering ivory handle is engraved and stained brown. A twisting ribbon runs down its length with the motto: THE LOVE THAT CHAST WILL NEVER WHAST. Amongst the attendant foliage is the profile of a woman in period dress and above her the figure of a bird. The handle is secured to the through-tang with a turned-brass ferrule and bell-shaped cap. English, c.1650. *B140*
Length: 15cm

51 (Left)

Knife
Probably silver, with blade of medieval form and handle with deep-cut decoration of seven petalled roses, pomegranates and a roundel showing an eight-pointed flower within a circle. Originally inlaid with enamel (traces remaining). Engraved with the date 1649 on the spine of the handle and a stylised sunflower on the cap. Possibly English. *B143*
Length: 13.5cm

The quality of the engraving is exceptional and in its original state would have been an outstanding example of its kind. There seems little doubt that the choice of symbols is deeply religious. In Christian philosophy, for example, pomegranate represented eternal life and spiritual fecundity. The sunflower represented worship and a seven petalled rosa alba signified not only purity and innocence, but to the Roman Catholics the seven sacraments or activities which confer grace. The most significant emblem, however, is the 'Rose of the Winds', with its double cross enclosed within a circle. Early Christians saw this as the symbol of the four cardinal and four intermediate directions which govern our journey through life.

51

50

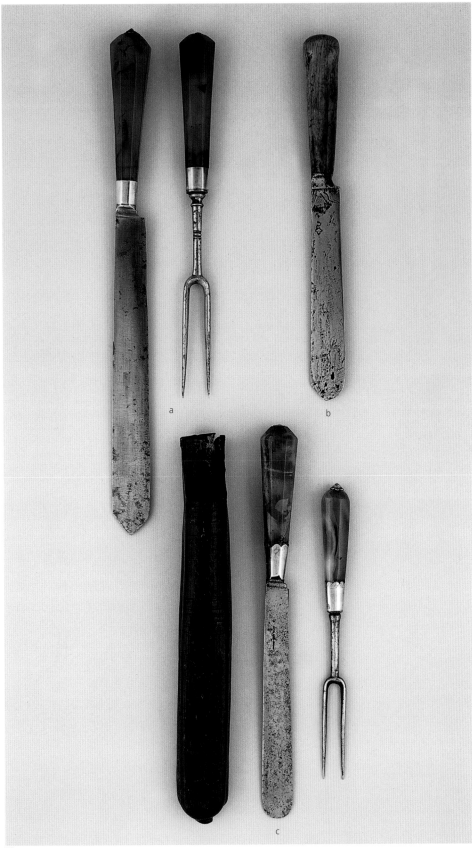

a   b

c

52 *(Left)*

a Knife and fork
Iron, the knife with tapered blade, square point tip and mean bolster. The fork with two steel tines of triangular section joined to a turned stem. Both handles, made of tapered faceted agate, are secured on the through-tang with silver ferrules and silver washered ends, no mark, English, c.1650.
B145
Length of knife: 27cm

b Knife
Iron, with tapered blade, pointed tip, mean bolster and knock-on tang. The mud stained ivory handle is of rounded rectangular section with a slight swell at the end. Marked on blade with fleur-de-lys and horseshoe, Thames find, possibly Sheffield, c.1650.
B141
Length: 19.5cm

c Knife and fork
Iron, the knife with tapered blade, round tip and mean bolster. The accompanying two-tine fork of rounded triangular section is joined to a plain round stem. Both handles, made of tapering faceted agate, are secured on the through-tang with scalloped silver ferrules and washered ends of silver and silver-gilt. Marked on blade with a crown for JEREMY KNOWLES, and the dagger mark of the Cutlers' Company of London, c.1657.
B146

The accompanying two-part leather slipcase is decorated with panels of thistles, vertical lines and banding that imitates a stave construction.
Length of knife: 21cm

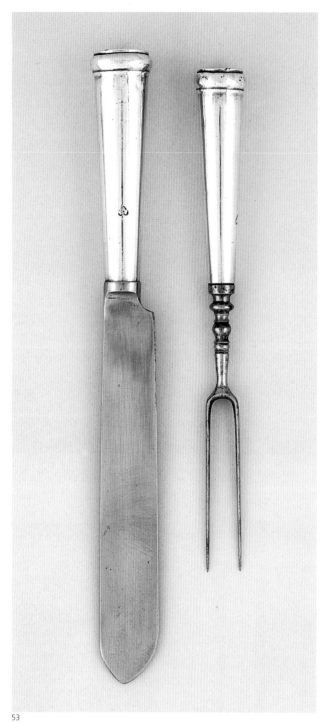

53

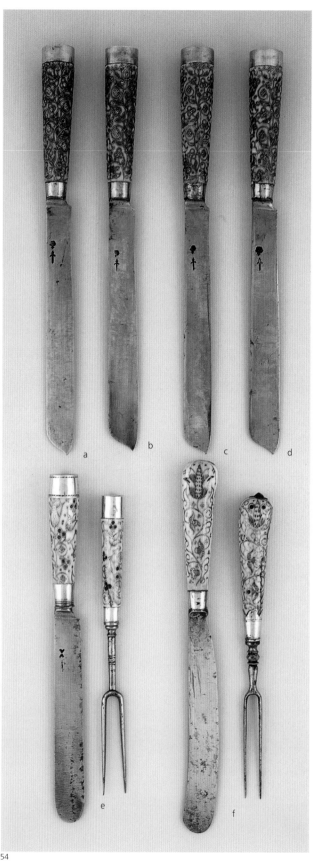

53 *(Above)*

Knife and fork
Iron, the knife with gently tapered blade, square point tip and small bolster is fitted with a silver handle of cartridge tapered round section. The matching two-tine fork is similarly constructed. Each handle is engraved on the 'seal-top' with the initials 'W W' within a roundel of leaves.
Obscure silver mark of a heart, English, c.1660. *B151*
Length of knife: 22.5cm
This example qualifies for what Bill Brown describes as a 'prime' knife.

54

54 *(Left)*

a, b, c, d Knives (4 of 6)

Iron, with near-parallel blades, dropped point tip and mean bolsters. The handles are tapered round-section ivory, in patterns of vine leaves and grapes. Fixed in place with plain ferrules and caps made of silver. Marked on five blades with a crown, probably the mark of Paul Browne, and the dagger for the Cutlers' Company of London, c.1677. *B153*
A sixth blade (not shown) bears a different maker's mark.
Length: 25.5m

The design of these blades is unusual and does not seem to conform with the majority of British blades in production at this time. The slight curve to the tip and the dropped point is reminiscent of designs for Italian knives from an earlier period (p. 30).

e Knife and fork

Iron, the knife with near parallel blade, round tip and mean bolster. Both implements have handles formed by tapered round section ivory, decorated in a more sophisticated manner than B153, with patterns of flowers and vines, inlaid with silver wire and green and red enamel. The knife has a silver ferrule and cap with some banded decoration, but those on the fork are plain. Marked on blade with a double heart for Bartholomew King and the dagger for the Cutlers' Company of London, c.1685. *B167*
Length of knife: 23.5m

f Knife and fork

Iron, the knife with transitional scimitar blade, small bolster, and through tang. The two-tine fork has a turned baluster stem. Both have ivory handles of slight pistol shape, decorated with elaborate silver inlaid arabesques of flower and leaf coloured with red and green enamel. English, c.1690. *B171*
Length of knife: 23.5cm

Note the slight curve of the blade and the lack of choil (chin of blade). The knife's blade is stamped with word 'HOW', but the absence of the London dagger mark indicates this is probably not the mark of Ephraim How, but more likely to be that of a Sheffield cutler.

55

55 *(Left)*

Spoon and fork

Silver, the folding four-tine fork with attachable spoon bowl is engraved on the octagonal faceted stem with alternating chevrons. Screwed into the handle is a silver toothpick decorated with the figure of Minerva in repose. A sliding sleeve holds the spoon in the opened position. Engraved with the letters 'S M' on the spoon bowl. Dutch or Italian, c.1620. *B156*
Length when open: 17cm

The painting by Gasper Van der Hocke (p. 20) seems to illustrate an example of this travelling cutlery.

For similar examples in the Victoria & Albert Museum Collection see Bailey, C. T. P., *Knives and Forks*, The Medici Society, 1927, fig. 20.

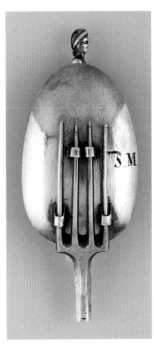

Above (detail)

The combined spoon and fork in closed position.

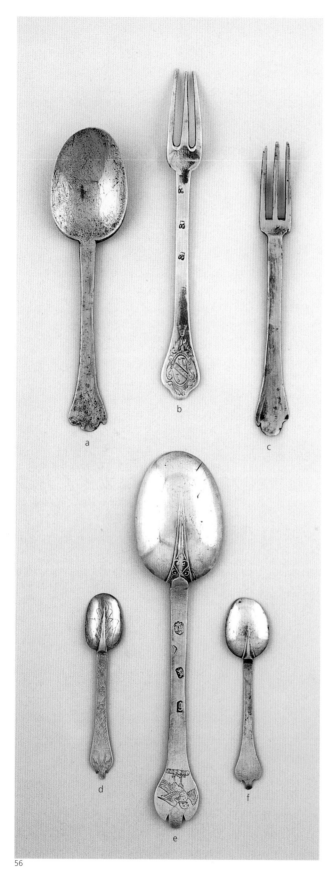

56

57

56 *(Left)*

a, c Spoon and fork
Latten, both showing considerable wear, the three-tine fork follows the shape set by the Puritan-style spoon. English, c.1680. *B158*
Length of spoon: 16cm

b Fork
Silver, a three-tine fork with dognose end engraved with a crest, possibly for Russell, marked three times on the stem with 'I P' beneath a heart with two pellets. English Provincial, c.1690. *B160*
Length: 17.5cm

The general use of armorial decoration on spoons and forks appears on British cutlery during the reign of Charles I (1625–49), although in wealthy households this was the practice much earlier. It was a useful identification method, but more importantly, it allowed the owner to display his bearings, for the 'dignity of the host and benefit of the guest'. The cutlery was displayed crest-up and this gives a clear indication of how the piece would be presented on the table.

d Spoon
Silver, small with trifid end, engraved stem and rat-tail bowl. The same leaf and cabachon decoration is repeated on the upper face of the steam. Marked with a crown over D S, London, c.1660. *B155*
Length: 10cm

e Spoon
Silver, with trifid end and decorated rat-tail decorated with scrolls and ribbing. Maker's mark of Edmund Hinton. London, c.1683. *B159*

The trifid end bears the crest of a falcon rising and belled, with ducal collar on a torse; for Powlett, the family name for the Dukes of Cleveland.
Length: 20cm

f Spoon
Silver, plain with trifid end, rat-tail bowl and obscure mark, probably English, c.1680. *B157*
Length: 10.5cm

57 *(Above)*

Knife
Silver, tapered blade with round end and mean bolster. The silver cannon handle fitted with blade mark for Barthomolew King. London, c.1680. B161
Length: 22.5cm

a

b

a Knife, fork and spoon

With filigree case, silver, the knife with tapered blade, square tip and no blade mark, the two-tine fork with baluster stem. Both knife and fork have silver cartridge handles with obscure marks. The trifid spoon is engraved in naive style with a flowering rat-tail on the underside of the bowl and a face amongst foliage on the trifid end.

The accompanying filigree case is decorated with a variety of flowers, trailing plants and scrollwork.

At the top, a hinged lid (the hinge made from twisted wire) is locked in place with a rotating clasp. England, c.1685. *B162*
Length of case: 11.5cm

David Mitchell has shown that the need for a personal set of cutlery, when travelling or visiting, was still very important at the end of the seventeenth century. There were some wealthy merchants who bought sets of knives and forks in the 1680s, but they are very much the exception. However, by the beginning of the eighteenth century the situation had changed significantly.

b Knife, fork and spoon

Iron and silver, the knife with transitional blade, small bolster, and blade mark of Ephraim How. The cartridge-style silver handle engraved with panels of feathered diamonds and a pomegranate on the cap, is stamped with the mark 'TT' below a crown. Both spoon and fork are marked for Peter Harrache and engraved with flowers and faces on the front, with the initials 'M O' in a panel on the reverse of the trifid ends. London, c.1690. *B164*
The attendant fitted case is covered in snakeskin.
Length of case: 13cm.

Ephraim How and his son John How had a blade mill at Southend, Lewisham, in the early part of the eighteenth century and a shop on Saffron Hill, London. They introduced a factory system and produced large quantities of pistol knives and forks for standing boxes.

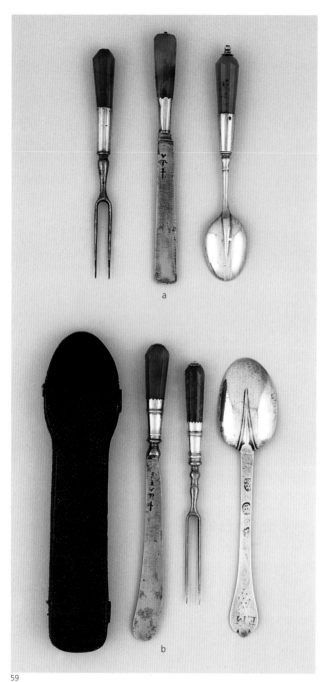

59

60

---

59 *(Above)*

a Knife, fork and spoon
Iron and silver, the knife with
tapered blade, square tip and
mean bolster, the two-tine steel
fork with baluster stem. An
associated spoon, with silver stem
and rat-tail bowl has French
marks. The three handles are
made of faceted and tapered
cornelian, with through-tang,
faceted silver ferrules, and
washered ends (one missing). The

knife with blade mark of Ephraim
How, and the dagger for the
Cutlers' Company of London,
c.1687. *B165*
Length of knife: 12.5cm

b Knife, fork and spoon
Iron and silver, the knife with
scimitar I blade, flying bolster and
through tang, bearing on the
blade the mark of Ephraim How.
The two-tine fork with turned
baluster stem is fitted like the
knife with faceted and tapered

cornelian handles, secured with
turned silver ferrules and
washered ends. A silver rat-tail
spoon of trifid form bears the
mark of 'SW' with no date letter.
The initials 'E M' are engraved on
the reverse and 'AS' on the front
of the trifid end.
    All these items fit neatly into
the attendant black fish-skin case.
All probably made in London,
c.1690. *B174*
Length of case: 16cm

60 (Left)

Knife and fork
Iron, the knife with near-parallel blade, round tip and mean bolster. The two-tine fork of triangular section has a turned baluster stem. Carved ivory handles of Jupiter and Juno are held in place with silver ferrules. Marked on the knife blade with a horseshoe for Robert Ashwood and dagger for the Cutlers' Company of London, c.1685. *B166*
Length of knife: 22.5cm

The representations of two senior gods of Olympus is exquisitely realised in these two carved figures. A crowned figure of Jupiter stands before an eagle, the bird which flew to him as he was about to make war on the Titans, and which he adopted as his messenger. He holds in one hand a representation of thunder and lightning, whilst in the other is a sceptre, a symbol of regal authority. His wife Juno, also in period costume, stands next to a peacock, a bird sacred to her and used to draw her chariot. Around her waist is the magic belt or girdle borrowed from Venus and said to make the wearer of it irresistible. She also holds a regal sceptre and wears a sprig of laurel at her breast.

These carved ivory handles exemplify a small but distinguished group of hafts which appear on cutlery in several European countries at this time. As well as mythological representations, the subjects employed are sometimes zoomorphic (p. 97) or even salacious (p. 102) and occasionally a male and female in period costume (p. 99), which seems to perpetuate the tradition of the marriage gift. It is still not clear where these handles were being made but possibilities include the Dieppe, St Petersburg or Augsburg in Germany.

61 Right)

a Knife and fork
Iron and silver, the knife with small, tapered blade, square tip and mean bolster, the two-tine fork of triangular section with lightly turned stem. Both silver-gilt handles of tapering octagonal form are engraved with alternating panels of chevrons and floral pendants. The beaked ends are engraved with roses. Marked on blade with the dagger of the Cutlers' Company of London, and on the handles with a silver mark 'RS' perhaps Richard Sheldon. London, c.1690. *B168*
Length of knife: 16.5cm

b Knife and fork
Iron and silver-gilt, the knife with tapering blade, square tip, mean bolster and silver-gilt octagonal-shaped handle decorated with panels of oak leaf engraving, marked on blade with a chalice, c.1680. The silver-gilt fork of trifid style has three tines and scrolling foliate engraving with the engraved mark of J. Phelps. London, c.1685. *B163*
Length of knife: 13.5cm

c Knife and fork
Iron. A dismantling knife and fork with extra quill blade. The knife with scimitar I blade, mean bolster, the two-tine fork with short turned baluster stem. Threaded to fit into solid iron bolsters fitted to ivory handles carved as standing dogs. Marked on knife's blade with a pipe. Sheffield, c.1700. *B178*
Length of knife: 19cm
A custom-made compartmentalised leather case is stamped on the body with panels of dot-and-dart decoration and diamond patterns on the cap.

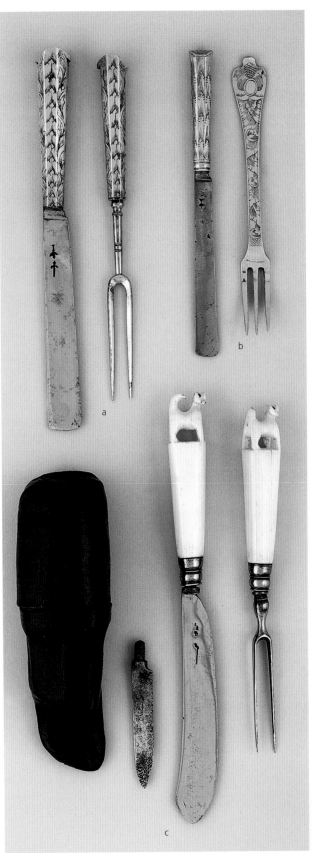

Portable cutlery was essential for the traveller who could not guarantee to be offered an acceptable range of eating implements when visiting in the country or staying at inns or taverns. Early English travelling sets date from the 1680s and are often small for easy storage in a satchel or saddlebag. The cases are usually leather or shagreen, although sometimes a more exotic material like silver filigree is employed (p. 95). It is not yet clear just how popular the English-made sets were at this time. They had stiff competition from Carlsbad in former Czechoslovakia where the workshops made a speciality of these novelty items (p. 15), but English production may have catered for a less affluent clientele.

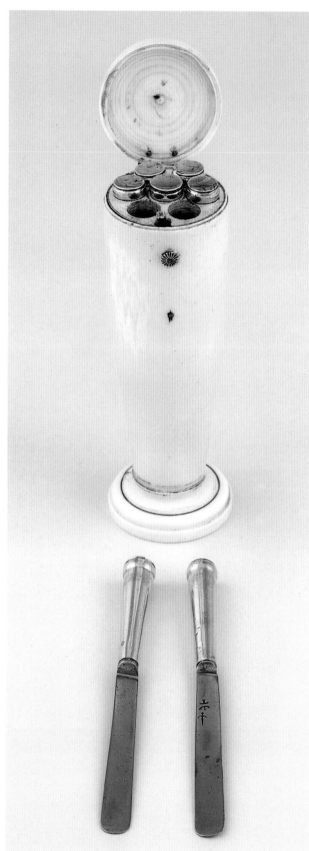

63

63 (*Above*)

Campaign set
Steel and silver, containing
dismantling cutlery, comprising
two sets of knives, forks and
spoons, with small combined
marrow scoop/spoon, a nutmeg
grater and a corkscrew. All set
into a partitioned papier-mâché

liner which sits within a silver
beaker of plain tapered form
marked for J. LINGUARD, London,
1726. *B473*
The purpose-made black fishskin
case fitted with lock and engraved
escutcheon plate. .
Height of case: 16cm (closed)
Length of knife: 22cm
(constructed)

62 (*Left*)

Knives (7)
Iron, the near-parallel blade with
rounded tips and bearing the
mark of a Crown and letter 'T',
perhaps for Joseph Stanhouse and
a dagger for the Cutler's Company
of London, c.1680. *B470*

All housed in a free-standing
turned ivory stock with hinged lid
and button clasp.
Height of case: 15cm (closed)
Length of knife: 11cm

Ivory stocks of this pattern are
rare, and mostly made of laquered
papier-mâché or fishskin.

62

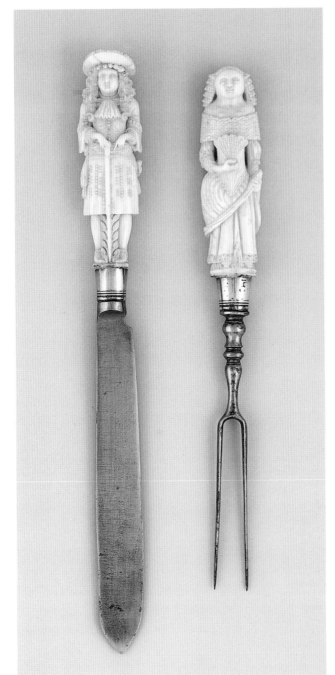

64

64 *(Left)*

Knife and fork
Iron, the knife with tapered blade, centre-point tip, and small bolster, (unmarked), the two-tine fork with turned baluster stem. The carved ivory handles are secured with silver ferrules and depict a man and a woman in period dress. English, c.1690.
B169
Length of knife: 25cm

The quality and accuracy of these carved figures suggests the artist was working from contemporary engravings. A number of these sources were produced, a popular one being the frontispiece to Ogilby and Morgan's *Map of London*, 1682 (see Ribeiro and Cumming, *The Visual History of Costume*, London, 1989).

The ivory gentleman has a gathered cravat and ruffed cuffs below his long, loose coat with its assemblage of buttons and wide cuffs. Around his waist is a sword and scabbard together with a fringed sash, a quasi-military style popular since the 1670s. On his head, he wears a curled wig and flat brimmed hat, a style which is entirely consistent with this period. The woman is also formally dressed with her stiff, long-fronted bodice and looped-up trained skirt over a fringed petticoat. Her hair is smooth at the temples and gathered at the sides with a tight bun at the back. She wears an embroidered shawl around her shoulders and holds an unfolded fan. Manuals of instruction on how to hold a fan illustrate this as the correct method in fashionable circles.

65 *(Right)*

Knife
Iron and brass, with small scimitar folding knife, and blade mark of W. Pepys. The pistol handle of brass is inscribed MARY BROOMHALL on one side, ALBRIGHTON on the reverse, London, c.1690. *B172*
Length when open: 13.5cm

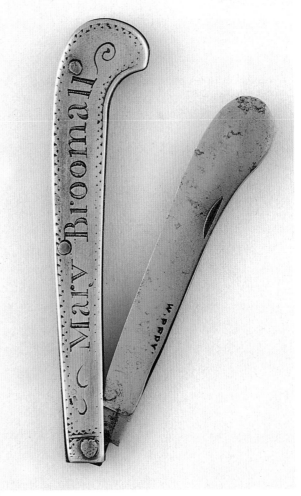

65

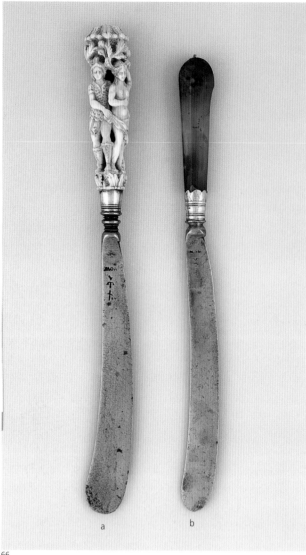

66

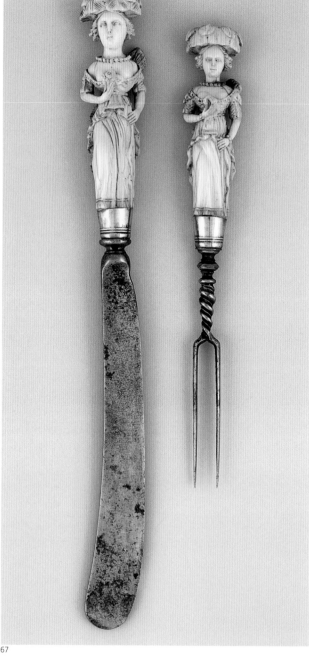

67

66 (Above)

a Knife
Iron, with large scimitar I blade, flying bolster and silver ferrules. The carved ivory handle tells the story of the illicit love of Mars and Venus in the forest. On the reverse is a kneeling Cupid clasping the Goddess's leg. Above, in the form of a canopy, is a plumed aigrette of feathers. Blade mark of Ephraim How with dagger of the Cutlers' Company of London, c.1690. *B175*
Length: 30.5cm.

b Knife
Iron, with large scimitar I blade, flying bolster, through tang and shaped silver ferrule. The semi-pistol handle of faceted agate fixed with washered end. Mark of

Ephraim How and dagger of Cutlers' Company of London, c.1690–1700. *B176*
Length: 28.5cm

See note on Ephraim How (B164, p. 94).It was not until about 1710 that the fully developed pistol handle became popular in England. This example and also that of B171, p. 93, must be early examples of a style in its formative years. It seems reasonable to assume this shape takes its inspiration from the weaponry of the period. The English gunsmiths were producing the so-called 'Queen-Anne pistol', in great numbers from the 1690s onwards, not only for the military but for the civilian market.

67 (Above)

Knife and fork
Iron, the knife with scimitar 1 blade and flying bolster, the two-tine fork with twisted baluster stem. Both fitted with exquisitely carved ivory handles in the form of the hunter goddess Diana, dressed in stylised classical costume with short sleeves and low, square-cut bodice trimmed

with lace. They hold a 'posie' in one hand and bow in the other, with a cap, or aigrette, of plumed feathers on their heads. On the reverse, the hair is banded and strung with pearls, and they carry a full quiver of arrows. Blade mark obscure, possibly London or Sheffield, c.1700. *B179*
Length of knife: 26.5cm

1700 – 1800

Table knives and forks at the end of the seventeenth and into the beginning of the eighteenth centuries were long, the knife usually measuring over twenty-six centimetres, with a scimitar, spatulated blade and a curved, pistol-grip handle. These scimitar knives qualify for 'prime' knife status, and although made 300 years ago they are still admired and are very pleasing to use and to hold.

The cutlers were particularly innovative in the choice of materials for handles at this time, with the most expensive being the 'massy' silver or agate and the cheapest examples coming from France and Sheffield. Other popular materials in use included ebony, ivory, green fishskin, amber and tortoiseshell, together with exotic glass imports of aventurine, millefiore and scrambled glass. The records of the English East India Trading Company show that by the 1720s ceramic handles were starting to be imported into England, arriving as straight-sided or pistol shapes and decorated in either Imari or blue-and-white colours.

The European manufacturers responded quickly to this competition with their own production, particularly Meissen in Germany and St Cloud in France. By the middle of the century the British factories at Bow, Chelsea, Worcester and in Staffordshire were also able to compete on quality and price. Given the quantities produced, we know these ceramic handles were very popular but few have survived due to the fragile nature of the material.

Other developments in the cutlery trade stand out in the eighteenth century, the most significant being the gradual movement of the heavier side of cutlery making to Sheffield. With better power supplies (the city had six rivers to call upon), an abundance of labour and a closer proximity to raw materials, the Sheffield manufacturers were much cheaper than their London counterparts.

The introduction of standing boxes for cutlery also stimulated a great increase in production. Households were now being fitted out with more cutlery than they could use themselves. Similarly, the development in the 1730s of knives and forks specifically for dessert must have been greeted with relish by the manufacturers.

By the middle of the century, a sudden change in fashion from scimitar to French-style blade and a rise in the neoclassical movement was a further stimulus to large-scale production. These spear-point blades and straight-sided handles dominated for some forty years, but although superseded by a transitional type of knife designed with the aim of rekindling an interest in the old-style scimitar form, they were quickly replaced by a simpler parallel-sided blade, a shape which dominated for some 150 years.

Fork and spoon design, especially in silver, changed slowly with only minor variations throughout the century. The so-called 'Hanoverian' pattern, with its distinctive rat-tail design on the end, gave way in the 1760s to an 'Old English' style with simplified shape and the ends turned down instead of up. As a result the crests and initials appear on the front of the spoon, causing the spoons and forks to be displayed face-up on the table.

By the end of this period, cutlery for specialised purposes made its appearance. Mechanical cheese scoops and 'masticating' knives were just two of the innovations introduced to cater for an increasingly affluent society.

68

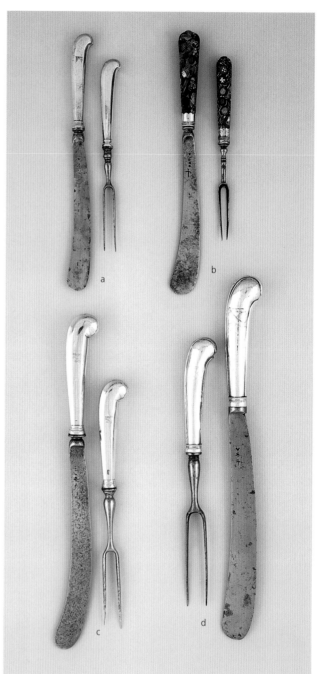

69

68 *(Left)*

Knife
Iron, scimitar I blade, the carved ivory handle sitting in a deep silver ferrule depicts at the front a pair of lovers embracing. At the rear is a shame-faced 'Peeping Tom' displaying false modesty. He partly covers his eyes with one hand whilst holding his genitals with the other. Probably London, c.1700. *B181*
Length: 18cm

69 *(Right)*

a Knife and fork
Iron, small 'prime' knife with scimitar I blade, and flying bolster, the two-tine fork with turned baluster stem. Both fitted with silver octagonal pistol handles marked with the initials 'W C' and an armorial crest of a pair of clasped hands between two wings erect on a torse, possibly for Crathorne. The blade marked with a heart and fleur-de-lys for Peter Spitzer and a dagger for the Cutlers' Company of London, c.1698. *B177*
Length of knife: 20.5cm

b Knife and fork
Iron, scimitar I blade, with flying bolster, the two-tine fork of splayed form has a turned baluster stem. Venetian *millefiore* glass handles of tapering section are secured with silver ferrules and end caps. The blade marked with PATCH and the dagger for the Cutlers' Company of London, c.1710. *B183*
Length of knife: 21cm

The technique of enclosing brightly coloured discs of *canna vitrea* within the body of glass was a technique known from Roman times but re-discovered and exploited by the Italian glass-makers at Murano.

c Knife and fork
Iron, scimitar I blade, with flying bolster, the two-tine fork with elegant baluster stem. Both fitted with resin-filled, cast-silver octagonal pistol handles, and bearing the mark for John Taylor and an armorial crest of a cockatrice on a torse, possibly for Jenkins or Reynolds. The blade marked with a heart and fleur-de-

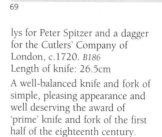

(Above)
Reverse view

lys for Peter Spitzer and a dagger for the Cutlers' Company of London, c.1720. *B186*
Length of knife: 26.5cm

A well-balanced knife and fork of simple, pleasing appearance and well deserving the award of 'prime' knife and fork of the first half of the eighteenth century.

d Knife and fork
Iron, scimitar I blade with haunched bolster, the two-tine fork with turned baluster stem. Both with plain-ribbed, resin-filled, cast-silver handles of pistol form bearing the armorial crest of two lions jambes in saltire on a torse, possibly for Bermingham of Warwickshire. The blade marked with a heart and fleur-de-lys for Peter Spitzer and a dagger for the Cutlers' Company of London, c.1720. *B188*
Length of knife: 28.5cm

70

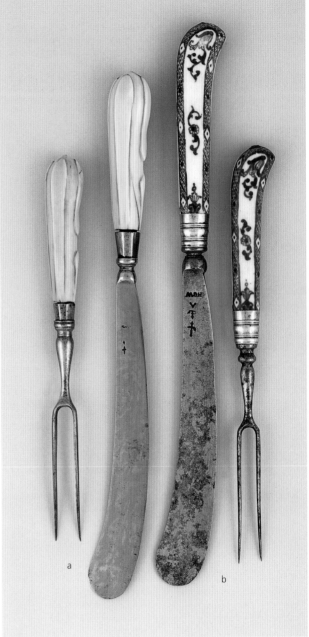

71

70 (Above)

a Knife
Iron, scimitar 1 blade with flying bolster and through-tang. The tapered Venetian *millefiore* glass handle fitted to a scalloped-edge silver ferrule. A blade mark of the letter 'D' and dagger for the Cutlers' Company of London, c.1710. *B182*
Length: 27.5cm

b Knife
Replacement silver scimitar II blade, with faceted Venetian 'scrambled' glass handle, secured with a short decorated silver ferrule. C.1720. *B184*
Length: 20.5cm

c Knife
Iron, scimitar blade, with flying bolster, and 'scrambled' aventurine glass handle secured with a decorated silver ferrule, blade probably London, handle probably Venetian import. Venetian, c.1720. B185
Length: 27cm

The technique of making aventurine involves sprinkling copper crystals into molten glass, a technique used in antiquity, but rediscovered by the Murano glass-makers in the sixteenth century. Normal exports from Italy at this time were usually a dark brown glass with coloured specks, which makes this 'scrambled' example of black, red, white and yellow glass an interesting variation.

71 (Above)

a Knife and fork
Iron, scimitar I blade, with flying bolster, the two-tine fork with simple baluster stem. Both with integral faceted bolsters. The ivory handles showing Chinese influence (plant form), perhaps imported. Blade mark for Cutlers' Company of London, c.1730. *B190*
Length of knife: 27.5cm

b Knife and fork
Iron, scimitar I blade, with flying bolster and through-tang, the two-tine fork with turned baluster stem. Two porcelain handles (probably Meissen) in blue-and-white Chinese style, secured with turned silver ferrules. Blade marked with spade and crown for Ephraim How and dagger for the Cutlers' Company of London, c.1730. *B191*
Length of knife: 29.5cm
See note on Ephraim How (B164, p. 94).

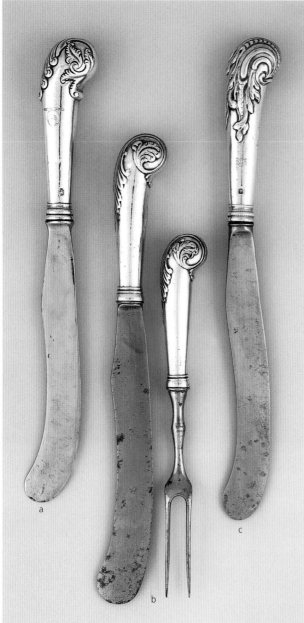

72

72 *(Left)*

a Knife
Iron, scimitar II blade, with cast-silver handle decorated on the butt with a short acanthus scroll. Bears the silver mark for William Alexander, London, c.1740, and the armorial crest of a crescent on a torse. *B197*
Length: 26.5cm

b Knife and fork
Iron, scimitar II blade, the two-tine fork with simple turned baluster stem. The cast silver handles decorated with a foliate pattern of scrolling acanthus on the butt and bearing the silver mark of Thomas Lawrence, London, c.1742. *B195*
Length of knife: 27cm

c Knife
Iron, scimitar II blade, with elaborate cast-silver handle decorated with an ornate acanthus scroll on the butt. Maker's mark is rubbed, with an armorial crest of a collared griffin's head between two raised wings on a torse. Probably London, c.1750. *B202*
Length: 27.5cm

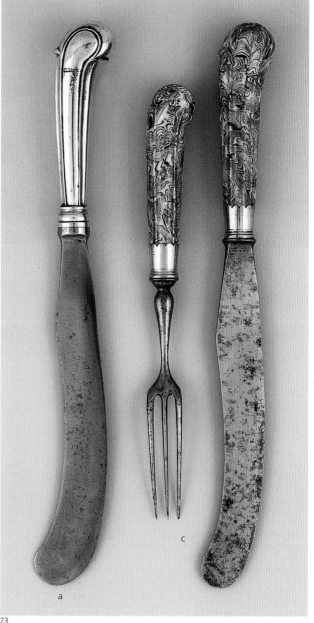

73

73 *(Right)*

a Knife
Scimitar II blade, with cast-silver handle of fluted, pistol shape. Maker's mark rubbed, with armorial crest of a dexter hand couped at wrist, holding a sword piercing a bear's head, probably for Forbes. Possibly London, c.1740. *B199*
Length: 27cm

b Knife and fork
Iron, scimitar II blade, the three-tine fork with simple baluster stem. Fitted with fluted Whieldon agate-ware pottery handles (note the similarity with B199) and secured with scalloped silver ferrules. Sheffield, c.1740. *B200*
Length of knife: 27cm

Thomas Whieldon established a factory at Fenton Low in 1740 making knife and fork handles in white stoneware and agate-ware for the Sheffield cutlers. He employed Josiah Spode as an apprentice and was in partnership with Josiah Wedgwood (1754–59).

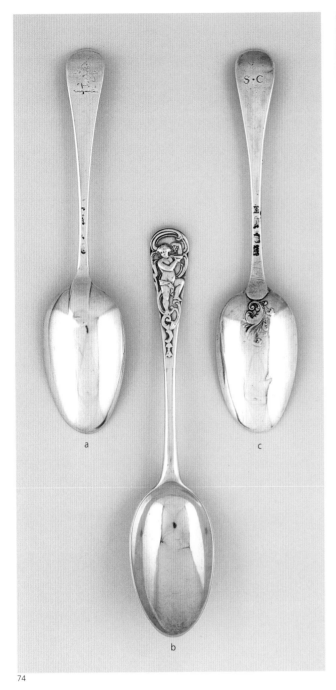

74

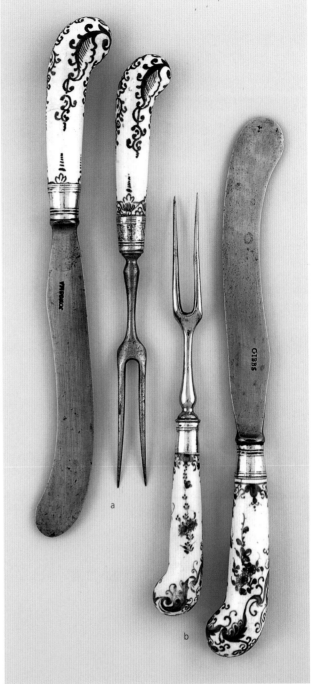

75

74 (Above)

a **Spoon**
Silver, Hanoverian style, bearing the mark of Elizabeth Oldfield, and an armorial crest of a lion rampant gardant holding an orb, for Lloyd Price. London, 1748. *B203*
Length: 20cm

b **Spoon**
Silver with gilt bowl. A Hanoverian style spoon having a cast figure of Bacchus within an elaborate rococo cartouche and bearing the mark of Thomas Mason. London, 1740. *B198*
Length: 21cm

c **Spoon**
Silver, Hanoverian 'Fancyback' style, with scrolling raffle leaf on the bowl, and marks on the stem for Ebenezer Coker. London, 1749. *B201*
Length: 20cm

75 (Above)

a **Knife and fork**
Iron, scimitar II blade, the two-tine fork with simple baluster stem. Fitted with Worcester blue-and-white ceramic handles and silver ferrules, blade mark for Gibbs. Probably London, c.1760. *B210*
Length of knife: 29cm

b **Knife and fork**
Iron, scimitar II blade, the two-tine fork with simple baluster stem. Fitted with Bow ceramic blue-and-white pistol handles set in silver ferrules, blade mark of Jongsma. Sheffield, c.1750. *B207*
Length of knife: 29.5cm

76

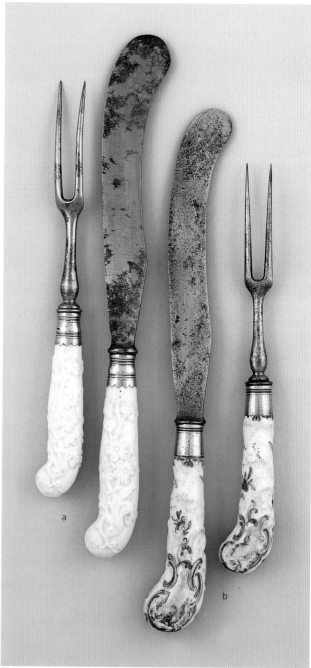

77

76 (*Left*)

a **Knife and fork**
Iron, scimitar II blade, the three-tine fork with simple baluster stem. Fitted with Bow white ceramic pistol handles painted in enamel colours and gilt, set in scalloped silver ferrules. London, 1760. *B208*
Length of knife: 28cm
The handles are decorated at the butt with an armorial crest of a ducal crown with plumed aigrette for Mendes.
Cf.: Tony Stevenson, *Linnean Society paper*, *Apr.16.1988*, English Ceramics Circle, Vol.1 3, pf. 3, 1989.

b **Knife**
Iron, scimitar II blade with Staffordshire enamel pistol handle set in scalloped silver ferrule. Probably Sheffield, c.1750. *B209*
Length: 28cm

77 (*Right*)

a **Knife and fork**
Iron, scimitar II blade, the two-tine blade with simple baluster stem. Fitted with moulded Chelsea ceramic handles set in banded and scalloped silver ferrules. Blade mark a pipe. Sheffield, c.1740. *B194*
Length of knife: 28cm

b **Knife and fork**
Iron, scimitar II blade, the two-tine fork with simple baluster stem. Fitted with moulded Bow white ceramic pistol handles, painted in enamel colours and set in silver ferrules. Blade unmarked. London, 1755. *B206*
Decorated at the base with the armorial crest of a hawkshead between two raised wings on a torse, possibly for Hawkins or Jervis.
Length of knife: 28cm

Early Georgian place setting, c.1740

Photograph: Jeremy Phillips for Fairfax House, York

The trade with the Far East had reached its zenith by the 1740s and huge quantities of porcelain were being imported. The Chinese dinner plate in this setting with a border of fruiting vines bears the arms of the Warren and De Lacey families, whilst the star-shaped sweetmeat bowl with rouge-de-feu and gold decoration on the inner border and an armorial bearing in the centre, was fashioned for the Belasyse family of York. This would be the centrepiece for a six-sided arrangement of shaped dishes. A handsome set of cutlery with Delft pistol-shaped handles (B193) flanks the plate and an engraved wine glass (with coat of arms of the Fairfax family) stands in readiness to receive wine. The linen damask napkin folded in the shape of a flower is woven with the arms of Erskine of Dun and has a field of flowers taken from an earlier Dutch pattern of the 1690s. Notice also the superb pair of rococo-style candlesticks by Paul de Lamerie, 1742. Table candlesticks were a rare commodity in seventeenth century-country house inventories, but by the middle of the eighteenth century they had become essential items, usually brought on for the dessert course when the light was failing.

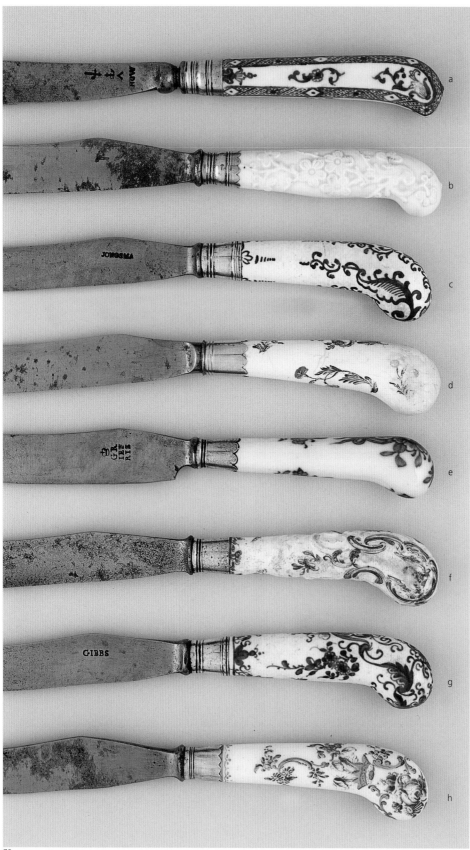

78 (Left)

Ceramic knife handles of pistol shape

a Blue-and-white hard-paste porcelain, in Chinese style. Probably Meissen, c.1730. *B191*

b White porcelain with relief trailing flower decoration. Chelsea, c.1740. *B194*

c Blue-and-white porcelain, Bow factory, c.1750. *B207*

d White porcelain with enamel floral decoration. Staffordshire, c.1750. *B209*

e Blue-and-white porcelain. Chinese, c.1760. *B227*

f White porcelain, Bow factory, moulded and decorated with enamel colours and crest of Hawkins or Jervis (partially erased). c.1760. *B206*

g Blue-and-white porcelain, Worcester, c.1760. *B210*

h White porcelain, Bow factory, decorated with enamel colours and armorial crest of a ducal crown with plumed aigrette for Mendes. c.1760. *B208*

Cf.: Stevenson, T., Review of Bow and Worcester knife and fork hafts, *English Ceramic Circle*, Vol.13, pf. 3, 1989.

Early ceramic handles for cutlery were being imported firstly from China through the East India trading companies of Holland and England and copied patterns from silver models, probably the popular canon style of the late seventeenth century.

The main competition for this type of exotic handle at the time was from the Italian glassmakers who were using millefiori, 'scrambled' and aventurine glass. However, Chinese imports were much cheaper and just as attractive, with their bright blue and white, Imari and *famille verte* colours.

The English ceramic companies like Chelsea, Bow and Worcester were unable to work out their own formula for true porcelain, but they devised something similar which allowed them to compete on colour and price.

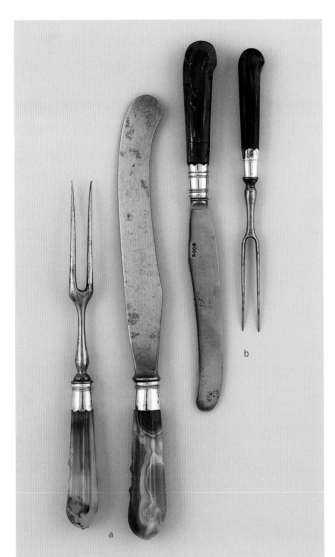

79

79 (Left)

a Knife and fork

Iron, scimitar II blade, two-tine fork with simple baluster stem. Fitted with carved fluted agate handles in imitation of Chinese plant forms (cf. with B190, p. 103) and plain silver ferrules. c.1750. *B213*
Length of knife: 27cm

b Knife and fork

Iron, scimitar II blade and two-tine fork with simple baluster stem. Fitted with faceted pistol-shape handles of blue aventurine glass, probably from Murano, and scalloped silver ferrules. Blade mark of BOOG, c.1750. *B212*
Length of knife: 22.5cm

Blocks of aventurine glass were being imported from Murano, near Venice at this time, then re-melted and fashioned into knife handles.

80

80 (Right)

a Knife and fork

Iron, scimitar II blade and two-tine fork with solid bolsters. The pistol handles made of stamped fused Sheffield plate, resin filled, unmarked blade. Sheffield, c.1760. *B225*
Length of knife: 24.5cm

b Knife and fork

Iron, scimitar III blade and three-tine fork fitted with stamped fused Sheffield plate handles, unmarked. Sheffield, c.1760. *B249*
Length of knife: 28cm

A vessel or object made of 'fused Sheffield plate' comprises a thin sheet of copper with a thinner covering of fused silver. The process begins with the bonding of a thick bar of copper onto a thinner bar of silver. After treating the interfaces with a flux the bar is heated in a furnace until the copper and silver fuse together. This block of fused copper and silver is then forged or rolled until it becomes a large thin sheet with the same proportion of silver to copper as in the original section. This can be used as a 'solid' silver sheet, but if the article being made needs to have silver showing on both sides, the original copper block would be bonded with silver on both sides. The edges of the bar were not coated, however, and this tended to restrict the complexity of construction. Both this Sheffield plate and the later electroplate were invented to satisfy a market of aspiring middle-class consumers with 'look-alike silver'.

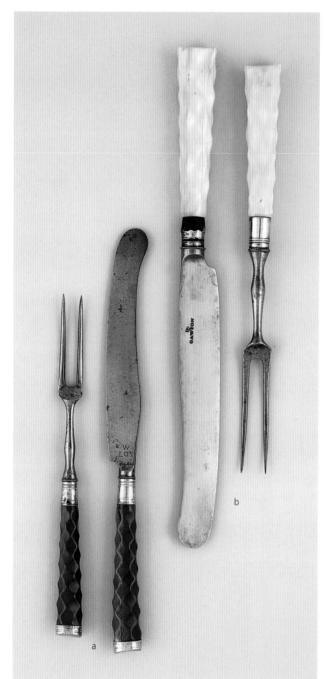

81

81 (Left)

a Knife and fork
Iron, scimitar III blade and two-tine fork with 'chip' carved, green-stained ivory handles set between silver ferrules and caps. Blade mark of John Green. Sheffield, c.1760. *B233*
Length of knife: 23cm

b Knife and fork
Iron, scimitar III blade and two-tine fork with 'chip' carved ivory handles and silver ferrules. Blade mark of Joshua Cawton. Sheffield, 1760. *B235*
Length of knife: 27cm

82 (Right)

a Knife and fork
Iron, scimitar III blade and two-tine fork fitted with green-stained ivory handles between scrolling silver caps and ferrules. Blade mark of a pistol and an 'L' for Broomhead & Ward. Sheffield, 1760. *B236*
Length of knife: 27.5cm

This type of scrolling cap was a distinctive feature of Sheffield knife handles at this time.

b Knife and fork
Iron, scimitar III blade and three-tine fork fitted with red-stained ivory handles between scrolling silver ferrules and caps. Probably Sheffield, c.1760. *B237*
Length: 22cm

A rare survivor, as are examples stained yellow or blue.

82

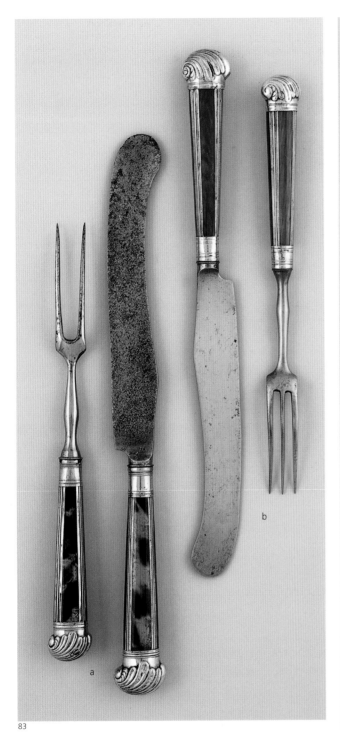

83

84

83 (Above)

a Knife and fork
Iron, scimitar III blade and two-tine fork fitted on a wooden core with composite handles of silver and tortoiseshell between silver ferrules and scrolling caps. Sheffield, c.1760. *B238*
Length of knife: 29cm

b Knife and fork
Iron, scimitar III blade and three-tine fork fitted on a wooden core with composite handles of silver and green-stained ivory between silver ferrules and scrolling caps. Sheffield, c.1760. *B239*
Length of knife: 27.5cm

84 (Above)

a Knife and fork
Iron, scimitar III blade and two-tine fork fitted with wrythen silver and blue enamel handles between silver ferrules and caps. Sheffield, c.1760. *B244*
Length of knife: 28cm

b Knife and fork
Iron, scimitar III blade and two-tine fork fitted with wrythen silver and blue enamel handles between silver ferrules and domed spiral caps. Sheffield, c.1760. *B245*
Length of knife: 30cm

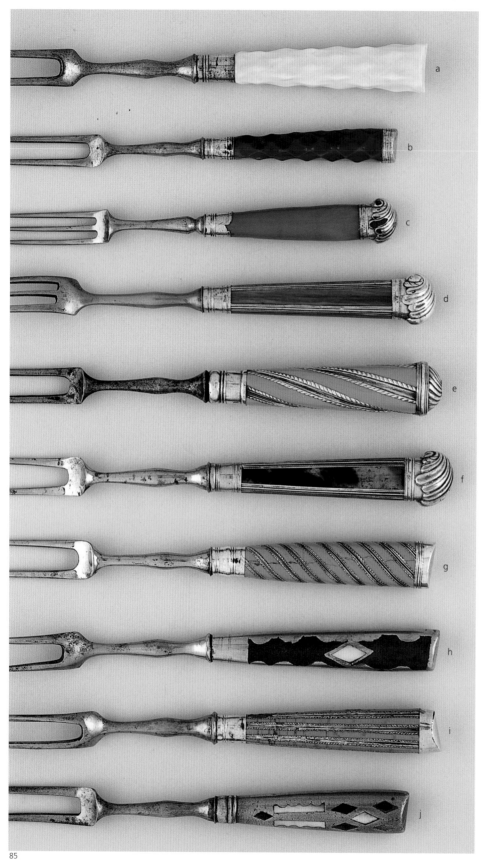

85 (Left)

Sheffield fork handles of the mid-eighteenth century

It was not normal practice to mark forks with a maker's mark. All references to makers, therefore, are those recorded on the matching knife blade.

a 'Chip' carved ivory handle and silver ferrule. Blade mark Joshua Cawton. Sheffield, 1760. *B235*

b 'Chip' carved, green-stained ivory handle set between silver ferrule and cap. Blade mark of John Green. Sheffield, c.1760. *B233*

c Scrolling red-stained ivory handle between silver ferrule and scrolling cap. Probably Sheffield, c.1760. Rare survivor. *B237*

d Composite handle of silver and green-stained ivory with silver ferrule and scrolling cap. Sheffield, c.1760. *B239*

e Wrythen silver and enamel handle between silver ferrule and domed spiral cap. Sheffield, c.1760. *B245*

f Composite handle of silver and tortoiseshell with silver ferrule and scrolling cap. Sheffield, c.1760. *B238*

g Handle of wrythen silver and enamel over copper sheath, with silver ferrules and truncated cap. Probably Sheffield, c.1780. *B265*

h White metal handle filled with lapped wooden scales and shell inserts. Sheffield, c.1760. *B252*

i Handle of enamel and silver over a copper sheath, with silver ferrules and caps. Probably Sheffield, c.1780. *B263*

j White metal handle inlaid with shell and green-stained ivory. Sheffield, c.1760. *B251*

Cutlery production in Sheffield has a long history. Chaucer, in the *Reeves Tale* (1387), tells us that the Miller of Trumpington had a 'Sheffield Thywtel baar in his hose'.

The area of Hallamshire (of which Sheffield was the centre) had an abundance of water (essential for the manufacturing process) and a large pool of cheap labour. By the eighteenth and nineteenth centuries their workshops had gained a reputation for inventiveness and good design.

85

86

86 *(Left)*

a Dessert knife and fork
Iron, French-style blade and
three-tine fork, the blade close
plated with silver, fitted with
silver ferrules and imported
Chinese porcelain handles.
London, 1760. *B254*
Length of knife: 22cm

b Knife and fork
Iron, French-style blade and
three-tine fork fitted with silver
ferrules and imported Chinese
porcelain handles, c.1760. *B255*
Length of knife: 28cm

87 *(Right)*

a Knife and fork
Iron, French-style blade and two-
tine fork with heavy silver 'bulb'
handles, decorated with shells
and wavy panels, resin filled.
Mark of John Dewsnip, Sheffield,
1781. *B262*
Length of knife: 27cm

b Knife and fork
Iron, French-style blade and
three-tine fork fitted with heavy
silver 'bulb' handles, decorated
with scallop shell and a pendant
graduated husk, resin filled. A
Scottish armorial crest of a tree on
a torse with the motto VIRESCO,
possibly for Montieth or Stewart.
Engraved date letter 'R' replicating
the silver hallmark date letter for
Sheffield, 1776. *B260*
Length of knife: 28cm

87

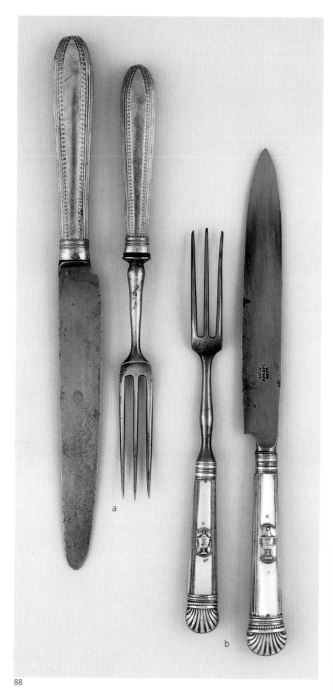

88

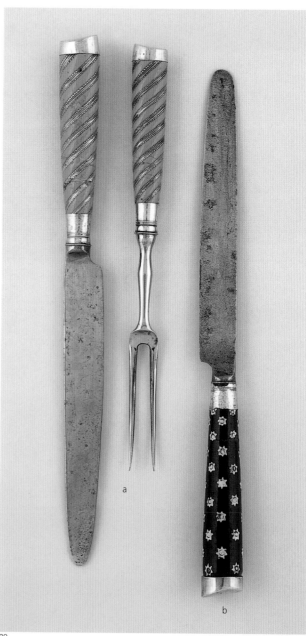

89

88 *(Left)*

a Knife and fork
Iron, French-style blade and three-tine fork fitted with beaded, fused Sheffield plate handles. Sheffield, c.1770. *B257*
Length of knife: 27cm

b Knife and fork
Iron, French-style spear-point blade and three-tine fork of imported style, the composite silver and shell handles decorated with a classical urn motif. Secured with ferrules and scallop-shell caps. Blade mark of London, hand made, c.1770. *B256*
Length: 26cm

This knife qualifies for the accolade of 'prime knife' for the last quarter of the eighteenth century.

89 *(Right)*

a Knife and fork
Iron, French-style blade and two-tine fork with simple baluster stem. The handles of wrythen silver and turquoise enamel over a copper sheath. Fitted with silver ferrules and caps, perhaps influenced by French small swords of the period. Probably Sheffield, c.1780. *B265*
Length of knife: 27.5cm

b Knife
Iron, French-style blade with handle of dark blue enamel and white stars over a copper sheath, silver ferrule and cap. Probably Sheffield, c.1780. *B264*
Length of knife: 27.5cm

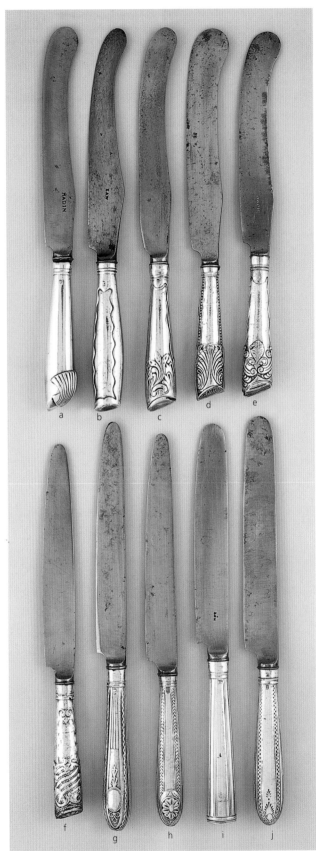

90

90 *(Top left)*

a Knife
Iron, scimitar III blade and cast silver handle decorated with unusual shell end, blade mark MADIN. Sheffield, 1760. *B241*
Length: 27.5cm

b Knife
Iron, scimitar III blade with stamped silver handle, resin filled, marked with T. L. Blade marked LAW: for Thomas Law, Sheffield, 1760. *B229*
A Scottish armorial crest of a hand couped at the wrist holding a dagger, and the motto VICERE VEL MORI, possibly for McNeill.
Length: 26cm

c Knife *(fork not shown)*
Iron, scimitar III blade fitted with truncated stamped silver handles, resin filled. 'Sterling' mark of MADIN & TRICKET, blade mark MADIN, Sheffield, c.1778. *B248*
Length: 26cm

d Knife
Iron, scimitar III blade, with truncated stamped silver foil handle, resin filled. Mark of T. Hoyland. Sheffield, 1776. *B247*
Length: 26.5cm

e Knife
Iron, scimitar III blade, with truncated, stamped silver handle, resin filled, marked I. B. Blade unmarked?. Sheffield, 1760. *B230*
Length: 27.5cm

90 *(Bottom left)*

f Knife *(fork not shown)*
Iron, French-style blade, with stamped silver handles, resin filled. Marked SYKES & CO. Sheffield, 1783. *B268*
Length: 26.5cm

g Knife
Iron, French-style blade with stamped bright-cut style silver handle. Mark of THOMAS LAW. Sheffield, 1783. *B269*
Length: 29cm

h Knife
Iron, French-style blade, with stamped bright-cut style silver handle. Mark of PHILIP MADIN & ROBERT TRICKET. Sheffield, 1785. *B270*
Length: 27.5cm

i Knife
Iron, transitional shape (more parallel and rounded tip) with silver handle in stamped bright-cut style. Mark of THOMAS LAW. Sheffield, 1794. *B275*
Length: 29cm

j Knife
Iron, transitional shape with silver handle in bright-cut style. Mark of SYKE & CO. Sheffield, c.1796. *B276*
Length: 29cm

The use of silver for knife handles is recorded in Italy, Germany and the Iberian Peninsula from medieval times but only became popular in England during the seventeenth century. Few early English examples survive but those that come down to us are usually cast in one piece, perhaps with *cire-perdue* decoration (B114, p. 83) or champleve enamelling (B143, p. 90). Silver has always been an expensive material, and most supplies at this time were under the control of the Spanish authorities, the great majority being imported from their mines in Mexico and Peru.

The inventory of the wealthy London cutler John Waters (pp. 26 and 27), who died in 1671, showed that the most expensive knives in his stock were those with silver handles. One dozen 'Graven Massy silver haft knives', for example, was valued at 30s., whilst other 'Massy silver hafted knives' were priced between 60s. and 70s. a dozen.

Waters' silver handles were probably still being made as a one-piece casting at this time, having a core placed inside during the casting process to create a cavity for the iron tang of the blade. The cartridge or cannon-style handles (B151, p. 92 and B161, p. 94) were solid and substantial and it was the weight of the silver which absorbed most of the cost. In order to reduce their overheads without compromising the finished product, cutlers introduced a two-part handle cast from a pair of moulds which was then silver-soldered together. These lighter, two-part handles were eventually superceded by the much thinner stamped handle in the 1760s.

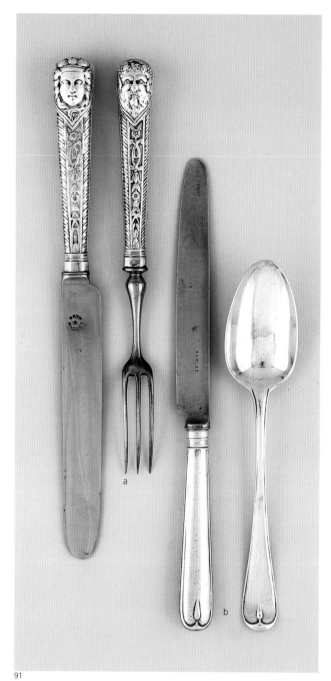

91

91 *(Left)*

a **Knife and fork**
Iron, transitional-style blade and three-tine fork with simple baluster stem. The silver handles decorated in antique manner with bearded satyr on the front and female face on the reverse.
Maker's mark for WILLIAM ABDY.
London, c.1780. *B274*
Length of knife: 28cm

b **Knife and spoon**
Iron and silver, French-style blade with Hanoverian thread and drop pattern. The silver spoon struck with the mark of GEORGE SMITH.
London, c.1782. *B272*
Length: 21cm
Knife in same style, but perhaps later date. Blade mark of HAMLET. Handle bears an armorial crest of a molet between two quills and the motto, NE CEDES MALIS for NEWEKE.
Length: 27cm

92 *(Right)*

a **Knife and fork**
Probably a carving set, iron, French-style blade and two-tine fork with shaped baluster stem. Fitted with green-stained ivory handles, plain silver ferrules and caps. c.1790. *B278*
Length of knife: 31.5cm

b **Knife and fork**
Silver, transitional-shape silver blade and three-tine fork with baluster stem. Fitted with blue-and-white Jasper ware handles, possibly by J. Wedgwood. Silver fork unmarked, blade mark for W. ELEY & W. FEARN. London, c.1798. *B277*
Length of knife: 22cm

92

93

94

93 (*Above*)

Knives, forks, carving knife and fork

Twelve green-stained ivory handled knives and twelve two-tine forks, plus matching carving knife and fork. The knives with near-parallel blades and rounded tips. The carving knife with French-style spear-shaped tip. Marked NOWIL, silver ferrules and caps, all housed in black fish-skin covered standing box. Sheffield, 1780. *B478*
Height of box: 36cm (closed)
Length of knife: 27cm
Length of carving knife: 32cm

94 (*Above*)

Small red leather cylindrical case containing silver dismantling set

Comprises a pair of knives, forks, spoons and beakers, also a corkscrew, an infuser, three glass containers with screw-on silver tops, marked with various dates and makers. From 1801–63, London. *B482*
The beakers engraved with two crests with ribbons, one with a swimming dolphin on a torse and the motto HONESTUM PRO PATRIA for the HAMILTON family, the other with a goat's head on a torse and the motto LET THE DEED SHOW for the Fleming family. The tooled leather case lid is stamped with 'W.C.S.H. Craighlaw, Kirkcowan, Scotland'.
Height: 17cm (closed)
Depth: 11cm

117

95

95 (Left)

a Knife and fork
Iron, transitional French-style blade and three-tine fork with solid bolsters. Fitted with reeded pressed horn handles. Sheffield, c.1790. *B279*
The blade shape with its shallow reverse taper and rounded tip is a significant development.
Length: 27.5cm

b Knife and fork
Iron, scimitar III blade, with four-tine fork fitted to wrythen carved green-stained ivory handles. The scallop shaped ferrules are silver, as are the tips of the fork tines. Blade mark of BAKER SALOP, Salisbury, c.1790. *B281*
Length of knife: 28.5cm

These pieces exemplify the return to the English style of blade and a rejection of the sharp, pointed French variety. Salisbury became an important centre for cutlery between the sixteenth and eighteenth centuries, although mention of the trade appears in records from the thirteenth century onwards.

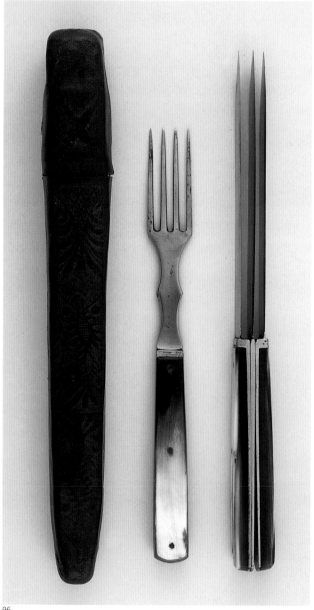

96

96 (Right)

a Knife and fork
Iron, the knife a three-part masticating utensil with French-style blades and scaled tangs. The fork similarly constructed with four tines. Fitted with horn scales. Blade mark of GRAY. Sheffield, c.1790. *B283*
The attendant leather carrying case is decorated on the body with elaborate foliate panels, whilst on the lid, an emblem showing a knife cutting some fish on one side, whilst on the front, a large crown, the town mark for Sheffield.
Length of knife: 26.5cm

This type of companion set was developed for medicinal use and to ease the problems of chewing food without teeth. The blades are slotted and can be parted for cleaning.

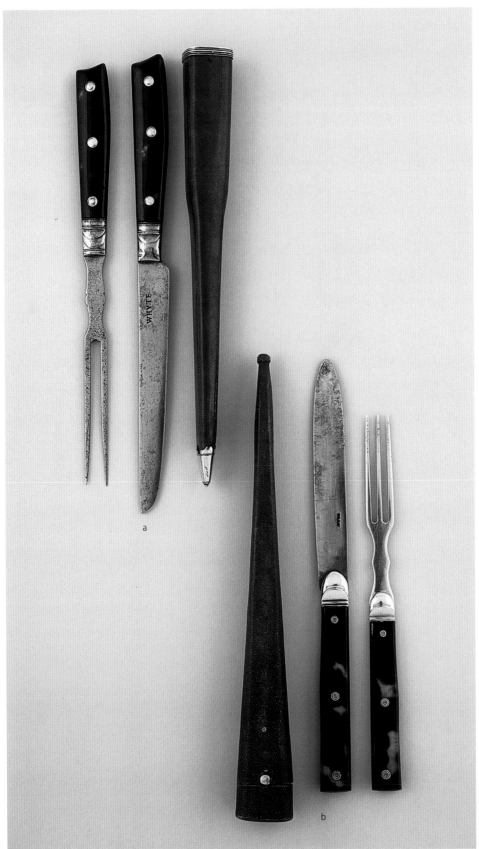

a

b

97

97 *(Left)*

a **Knife and fork**
Iron, French-style blade and two-tine fork with scale tang. Fitted with 'riding boot'-shaped tortoiseshell scale handles, and imbricated solid bolsters. Blade mark WHYTE, probably London, c.1790. *B285*
The attendant green reptile skin sheath with silver guard and scallop edged tip.
Length of knife: 23cm.

This set and B286 have a distinct French feel although the handles are more solid and robust than their French equivalents.

b **Knife and fork**
Iron and silver, French style blade and three-tine fork with scale tangs. Fitted with slightly shaped tortoiseshell scale handles. Silver fork and bolsters unmarked. Blade mark for GRAY, Sheffield, c.1790. *B286*
The original fish skin sheath with brass hinged lid.
Length of knife: 21.5cm

French cutlery production, and in particular the innovative folding knife and fork, was the subject of English imitation during the latter part of the eighteenth century.

It is likely, however, that only the blades were being made in England: the scales for the handles were probably supplied by the highly skilled French 'pearlers' and workers in tortoiseshell. The shape of blade at this time was usually spear shaped with a point, a profile that fitted safely in the handle when folded, but proved difficult to open. The problem was solved by the stamping of nail nicks onto the blades, a feature which appears from about 1790. Gold and silver were often used for the blades (see p. 121), which defines these utensils as being intended for fruit or dessert.

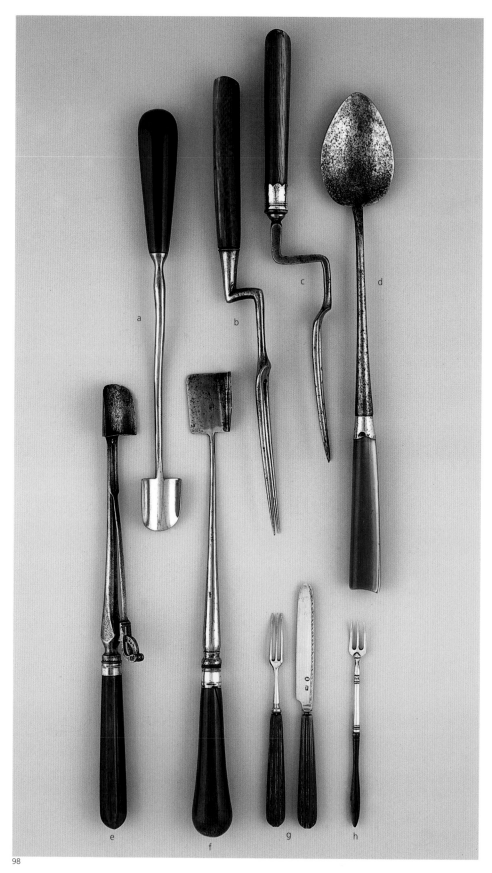

98

98 *(Left)*

a Cheese scoop
Steel, the curved scoop and bent stem fitted with green-stained ivory handle. c.1750–1800. *B294*
Length: 25cm

b Carving fork
Steel, trowel-shaped carving fork with two parallel tines and solid bolster fitted with green-stained ivory handle. c.1750–1800. *B295*
Length: 27cm

c Carving fork
Steel, trowel-shaped carving fork with two slightly splaying tines fitted with green-stained ivory handle and silver ferrule. 1750–1800. *B289*
Length: 25.5cm

d Serving spoon
Steel, the leaf-shaped bowl and long, tapering stem fitted with green-stained ivory handle and silver ferrule. c.1750–1800. *B292*
Length: 29.5cm

e Cheese scoop
Steel, the curved scoop and tapered stem fitted with a push mechanism which places the cheese on the plate. Fitted with octagonal green-stained ivory handle and silver ferrule. c.1780. *B290*
Length: 27cm

f Cheese scoop
Steel, the hod-like scoop and long, tapering baluster stem fitted with green-stained ivory handle and silver ferrule. c.1750–1800. *B293*
Length: 28cm

g Knife and fork
Silver, French-style decorated blade and three-tine fork marked with assay only. Fitted with oval, reeded, green-stained ivory handles, c.1790. *B300*
Length of knife: 15cm

Perhaps a lady or child's travelling set, usually stored in a flat case.

h Fork
Silver, three-tine fork and long turned stem fitted with green-stained ivory handle. c.1750–1800. *B291*
Length: 12.5cm

99 (Right)

Folding cutlery of the late eighteenth century

a Knife and fork
Silver, folding, French-style blade and two-tine fork fitted with shell scales and silver inserts (initials of L.A.M.) assay marks only. Probably Sheffield, c.1790. *B296*
Length of knife: 16.5cm (open)
Probably cased and carried in the pocket for the eating of fruit on a picnic.

b Knife
Silver-gilt, folding, French-style blade decorated with husks and banding. Fitted to a reeded, green-stained ivory handle. Marked Sheffield, 1779. *B299*
Length of knife: 17cm (open)

c Knife and fork
Unmarked gold, folding French-style blade and two-tine fork with shell scales, scalloped caps and gilt inserts (initials of G.K.). Probably Sheffield, c.1790. *B297*
Length of knife: 14cm (open)

d Knife and fork
Silver, folding, French-style blade and three-tine fork. Handle with shell scales, silver caps and inserts (initials of M.H.), silver handles, silver caps, assay mark only. c.1780. *B301*
Length: 22cm

e Knife and fork
Iron, folding, 'slotted' knife, with scimitar-style blade and two-tine fork. The pistol handles have buffalo horn scales. Blade mark for JEFFERYS, c.1740. *B287*
Length of knife: 25.5cm (open)

f Knife
Silver, folding, French-style blade with bright-cut decoration. The handle with engraved shell scales, silver pins, end caps and inserts (initials of H. L.). Blade has assay marks and an armorial crest of a centaur passant drawing a bow and arrow, for LAMBERT. Sheffield, 1790. *B303*
Length: 21.5cm (open)

g Knife
Close plate, folding, French style locking blade, marked COLMORE PATENT and showing a hunting scene of a chase with dogs and rabbit. The handle fitted with tortoiseshell scales, silver cap and pins, Sheffield, 1791. *B302*
Length: 24cm (open)

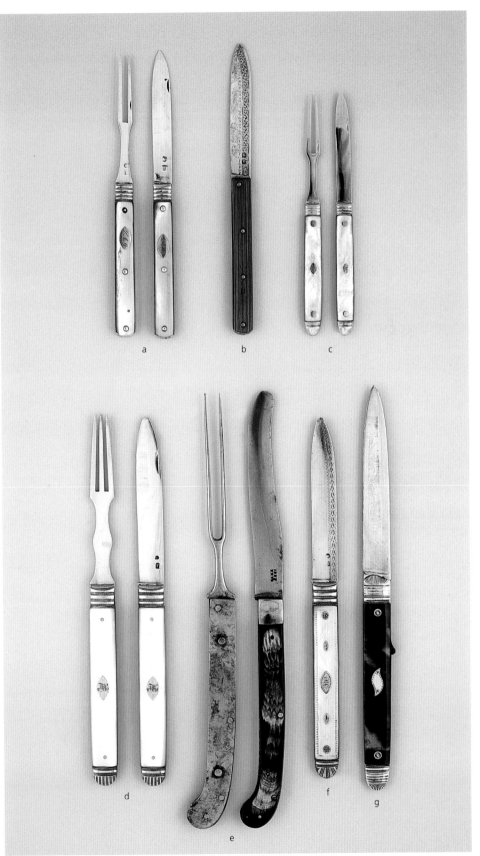

a b c

d e f g

99

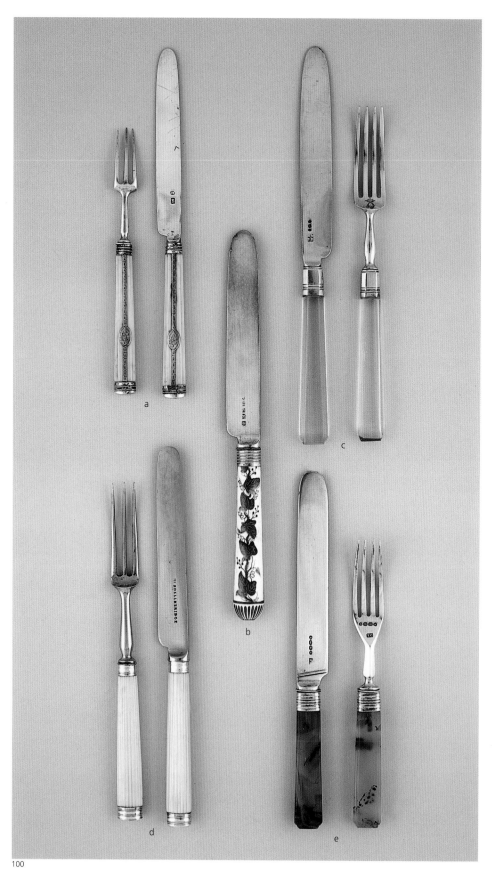

100 (Left)

a Knife and fork
Silver and ivory, French-style silver blade, and two-tine fork, both with ivory handles with silver inlay. The blade with assay mark only, the fork with maker's mark for I. BAILEY. Sheffield, 1791. *B298*
Length of knife: 19cm

b Knife
Close-plated blade marked SILK, and painted creamware ceramic handle. Staffordshire, c.1800. *B311*
Length of knife: 21cm

c Knife and fork
Silver-gilt and cut glass, the silver-gilt blade marked W. M. ELEY & W. FEARNS. London, c.1806. *B310*
Length of knife: 21.5cm

d Knife and fork
For dinner and dessert, steel blades marked RUNDELL & BRIDGE. The ribbed ivory handles have silver ferrules and caps, London, c.1820. *B325*
Length of knife: 27cm

e Dessert knife and fork
Silver, blade and three-tine fitted fork with handles of moss agate, by THOMAS CORDING. London, 1841. *B345*
Length of knife: 19.5cm

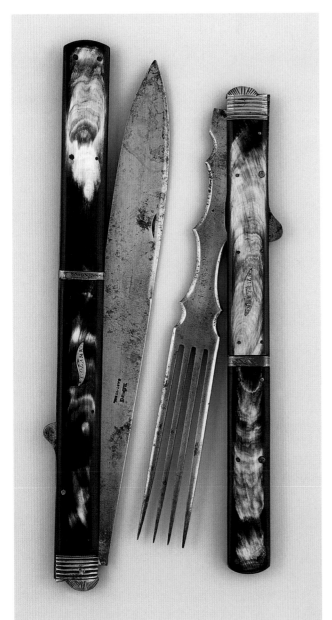

101

Carving knife and fork
Steel, large and locking, folding
French-style blade and four-tine
fork with shaped stem. The
handle with horn scales, brass
ribbed and silver inserts (name of
T. CLARKE). Blade marked with
L .G. and CAST STEEL. Sheffield,
c.1770. *B304*
Length of knife: 61.5cm (open)

Perhaps for campaign use.

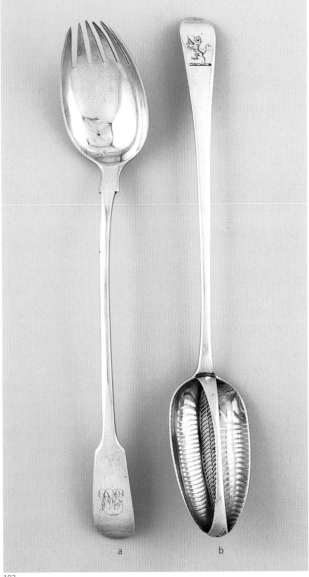

102

102 (Right)

a **Salad Server**
Silver, by C & T BARKER, London,
1804. *B312*
The handle engraved with the
monogram of GAP.
Length: 30cm

b **Strainer spoon,**
Silver. Mark for GEORGE SMITH and
WILLIAM FEARN. London, 1792.
B305
The handle with an armorial crest
of a lion rampant holding in its
forepaws a sword erect.
Length: 30cm

1800 – 1900

With the support of the Prince of Wales, who reigned as Prince Regent (1811–20) and as George IV (1820–30), British manufacturers received a greater recognition both at home and abroad. By the middle of the nineteenth century, during the reign of Queen Victoria, new developments also helped strengthen British manufacturing growth.

A turning point for the cutlery trade, and for metalwork in general, was the invention of silver plating by electrolysis, patented in 1840 by the Birmingham firm of Elkington. This coincided with the expansion of the cities, the movement of people into towns, and the increasing demand for more sophisticated, but not too expensive, com-modities enjoyed by a more affluent middle class. Marketing these products became an imperative for the manufacturers. Trade journals, directories and newspapers were used for this purpose, as were expensive and elaborate catalogues finely illustrated with exquisite engravings. But probably the best form of promotion was to exhibit at the numerous trade fairs and exhibitions which became popular during the nineteenth century.

Although during the latter part of the eighteenth century Sheffield had taken most of the cutlery manufacturing away from London, the capital still maintained its role as the main showcase for the domestic market. Many of the cutlery companies of Sheffield and Birmingham felt obliged to have London showrooms.

In the earlier part of the century, the extravagant taste of the Prince Regent and his love of food reflected itself in the gifts he gave to members of his court and to his friends. Beautiful sets of cutlery, such as oyster knives, personalised with his crest and contained in a sumptuous box lined with tinsel paper, were among his favoured presents. The box-making industry, as part of the expanding gift business, was one of the most important ancillary trades in Sheffield. A number of companies made boxes for sets of dessert knives and forks, given as presents but seldom used by the recipient.

Carving sets were another popular nineteenth-century gift. In earlier times to be assigned the office of 'Carver' at a rich man's table was considered a honour, a position of great importance which required skill and dexterity. It was a tradition which lasted until quite recently, although to a much lesser degree, when even in modest households the task of carving the joint (however small) on a Sunday was a ritual accomplished by the head of the family.

The market for carving sets flourished in the nineteenth century and once again the Sheffield cutlery trade met the demand, manufacturing attractive cased sets of carving knife, fork with patented finger-guard and sharpening hone and sometimes specialist game carvers. These sets, often of huge proportions, would have handles of stag or ivory, although later on in the century this was substituted by Ivorine, a trade name for Celluloid. Commemorative carving sets made for the upper end of the market, had ivory handles often carved in the likeness of Victoria and Albert, or of other famous people, such as Wellington and Shakespeare.

New materials like Celluloid were being developed during the nineteenth century as an alternative to the diminishing supplies of increasingly expensive ivory. By 1900 it is estimated that the Sheffield cutlers required some twenty million Celluloid knife handles each year in order to satisfy demand.

Victorian place setting, c.1890
Photograph: Jeremy Phillips for Fairfax House, York
When Lord Milton returned from a successful exploration of a north-west passage across Canada, he commissioned Minton to produce a commemorative dessert service showing the highlights of the expedition. Attending the compote and plate are examples of Stourbridge glass in the rock-crystal style and cutlery by Elkington (B396, p. 158) which follows the popular aesthetic movement, with Oriental motifs on the Japanese 'Shibayama' handles. The napkin, which bears the coat of arms of the Duke of Newcastle-under-Lyme, is folded in a popular mitre design illustrated in household manuals by Mrs Beeton and others at that time.

103

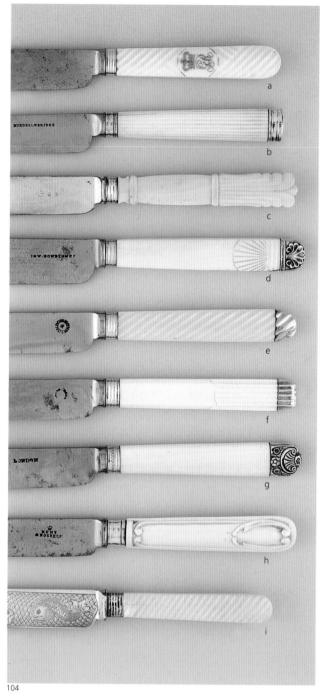

104

---

103 *(Above)*

a Knife and fork
Steel, wide blade with round tip and two-tine fork, both with solid bolsters and scale-tang. The scales of chequered bone with iron plate ends. Sheffield, c.1800. *B307*
Length of knife: 26.5cm

b Knife and fork
Steel, parallel-sided blade and three-tine fork with plain green-stained ivory handles. Marked G.R., London, c.1800. *B309*
Length of knife: 26.5cm

Deserves the accolade of being a 'prime' knife. Both sets are good examples of the cutlery available to the great majority of the population at this time.

---

104 *(Above)*

Carved ivory handles of the first half of nineteenth century

a Knife
Steel blade with cross-banded ivory handle showing the Royal cypher in gold piqué work. Mark of MORTIMER & HUNT. London, c.1820. *B322*
Length: 27cm

This is probably a sample knife from the stock of Paul Storr, a former partner of Mortimer & Hunt.

b Knife (fork not shown)
Steel blade marked RUNDELL & BRIDGE. The reeded ivory handle with ribbed silver ferrule and cap. A monogram on the cap for R. P. R. London, c.1820. *B325*
Length: 27cm

104 cont. *(left)*

c Knife (fork not shown)
Close plate on iron, with carved ivory handle in the form of a gathered fluted plume. The design is closely related to illustrations of four-inch hafts in Maleham and Yeoman's Daybook, c.1850. Mark of JOHN GILBERT. Birmingham, c.1820. *B331*
Length: 27cm

d Knife
Steel blade, marked HOWDEN & CO. The ivory handle carved in the form of a fan with a silver ferrule and scallop-shaped end cap. London, c.1835. *B336A*
Length: 29cm

The four knives in B336 are probably manufacturer's samples.

e Knife
Steel blade, marked LONDONMADE. The ivory handle with diagonal fluting, silver ferrule and matching end cap. London, c.1835. *B336B*
Length: 28cm

f Knife
Steel blade, marked LONDONMADE. The carved ivory handle partly reeded with silver ferrule and matching end cap. London, c.1835. *B336C*
Length: 28cm

g Knife
Steel blade, marked LONDON. The plain ivory handle with decorated silver ferrule and end cap. London, c.1835. *B336D*
Length: 29cm

h Knife
Steel blade marked HUNT & ROSKELL with carved ivory handle and silver ferrule. London, c.1840. *B339*
Length: 27cm

From a set of numbered sample knives.
Cf: No. 2257 in Maleham and Yeoman's Daybook.

i Knife
Close plate on iron, blade engraved with fish and marine motifs with carved ivory handle and silver ferrule. c.1840. *B340*
Length: 25.5cm

105 *(Right)*

a Knife
Steel blade marked I. & S. W., King's pattern silver handle, E & ? Sheffield, 1821. *B327*
Length: 27cm

b Knife
Steel blade marked LAW, the silver handle with Dublin hallmarks (perhaps both by LAW of Dublin), c.1822. *B324*
Length: 28cm

c Knife
Steel blade marked GARRARD, surmounted by crown G. R., King's pattern silver handle by W. M. Chawner, London, 1822. *B329* Marked with the armorial crest of a boar's head on a torse below a coronet, for the Earl of Breadalbane.
Length: 27cm

d Knife
Steel blade marked DANIEL, the silver handle figured with a coronet and letter C. Made by W. M. Eaton. London, 1830. *B338*
Length: 27mm

From a service made for the second Marquis of Cholmondeley to commemorate his wedding on 11 May 1830.

e–h Knives
Four with parallel steel blades and silver handles from a quantity of sample knives by HUNT & ROSKELL, London, dating from 1840–49. *B342*
Length: 27.5cm–28cm

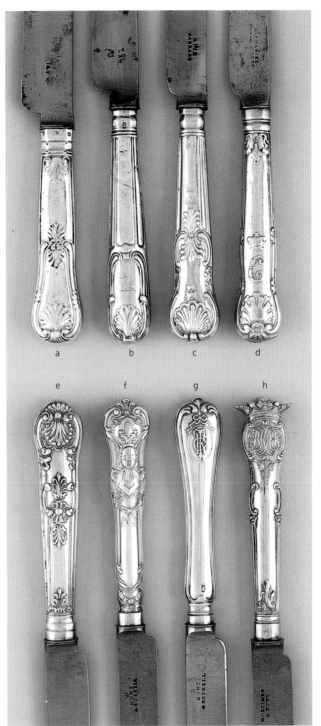

105

106

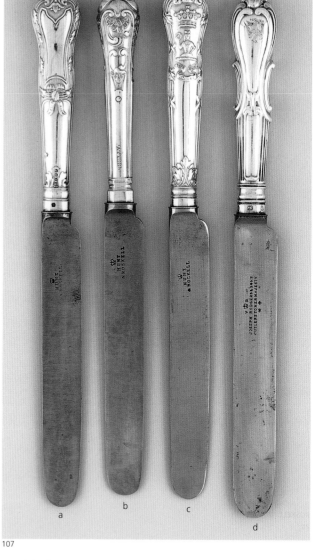

a   b   c

d

107

106 (Above)

Knives and fork (one not shown)
Steel blades and two-tine carving
fork by Mappin Bros, Sheffield, all
fitted with gilded, bone china
handles. Staffordshire, c.1850.
B346
Length of large carving knife:
31cm

These are probably factory
samples.

107 (Above)

a Knife
Steel, the blade marked HUNT &
ROSKELL, the silver handle London,
1850. *B349a*
Length: 27.5cm

b Knife
Steel, the blade marked HUNT &
ROSKELL, the silver handle marked
PATTERN. London, 1855. *B349b*
Length: 27.5cm

c Knife
Steel, the blade marked HUNT &
ROSKELL, silver handle in style of
reed and ribbon, stamped with an
earls' crown and crest. London,
1850. *B350*
Length: 27.5cm

d Knife
Steel, the blade marked JOSEPH
RODGERS, the silver handle, of
Victoria pattern, also by Joseph
Rodgers, Sheffield, 1850. *B351*
Length: 28cm

Joseph Rodgers & Sons Ltd can
rightly claim the title of being the
foremost cutlers, not only in
Sheffield but probably throughout
the world. Their blade marks
were granted numerous Royal
Warrants throughout their
distinguished working life.

108

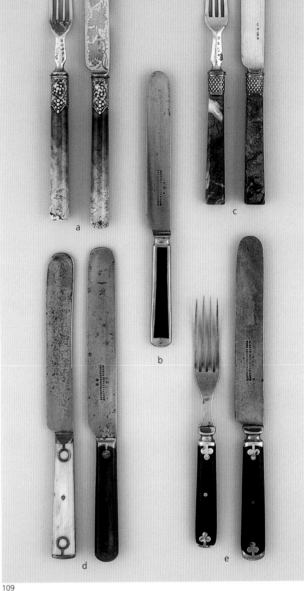

109

108 (Above)

Knife, fork and spoon
Electroplated nickel silver,
Sheffield, from 1840 onwards.
B352
Length of knife: 28cm

Elkington & Co., a Birmingham company, patented 'Electroplate' in 1840. This was a chemical process that involved depositing a thin layer of silver onto a base metal by means of electrolysis. The base metal was usually nickel silver (sometimes called German silver), an alloy of copper, zinc and nickel. Because it used a thin layer of silver only microns thick, it was relatively inexpensive and provided an opportunity for everyone to use and to own 'silver' cutlery.

109 (Right)

a Dessert knife and fork
Blade and four-tine fork close-plated on iron, with hardstone handles. Engraved and plated ferrules decorated with vine and trellis pattern. *B356*
Length of knife: 23cm

b Dessert knife
Steel blade and scale tang with cast copper alloy bolster and handle frame. Ebony scales as inserts by Joseph Rodgers. Sheffield, c.1850. *B355*
Length: 21cm

c Dessert knife and fork
Blade and four-tine fork close-plated on iron, with stone handles, c.1850. *B362*
Length of knife: 21.5cm

d Dessert knives (2)
Steel blades and scale-tangs, both with block tin run-on bolsters, one with plain bone handle decorated with ringlet pattern, the other with a green-stained bone scale handle, by Joseph Rodgers. Sheffield, c.1850. *B354*
Length: 23cm and 24cm

e Dessert knife and fork
Steel blade and four-tine fork with scale-tangs, both with block tin run-on bolsters and ebony scales decorated with clover-leaf pattern, by Joseph Rodgers, Sheffield, with run-on bolsters, c.1850. *B353*
Length of knife: 24.5cm

This method of construction with run-on bosters has been in use since medieval times.

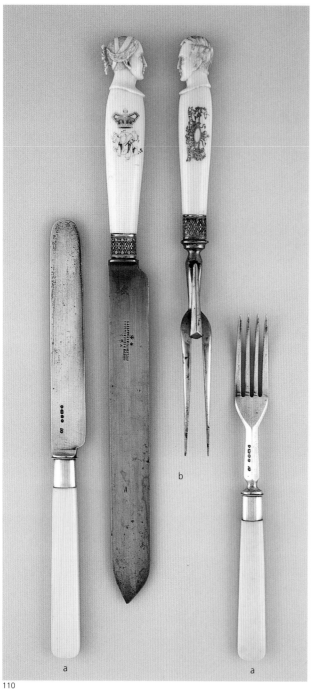

110

111

---

110 *(Above)*

a Large knife and fork
Silver blade and four-tine fork
with triangular-section stem.
The ivory handles secured with
silver ferrules, Elizabeth Eaton.
London, 1851. *B358*
Length of knife: 30cm

b Carving knife and fork
Steel knife and two-tine fork with
carved ivory handles of Queen
Victoria & Prince Albert, both
engraved with their own Royal
Cyphers. By Joseph Rodgers,
Sheffield, c.1850. *B361*
Length of knife: 38cm

---

111 *(Above)*

a Spoon and pickle fork
Cast iron, 'rustic' style, c.1850. .
B359
Length of fork: 18.5cm

Not a very satisfactory material or
method of construction for such
fine objects.

b Dessert knife and fork
Cast paktong (nickel alloy) blade
and tines, decorated with wavy

starbursts, fitted with ivory
handles, blade mark 'L & W'.
Probably Sheffield, 1850. *B364*
Length of knife: 21cm
See: Pinn, K., *Paktong*, Antique
Collectors' Club, 1999.

c Dessert knife and fork
Close plate on iron with engraved
blade and tines. The carved ivory
handles are stained brown.
Sheffield, c.1850. *B363*
Length of knife: 21.5cm

112 (Right)

a Knife
Steel blade, with straight ivory handle and silver ferrule. Engraved with an armorial crest of an owl above the initials H.C. possibly for Calverley. Joseph Rodgers, Sheffield, c.1840. *B341*
Length: 27cm

This is a good example of a quality knife of the nineteenth century, having a parallel steel blade, a pattern which lasted throughout this century and well into the next.

b Knife
Close-plated on iron with an elephant tooth handle. Sheffield, c.1860. *B367*
Length: 22.5cm

With the huge quantities of ivory being used, and supplies becoming scarce, the price was increasing dramatically. The cutlers were experimenting with other materials as suitable alternatives.

c Knife
Steel parallel blade of 'prime' design by Maleham & Yeomans. Fitted with a rectangular section celluloid handle in imitation of ivory. Sheffield, c.1850. *B368*
Length: 26cm

Celluloid was an invention of Alexander Parkes in the 1840s. Originally called Parkesine, it was made from cotton dissolved in nitric and sulphuric acid but proved very brittle. This process was subsequently improved by the Hyatt brothers from the USA by mixing it with camphor. It was finally patented as Celluloid in 1869 and found a ready market in knife handles as imitation ivory. In 1947 it was estimated that 24 million celluloid knife handles were required annually by Sheffield cutlers.

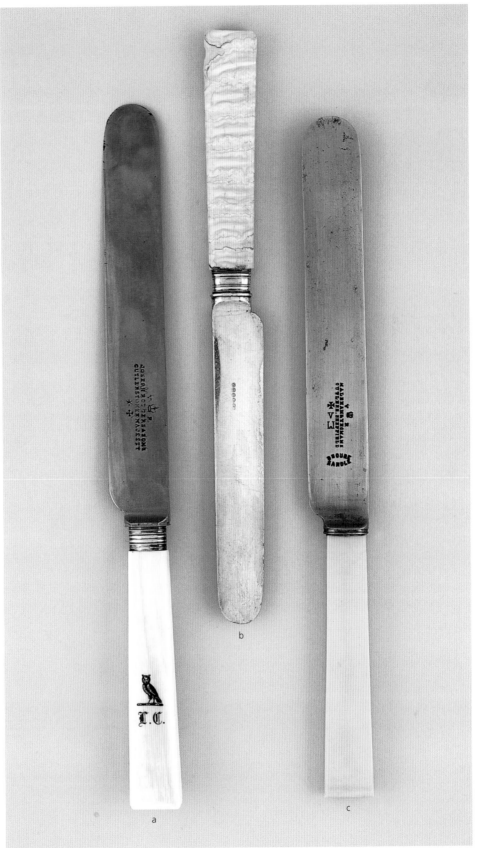

a

b

c

112

113

113 (Above)

a Bread knife
Steel blade marked JOSEPH
RODGERS, CUTLERS TO HER MAJESTY V
R crowned, carved ivory handle in
the form of an open corn cob.
Sheffield, c.1850. *B360*
Length: 34cm

Cf.: A design for an ivory handle in
Maleham & Yeomans pattern book,
No. 2571. The exact shape of this
blade is also drawn in profile at the
beginning of the book referred to as
'large bread knife'. Other blades of
smaller size, but exactly the same
profile, are recorded, i.e., 'Small Bread
knife, Cheese knife, Table knife, Plated
Fish eating knife and Plated Dessert'.

This example may have been a
later production model of a
design by John Bell (1811–1996),
who created a similar knife for
Felix Summerleys Art
Manufacturers. Produced by
Joseph Rodgers, Sheffield,
probably for exhibition purposes.

b Cake knife
Close plate on iron, the engraved
blade marked JOHN ROUND & SON,
with engraved ferrule, carved
ivory handle in the form of a
bound sheath of bamboo
(remnants of the original green
stain survive). Sheffield, c.1850.
B357
Length: 29cm

114

114 (Above)

a Gravy spoon
Electroplated nickel on nickel
silver, with detachable hollow
bowl. This was apparently filled
with hot water and may have
been intended to help with the
service of ice cream. Registered
design mark for 1872, maker's
mark H. B. *B378*
Length: 35cm

b Salad servers
Silver and ebony, by George
Adams. London, 1873. *B377*
Length: 31.5cm

c Gravy spoon
Electroplated silver on a base of
nickel silver, maker Joseph
Rodgers, Sheffield, registered
design mark for 1866. *B381*
Length: 34cm

115 (Right)

a **Knife**
With steel blade by Joseph Rodgers & Sons, Sheffield, and encaustic earthenware handle decorated in Renaissance Revival style, incorporating scrolls and animal figures, probably designed by Richard Redgrave RA. Made by Minton & Co., Stoke-on-Trent, c.1850–60. *B365*
Length: 27.5cm

Richard Redgrave was a painter and designer who worked at Minton. He designed many objects for the Staffordshire firm, including table knife handles.
Cf.: Atterbury, P. and Batkin, M., *The Dictionary of Minton*, Antique Collectors' Club, 1990.

b **Knife**
The close-plated blade engraved with scrolled foliate motifs, the encaustic earthenware handle decorated with two contrasting coloured inlays of clay forming a lozenge pattern along the sides and a dotted border decoration on the spine. (Identical handles of the same design but of different colour are also illustrated.) Perhaps samples produced by Minton & Co, Stoke-on-Trent, c.1860. *B366*
Length of knife: 27cm

The word encaustic refers to the technique and process of firing medieval inlaid tiles, a practice renewed and perfected by Herbert Minton in the mid-nineteenth century. A revived interest in Medieval tiles, linked also to the rediscovery of old kilns in various part of Britain, convinced Minton, who had A. W. N. Pugin as his collaborator and designer, to undertake a new commercial venture. In 1832 he purchased from Samuel Wright his patent for manufacturing ornamental tiles and soon commenced production.

This proved to be very popular, and encaustic tiles were used not only in the decorative scheme of prestigious public places and private manors, but also in more modest domestic interiors. Minton extended the encaustic technique even to include the manufacture of buttons.

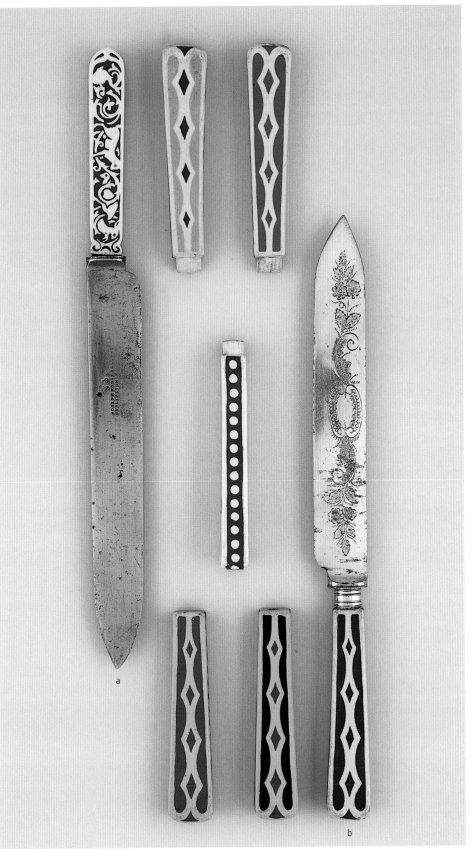

a

b

115

116 (Right)

a Fork and spoon
Silver-gilt, the handles with pierced arabesque motifs and a crown as finial. By Henry Wilkinson & Co., Sheffield, 1864. *B374*
Length of spoon: 19cm

In a curious Near Eastern fashion, not completely unusual at that time, these pieces may have been intended to commemorate the marriage of Edward, eldest son of Queen Victoria, to Princess Alexandra of Denmark in March 1863.

b Spoon
Silver, the bowl and top of handle pierced with *entrelac* motif, the centre of the bowl inscribed in relief AC ER·VII below a crown, stamped 'L. & Co' within three lozenges for Liberty & Co., 'Cymric', Birmingham, 1901. *B418*
Designed by Archibald Knox.
Length: 17cm

Cf.: Tilbrook, A. J., *The Designs of Archibald Knox for Liberty*, London, 1976, p.125.

c Fork and spoon
Silver, in the Art Nouveau style, the slender stem formed as a stylised plant inscribed EMPIRE CANADA, AFRICA and INDIA, and surmounted by a portrait of Edward VII and a crown. On the reverse a chased shield contained within stylised gnarled roots and divided into four sections bears the symbols of England, Scotland, Ireland and Wales, the stem also inscribed with EMPIRE, AUSTRALIA, NEW ZEALAND and WEST INDIES, Pearce & Sons Ltd, Sheffield, 1901. *B419*
Length: 16cm

d Tea and caddy spoons
Silver and enamel, the tea spoon of slender form, the stem inscribed with the date '1911', the finial shaped as a shield representing Great Britain and terminating in the entwined and crowned letters 'G R', on a blue and green enamelled ground. The tea caddy of similar design, also inscribed with the date '1911' below the entwined and crowned letters 'G R', on a blue and green enamelled ground, both pieces stamped 'L & Co' within three lozenges for Liberty & Co. Birmingham, 1911. *B433*
Length: 9.5cm and 13cm
These pieces were introduced to commemorate the Coronation of George V.

116

117 (Right)

a Dessert knife and fork
Silver-gilt, decorated with shell and scrolling foliate pattern by George Adams, London. Knife blade dated 1867, knife handle and fork dated 1872. *B384*
Length of knife: 21.5cm

b Dessert knife and fork
Gilded white metal, the blade and three-tine fork marked ATKINS BROS. The cast handles in gilded copper are mystical representations of Time, with his hour glass and sickle, and Flora holding her overflowing cornucopia of fruit and flowers. Almost certainly modelled from drawings by William Blake (1757–1827). Sheffield, c.1870. *B385*
Length of knife: 20.5cm

c Dessert knife and fork
Silver-gilt, blade and three-tine fork by Harrison Bros & Howson, Sheffield, 1877. Handles decorated with strapwork panels and bearing a crest of a lion rampant marked FBT. London, 1877. *B386*
Length of knife: 20.5cm

The famous London shop Liberty's takes its name from the founder and owner, Sir Arthur Lasenby Liberty, who played an important role in the promotion of the Arts & Crafts Movement and of the Art Nouveau decorative styles both at home and abroad.

The Regent Street store opened in 1875, selling a wide range of objects, furniture and textiles, many of which he imported from Japan.

Famous designers such as E. W. Godwin, C. F. A. Voysey, C. Dresser, A. Knox and R. Silver were associated with Liberty's.

In jewellery and metalwork Liberty's established a distinctive Celtic style of its own, retailed under the trademark 'Cymric' (silver) and 'Tudric' (pewter).

Launched in 1899, the 'Cymric' range was primarily manufactured by the Birmingham firm of W. H. Haseler and, from 1901, an ancillary company, known as Liberty & Co., was also registered.

Among the varied and extensive production, spoons proved particularly successful as gifts. The examples illustrated commemorate the coronation of Edward VII and George V.

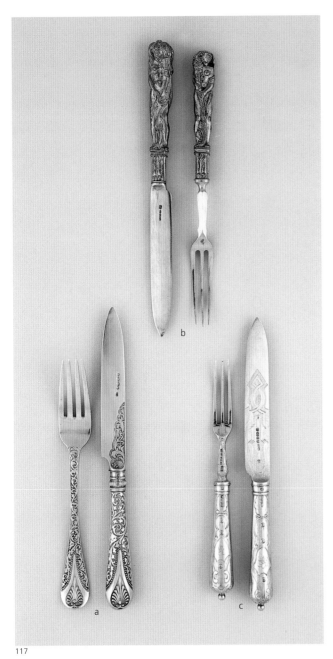

117

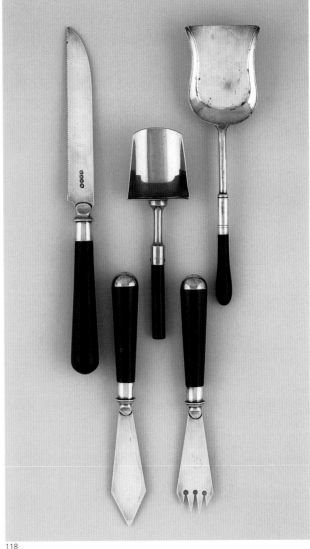

118

118 (Above right)

Scoops (2), knife, fork and lemon knives

Electroplate, in the style of Dr C. Dresser, with ebony handles and plated ferrules, marked H & H for Hukin & Heath. Birmingham, c.1878. *B391*
Length of lemon knife: 23cm
Christopher Dresser (1834–1904), a botanist by training, was one of the most prolific and eclectic designers of the Victorian era, a major exponent of Japonism and an art

adviser to many commercial ventures. After floundering unrecognised for most of the first part of the twentieth century, the modernity of his designs was finally appreciated by Sir Nikolaus Pevsner.

Although he remains a son of his times, his simple and innovative metalwork designs and his collaboration with various manufacturers place him among the first of the industrial designers. Dresser was the art adviser of the Birmingham and London firm of Hukin & Heath,

for whom, from 1878, he also designed various pieces. Those which do not bear his facsimile signature or are not stamped with his name have been attributed to him on stylistic grounds. This is the case of the pieces in Bill Brown's collection.The little shovel spoon in the centre is often associated with a sugar bowl shaped as a basket with an ebonised wooden rod handle, similar to the one seen in this example. This particular style of cylindrical handle is unequivocally a Dresser's design.
Cf.: Halén, W., *Christopher Dresser: a pioneer of modern design*, Phaidon Press Limited, 1990.

From the early 1860s Dresser's designs had progressed towards a more geometrical treatment of shape, characterised by symmetrically disposed lines, as seen here in the fork and lemon knives. His designs for Hutkin & Heath proved particularly popular, not only because they met the taste of a trendy section of consumers in love with Japanese-inspired objects, but also because they were small, indispensable everyday objects, like toast-racks and condiment sets, sold at affordable prices. Moreover, they could be easily readapted to please the taste and pocket of their clientele.

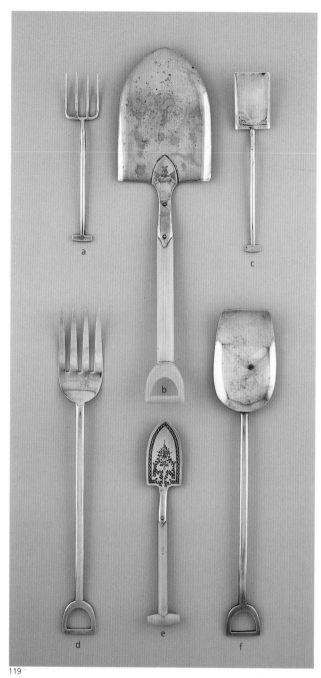

119

120

119 (Above)

a, c Sardine fork and spade
Electroplated silver, maker's mark
W. W. H. S., Sheffield. Registered
design mark for 1871. *B395*
Length: 13.5cm

b Serving spade
Large, electroplated silver blade
with ivory handle, no mark, but
bearing an armorial crest of a
plumed horse's head between two
crossed flags above the motto

IDLER, probably for use by a ships
company, c.1880. *B394*
Length: 28.5cm

d, f Salad servers
Electroplated silver by Briddon
Bros. Sheffield, c.1880. *B392*
Length: 26cm

e Butter spade
Electroplated silver, the pointed
blade engraved with foliate design
and fitted with ivory handle.
c.1880. *B393*
Length: 16cm

120 (*Left*)

a Dessert knife, fork and spoon
Silver, open-work handles marked
HENRY WILLIAM CURRY. London,
1883. *B401*
Length of knife: 19.5cm

c Spoon
Silver, with hollow handle fitted
as a rattle, marked H C & Co,
Edinburgh, 1878. *B379*
Length: 19cm

b, d Dessert knife and fork
Close-plated engraved blade and
three-tine fork. The handles are
black horn inlaid with shell
foliage and a silver cross, perhaps
as a *memento mori* gift or for use
at religious festivals, c.1880. *B400*
Length: 28.5cm

Dessert knife (*Above*)
Silver, in early Art Nouveau style,
originally gilded, silver blade and
handle by John Lias & Son,
London, 1871. *B376*
Length: 21cm

121 (*Right*)

a Dessert knife and fork
Electroplated blade and tines, the
kozuka-style handles of burnished
copper with gilt decorative motifs
in relief, the knife with a tiger
hidden behind a bamboo tree, the
fork with a branch of flowering
prunus and a stylised
representation of a *koto* (Japanese
lateral harp), the blade stamped
with a pseudo Japanese hallmark
on one side and the maker's mark
for Hukin & Heath on the
reverse. c.1880. *B399*
Length of knife: 20cm

In Japanese the word *kozuka*
refers both to a small sword and
to its decorated handle. It is
possible that the handles used in
these pieces were imported
directly from Japan and, on
arrival, struck with the
manufacturer's mark. This practice
was not uncommon. Similarly,
silverware imported from Japan
would often appear to have been
overstruck with the retailer's
stamp (e.g., Liberty) and the
import hallmark.

However, the possibility that
they may have been made by
Hukin & Heath of Birmingham
and London should not be
rejected. An enthusiastic review of
the firm in *The Art Journal*
(October 1879) states '*Messrs.
Hukin and Heath reproduce several
of the Persian and Japanese Art
works with accuracy unsurpassed –
perfect copies indeed – by electric
process: such specimens, being
selected for reproduction by Dr.
Dresser, are of course always
beautiful examples of Art*'.

As the firm's Art Adviser,
Dresser might have provided
Hukin & Heath with original
examples to reproduce.
(See Ill.124, p. 138 for a similar
example.)

b Serving knife and fork
The silver blade and tines
engraved with Japanese motifs of
birds and blossoming trees, both
fitted with ebony handles and
ivory finials. Walter & John
Barnard, London, 1880. *B397*
Length of knife: 30.5cm

The presence of birds perched on
trees are a popular theme in
Japanese art. Particular trees and
birds like the willow and the
swallow are commonly used to
represent the seasons. Here,
however, these motifs are used
more for their decorative effect
than for their symbolic meaning.

121

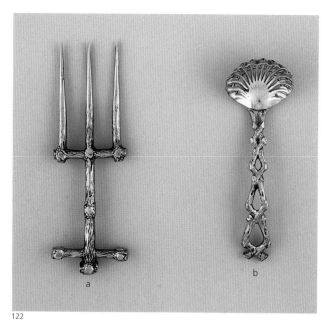

122

122 (Above)

a Bread fork
Electroplated nickel silver, 'Rustic' style, c.1870. *B389*
Length: 14.5cm

b Sugar sifter
Electroplated nickel silver, 'Rustic' style, c.1870. *B390*
Length: 13.5cm

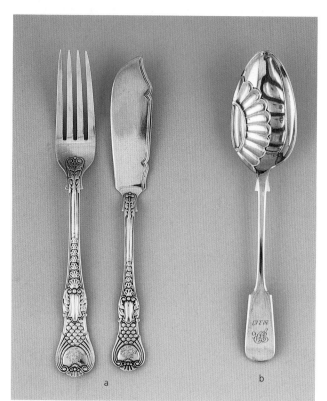

123

123 (Left)

a Table fork and fish knife
Silver, in Coburg pattern, both by Francis Higgins. London, 1884. *B403*
Length of fork: 21.5cm
Length of knife: 21cm

Cf.: Pickford, I., *Silver Flatware*, Antique Collectors' Club, 1983, (frontispiece).

b 'Moustache' table spoon
Electroplated silver on nickel silver, maker's mark W & W, with registered design mark for 1883. *B410*
Length: 20.5cm

An ingenious design intended to protect the moustache from being soiled.

124

124 (Left)

Dessert knife
Electroplated silver blade, the handle a re-used *kozuka* (Japanese small sword handle) in silver and copper, inlaid in relief with carps leaping out of water, also bearing a signature on the reverse, possibly for the Japanese maker, the blade stamped with marks for ATKIN BROS. Sheffield, 1880. *B398*
Length: 22cm

The leaping carp is a traditional motif in Japanese iconography and signified perseverance. In recent times the representation of the carp climbing up a rapid river has been associated with young boys, whose day (Boys' Day) is celebrated on 5 May. It is an auspicious symbol for their good health and strength and a reminder of the difficulties the boys have to overcome. This symbolism would be entirely lost to western eyes and only appreciated for the pleasant aesthetics.

It seems likely this handle was imported directly from Japan in the 1870s–80s, when the rage for *japonaiserie* was at its height, and then re-adapted as part of a knife. At that time Japanese artefacts were sold throughout Britain in major retailers, such as Liberty, London.

Dr Christopher Dresser (see B391, p. 135) played a major role in the diffusion of the 'cult of Japan' with his writings, lectures and also with his commercial ventures. In 1879, with a business partner, Charles Holmes, he started an import company of goods from Japan.

Cf.: Glanville, P., *Silver*, V&A, London, 1996, p. 67 (similar knives manufactured in the USA are illustrated). See also Ill.121, p. 137, for a *kozuka* handle.

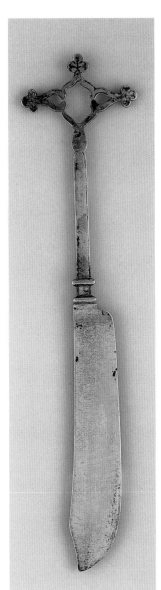

125

125 *(Above)*

Knife
Silver-gilt, the handle terminating in a pierced finial shaped as a stylised cross incorporating a trefoil. George Adams, London, 1881. *B404*
Length: 20cm

The mixture of Gothic and Celtic motifs shown in this piece demonstrates a continuing demand for historically inspired silver.

126 *(Right)*

a Bread knife
Steel blade with handle of a moulded hard polymer (probably gutta-percha) or rubber. Sheffield, c.1880. *B407*
Length: 28cm

b Bread knife
Steel blade marked JOSEPH HAYWOOD CO, with handle of moulded hard polymer (probably gutta-percha) or rubber. Sheffield, c.1880. *B408*
Length: 33cm

Gutta percha is a natural plastic similar to rubber, taken from the tree Palaqium Gutta and Palaquium Oblongifolia, both native to Malaya, where the material was used for tools and knife handles. Although introduced to Europe in the seventeenth century, it was not widely known until 1844 when the British inventor Thomas Hancock patented its use for stoppers.

Gutta percha was used widely in the late nineteenth century for a variety of both decorative and practical purposes. Unfortunately, not many gutta percha objects have survived, because with ageing the material loses its elasticity, become very fragile and is prone to cracking.

On the other hand, vulcanite or hard rubber, as it was known in the USA, is a substance obtained by a process of vulcanisation first experimented in the early part of the nineteenth century. Vulcanite was first patented in 1839 in the USA by Charles Goodyear and, a few years later, by Thomas Hancock in Britain. Widely used for dentures, buttons and pneumatic tyres, vulcanite was also used for manufacturing small everyday items such as vesta cases, fountain pens and cutlery handles.

Cf.: Katz, S., *Classic Plastics*, Thames & Hudson, 1984; Sparke, P., (ed.), *The Plastic Age*, Victoria & Albert Museum, 1990, (Part One, *Plastics Pre-History 1860–1914* for detailed information on early plastics).

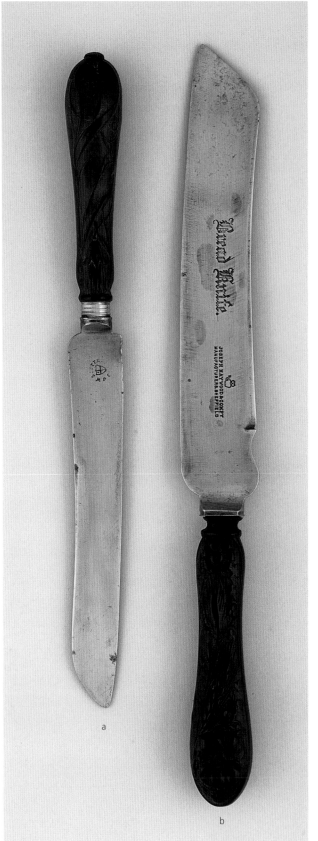

a

b

126

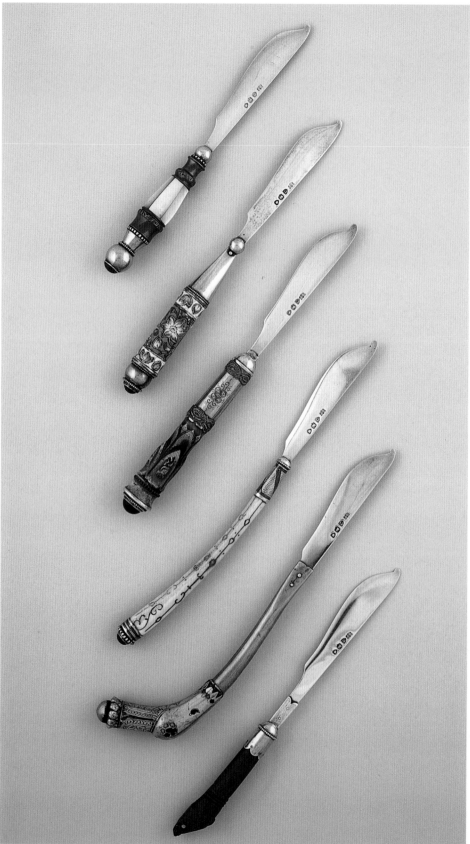

127

127 *(Left)*

Knives
Six from a set of twelve, all with silver blades bearing the mark of Robert Pringle, London, 1895.
B412
Length: 20–24cm
These handles appear to have been adapted from various items, including a cheroot holder, a parasol handle, a stone hone and the handle of a pen.

(Right)

Salon de Luxe, Willow Tea Rooms, Sauchiehall Street, Glasgow, c.1904
Photograph: Hunterian Art Gallery, University of Glasgow, Mackintosh Collection

Between 1896 and 1917 the Scottish architect Charles Rennie Mackintosh was commissioned to design and in some instances refurbish a series of tearooms owned by Miss Catherine Cranston. The commission was not restricted to interior decoration, but included furniture and fittings.

The result was to be a remarkable work of unity from conception to completion. The evolution from the Art Nouveau style of Macintosh's early interiors to the more austere geometrical patterns of the Modern Movement are found in his work for Miss Cranston's tearooms.

As Pevsner points out in his *Pioneers of Modern Design* (1936), Miss Cranston's tearooms were *'the first monument of the British movement, a movement in opposition to the snugness and stiffness of the pub, again typical of the new desire for health and daintiness'*.

The carefully starched white tablecloths, the tableware and the flower decoration, embody the desire for elegance and style to which the urban middle classes aspire.

1900 – 1950

At the start of the last century, a standard table knife was almost identical in design to one made a century earlier. Several versions of the same design were being produced in large, affordable quantities to satisfy a fast-growing population both at home and abroad. Most popular were those with celluloid handles, imitating natural materials, with silver-plated or nickel silver blades.

The concept of commemoration gained ground in this period. Special occasions, such as Edward VII succeeding Queen Victoria to the throne, were a great opportunity for silversmith designers, like Archibald Knox, working for Liberty & Co., and A. E. Jones of Birmingham to produce commemorative spoons and other items which, because of their nature, reflect best the prevalent style and design of that period.

Charles Rennie Mackintosh was also a designer whose innovative style had a huge impact early in the century both in Britain and abroad. Amongst the designers he inspired was Josef Hoffmann, one of the founders of the Wiener Werkstätte, a design workshop inspired by C. R. Ashbee's Guild of Handicraft.

The discovery of stainless steel by W. Brearley in Sheffield in 1914 was destined to change the production, design and durability of cutlery. The First World War, although it interrupted the production of stainless steel, probably allowed the necessary time to research how to apply this new metal for knife manufacturing. In 1920 a small number of cutlers started to produce knives with blades of stainless steel. It soon became obvious, however, that the old methods would not work with the new material and that a radical change in the approach to design was needed. It was only after a period of trial and error that new knife blade shapes appeared. Called 'finger point' and 'slipper', these had dark green, brown or ivory-coloured, slightly tapered handles.

Change and development was not limited to the domestic dining room. Hotel cutlery underwent a conscious effort to reflect the current style in design and large establishments had their own tableware designed for them. The same happened for those large 'travelling' hotels, the super ocean liners.

With the outbreak of the Second World War in 1939, the pace of change in Britain slowed and cutlery manufacturing gave in to the requirements of the war industry. Countries such as Sweden, whilst not taking an active part in the conflict, could experiment and expand their production of cutlery. This was the case for the Swedish firm Gense of Eskilstuna, a major manufacturer of stainless steel. In 1944 Gense produced a high-quality cutlery set called Thebe, which was designed by their leading in-house designer Folke Arström. This set was introduced to Britain by Heals, together with furniture from other Scandinavian countries. A 'one piece' set of stainless steel table cutlery, matched and sold with the designer's name, was a concept that British designers were able to compete with once peace was restored.

By the mid-1950s designers like G. Benney, R. Welsh and David Mellor were also producing successful designs for mass production in silver, which did not undermine the importance of the silversmithing craft.

128

129

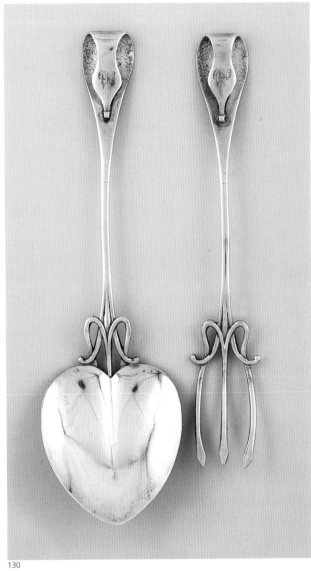

130

128 (*Above*)

Spoon
Silver and enamel, designed by
Archibald Knox, the bowl with
entrelac motif on a turquoise and
green enamelled ground below
inscription ANNO. CORON: ER VII,
the tapering pointed stem with
pierced symmetrical knot
decoration to sides, stamped 'L. &
Co.' within three lozenges for
Liberty & Co., Birmingham,
hallmark for 1901. *B417*
Length: 16cm

This spoon commemorates the
Coronation of Edward VII (see
also B418, p. 134). An identical
piece is in The British Museum,
but non-enamelled examples of
the same design are also known to
have been made at the same time.

Cf.: Tilbrook, A. J., *The Designs of
Archibald Knox for Liberty*, London,
1976, p. 127; *Style Liberty*, Victoria &
Albert Museum Publications, London,
1975, D.81D.

129 (*Above*)

Spoon
Silver, of slender form and
hammered effect, with oval-
shaped bowl, the finial with three
stylised heart-shaped leaves. A. E.
Jones, Birmingham, 1919. *B441*
Length: 11.5cm

To satisfy the demand for
fashionable items, some firms
like the Birmingham based
A. E. Jones, manufactured
pieces similar in style to the
ones retailed through Liberty.

Cf.: Pickford, I., *Silver Flatware*,
Antique Collectors' Club, p. 156
(for illustrations of related enamelled
cutlery by Liberty & Co.), similar
in design but with a highly
polished finish.

130 (*Above*)

Serving spoon and fork
Silver, the spoon with heart-
shaped bowl, both fork and
spoon with knot motif to the base
of stem continuing at the back of
the bowl, the handle terminating
in an inward-shaped loop
engraved with the letter 'M',
maker's mark for Walker & Hall,
Birmingham, 1902. *B422*
Length: 24.5cm

The design of this serving fork
and spoon is stylistically
transitional. The Art Nouveau
motif of organic interlacing forms
is rather restrained and confined
to the base of the stem.

The Arts and Crafts philosophy
of beauty linked to 'hand' making
lingered on as an ideal for a time.
Notice how pseudo-hammering
marks have been deliberately
created and left on the flat surface
of the handle, below the loop, in
order to give the impression that
the pieces were hand-crafted.

131

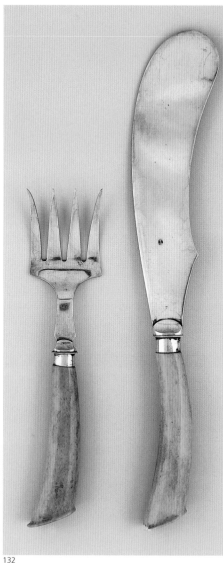

132

131 *(Above)*

Serving knife and spoon
Silver, in the Art Nouveau style, the elaborate whiplash motif of the handle similarly repeated on the bowl and on the lower part of the knife blade. Lee & Wigfull, Sheffield, 1901. *B423*
Length of knife: 28.5cm

The whiplash design is the most popular decorative pattern of the Art Nouveau style, characterised by a double, soft and flowing curve, often very intricate and elaborate. This motif was adapted from the much simpler organic forms used by the Arts and Crafts designers. The pleasing curvilinear shape was adopted and re-elaborated by the Art Nouveau artists, who made it the *leitmotif* of their works. It gave them freedom to interpret nature and adapt it in a very personal manner.

132 *(Above)*

Fish carvers
Electroplated silver on nickel silver, with silver ferrules and green-stained bone handles, by Spurrier & Co Ltd, Birmingham, c.1903. *B425*
Length of knife: 32.5cm

133 *(Right)*

a **Spoon**
Silver, with heart-shaped bowl and a stem decorated with stylised husk, the round-shaped pierced finial incorporating the figure of a deer. Maker's mark of A. E. Jones, Birmingham, 1906. *B426*
Length: 13.5
Cf.: Sutton, A., *A. Edward Jones, Birmingham*, 1980, p. 21, illustrates a similar spoon described as 'a souvenir of Oxford'.

b **Spoon**
Electroplated silver, of classical design, with lotus-shaped bowl, the stepped handle with zoomorphic forms to both ends, the scrolled finial shaped as a ram's head. c.1900. *B415*
Length: 27cm.

c **Spoon**
Silver, with round hammered bowl, the stem formed as twisted flattened tendrils terminating in honesty plant seed pods. Maker's mark of Ramsden & Carr, London, 1910. *B428*
Length: 16cm

d **Spoon**
Silver, with fig-shaped hammered bowl, the partly-twisted and curved stem terminating in a round finial mounted with a turquoise cabochon, by A. E. Jones. Birmingham, 1906. *B430*
Length: 17.5cm

e **Spoon**
Silver, with large hammered pear-shaped bowl engraved on the reverse, the long rope-twisted stem terminating in a pierced finial densely decorated in relief to imitate an armorial, the oval cartouche in the centre bearing the initial 'N' on a blue enamelled ground. Maker unknown, c.1900. *B416*
Length: 27cm

f **Spoon**
Silver, with round hammered bowl, the long stem with dot and elliptical decoration, the pierced heart-shaped finial surmounted by a malachite cabochon. Maker's mark 'A. E. B.' possibly for A. E. Bonner. London, 1909. *B431*
Length: 20cm

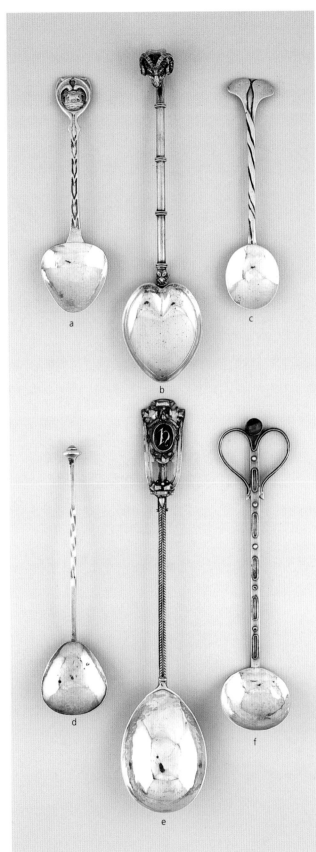

133

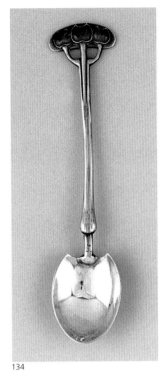

134

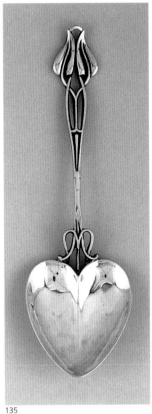

135

134 (Above)

Coffee spoon
Enamelled silver, the slender stem
terminating in stylised seedpods
on enamelled ground, stamped 'L
& Co' within three lozenges for
Liberty & Co., Birmingham,
1905. *B420*
Length: 10cm

For centuries seedpods have been
used as decorative motifs, often to
symbolise fecundity and life. In
the late nineteenth century, Art
Nouveau artists and designers
readapted this organic form and
used it in a variety of ways,
particularly in metalwork and
jewellery, where it was often
adorned with enamels or
semiprecious stones. The
pod of the honesty plant was
characteristic of Archibald
Knox's designs for Liberty's,
but was also used by many of
his contemporaries.

135 (Above)

Spoon
Silver, in Art Nouveau style, of
slender form, with heart-shaped
bowl, the stem with *entrelac*
motifs terminating in a bud-
shaped finial. Maker's mark
L. & S. Birmingham, 1902. *B421*
Length: 13.5cm

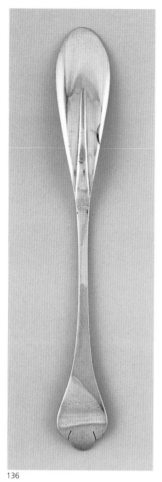

136

136 (Above)

Fish knife
Electroplated nickel silver, of trifid end pattern, designed by Charles Rennie Mackintosh, c.1905. *B434* (The piece appears unmarked. It is possible that the stamp *Miss Cranston's* has been removed at some stage.)
Length: 21cm

The prolific architect and designer Charles Rennie Macintosh (1868–1928) was the major exponent of the Glasgow School, whose work received international acclamation in 1900 at an exhibition in Vienna and in 1902 in Turin. He had a great influence on the international Art Nouveau circles and, in particular, on the Vienna Secessionists. Having designed the interiors of Miss Cranston's Tearooms in Glasgow (1904), he also furnished and completed them with his especially designed cutlery set.

Cf.: Rudoe, J., *Decorative Arts 1850-1950. A Catalogue of The British Museum Collection*, London, 1991, p. 68, pl. 66.

137

137 (Above)

Knife
Silver, small, the v-shaped stem with a cabochon cast in relief with fruit motif. maker's mark W.H.G. Birmingham, 1934. *B460*
Length: 17cm

138

138 (Above)

Knife
Silver, hammer-shaped from one single piece, with octagonal terminal. Omar Ramsden, London, 1928. *B451*
Length: 17.5cm

Omar Ramsden (1873–1939) studied at Sheffield School of Art, where in the early 1890s he met his future business associate Alwyn Carr (1872–1940). Their partnership lasted from 1898, the year when they registered their mark in London, to 1919. After the partnership was dissolved Ramsden continued to run the firm on his own until his death in 1939.

Ramsden owed his success mainly to his entrepreneurial approach to work. The decorative and domestic pieces made in the workshop were often personalised by the maker's signature which, combined with a very obvious 'hand-crafted' style proved very desirable. On the other hand, his interest in fifteenth- and sixteenth-century styles of ornamentation made his pieces even more popular.

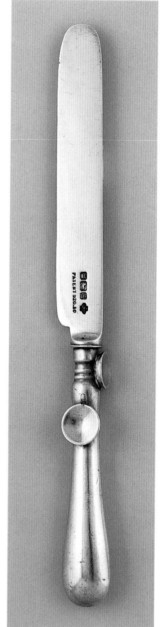

139

139 (Above)

Knife
Silver, patented child's training knife, silver blade and handle, mark of William Hutton. For training a child to place their fingers in the correct position. Sheffield, 1910. *B436*
Length: 19cm

At the same time as this knife, the Sheffield firm of W. Hutton & Sons was also manufacturing pieces in the Art Nouveau style, having employed Kate Harris as their designer in 1901.

140 (Left)

a Crab knife and fork and fruit knife

Crab knife with square hole cut into the plated steel blade. Fork with two steel tines, probably originally plated. Both with flattened oval-section silver handles with rounded ends. Fruit knife with silver blade and similar handle. The design attributed to Josef Hoffmann, marked with the monogram 'WW' for Wiener Werkstätte, Vienna, c.1910. *B438*
Length: 17.5–19cm

The Austrian architect and designer Josef Hoffmann (1870–1956) was one of the founding members of the Vienna Secession (1897) and of the Wiener Werkstätte (1903). The Wiener Werkstätte was a group of workshops set up to establish a relationship between designers, craftsmen and society. Hoffmann was a friend and admirer of C. R. Mackintosh, who had a powerful influence on his designs.

His early work is characterised by geometrical lines and forms of modern design. A pair of knife and fork similar to B438 are said to be used for eating crab.

Cf.: Fahr-Becker, G., *Wiener Werkstætte*, Taschen, 1995.
Decorative Arts from 1880 to the Present Day, Christie's London, auction catalogue, 18 April 1986, p. 36, lot 75 (illus.).

b Fish knife and fork and butter knife

Electro silver plate, of simple shape with rectangular flaring handles, 'Noreen' pattern, Roberts & Belk, London and Sheffield, c.1950. *B469*
Length: 19cm

See p. 151 b and 153 b&c for more information about the firm Roberts & Belk of Sheffield.
Cf.: Nevwith, W. & Hoffman. J., *Bestecke Für Die Wiener Werkstatte*, Wein, 1982, pp. 79 and 101.

c Part place setting (10 pieces)

Silver, of plain shape, with rectangular flaring handles. Charles Boyton, London, 1933. *B458*
Length of large knife: 21cm

Charles Boyton (1885–1958) first worked in his family's firm and later set up his own workshop. His designs increasingly conformed to the popular Art Deco style of the 1930s. Tableware seems to have been his passion, and some of his designs were a commercial success.

Cf.: Krekel-Aalberse, *Art Nouveau and Art Déco*, Abrams, 1989, p. 252.

a

b

c

d

140

141 (Right)

a Spoon
Silver, of simple design, the heart-shaped and rat-tailed hammered bowl continuing in a ribbed slightly flaring stem. Ramsden & Carr, London, 1912. *B440*
Length: 17.5cm

b Serving spoon
Silver, the oval bowl with a hammered finish, the plain tapered stem with a plain seal terminal, maker's mark A. I. S. London, 1926. *B447*
Length: 26cm

c Spoon
Silver, the flaring stem terminating in a splayed finial. Omar Ramsden, London, 1919. *B439*
Length: 17.5cm

In 1919, after his partnership with Alwyn Carr was dissolved, Omar Ramsden registered his famous mark *Omar Ramsden me fecit*. It is believed, however, that Ramsden had little to do with the actual making of the pieces both during and after his partnership with Carr.

d Spoon
Silver with hammered, round-shaped bowl with rat-tail, the flaring stem with pierced wrythen knop at the middle, terminating in a square finial. Omar Ramsden, London, 1927. *B452*
Length: 16cm

e Spoon
Silver, with large fig-shaped hammered bowl and short tapering stem with square terminal. Guild of Handicraft, London, 1927. *B454*
Length: 16.5cm

f Spoon
Silver, with oval hammered bowl and diamond-shaped terminal. Cecil R. Walker, London, 1928. *B453*
Length: 16cm

It is evident from the style of these simple but elegant spoons that they draw their inspiration from Middle Ages cutlery. The Arts and Crafts movement had adopted these fundamental principles of design and ornamentation, and this traditional style remained in vogue well into the 1920s.

141

142

142 *(Left)*

a Spoon
Silver, with pear-shaped hammered bowl and stem with relief decoration of entwined tendrils, the round-shaped finial with a thistle on matted ground. Ramsden & Carr, London, 1918. *B448*
Length: 16cm

Whilst Ramsden run the firm and Carr carried out most of the design, the fourteen craftsmen employed in the London workshop were executing most of the work.

Parallel to the domestic pieces Ramsden also received many commissions for ecclesiastical and ceremonial silver, for which they were highly renowned.

b Spoon
Silver, the stem cast as a column surmounted by the figure of Nelson. J. W. Ballatine, Chester, 1905. *B432*
Length: 20cm

The handle is fashioned as a replica of Nelson's column, erected in 1867 to commemorate the Battle of Trafalgar. This spoon marks the centenary of Nelson's death (1805).

c Spoon
Silver, with round hammered bowl and rat tail, the stem cast with stylised husk and scrolls, the finial formed as a sailing ship above Neptune's trident. Initialled J. R. on sail, Ramsden & Carr, London, 1912. *B437*
Length: 17.5cm

The galleon was a popular motif in the Arts & Crafts and in the early twentieth-century Elizabethan Revival. This motif is found not only in metalwork and jewellery but also in ceramics (tiles in particular) and in stained glass.

The galleon is often found in the work of the Guild of Handicraft, which used it as a play on the words for their name and to indicate craft.

Ramsden & Carr also used this motif either in solid silver of in enamels.

d Spoon
Silver, the pear-shaped hammered bowl with relief scrolls on reverse, the stem cast with key pattern and grape decoration terminating in a finial with stylised *entrelac* foliage motif. Ramdsen & Carr, London, 1910. *B427*
Length: 16.5cm

e Spoon
Silver, with pear-shaped hammered bowl, the upper part of the stem partly decorated with stylised tendrils and flowers and initialled A.E.A.G.S. In medieval style, Omar Ramsden, London, 1928. *B450*
Length: 16cm

f Spoon
Silver, of slender form, with fig-shaped hammered bowl and slightly curved stem terminating in a circular pierced finial, A. E. Jones, Birmingham, 1908. *B429*
Length: 16.5cm

g Spoon
Silver, the deep, round bowl engraved with a laurel leaf and ribbon cartouche on reverse, the crown-shaped finial engraved with pseudo armorial motif. Maker's mark of A. E. Jones, Birmingham, 1908. *B435*
Length: 19cm

Spoons of this type and quality by named designer silversmiths were given as gifts for special occasions.

h Spoon
Silver, with oval hammered bowl, the stem formed as tendrils with stylised seed pods. Maker's mark of Omar Ramsden, London, 1920. *B449*
Length: 15.5cm

Albert Edward Jones (1879–1954) trained at the Central School of Art in Birmingham, where he came into contact with the Birmingham Guild of Handicrafts, a great influence in his work. The workshop specialised in ecclesiastical silver, but also produced domestic silver and metalwork objects in the popular arts and crafts style, including tea sets, trays, butter dishes, condiment sets, caskets and clocks.

A. E. Jones was assisted by talented craftsmen and designers, such as Bernard Cuzner, who also designed silverware for Liberty's & Co.

In 1934 his son, Kenneth, joined the firm, which still survives today. Their success was due to the adaptability and diversification of their production.

143

143 (*Left*)

a Knife and fork
Stainless steel knife blade and fork with silver tines, both with Art Deco style carved ivory handles. French hallmarks and English import marks, imported by Goldsmiths & Silversmiths Co. Ltd, London, 1930. *B456*
Length: 24cm

b Table and dessert forks
Silver, by Francis Higgins & Son Ltd, London, 1932. *B455*
Length: 19cm
A child's cutlery set of the same pattern, also by Higgins, which comprised a knife, fork, spoon and pusher, is illustrated in *The Studio*, (vol. 110, 1935, p. 89) with other silverware for the nursery. The set was exhibited by the Worshipful Company of Goldsmiths at the *Universal and International Exhibition*, held in Brussels in 1935.

c Fish knife and fork
Marked 'Chrome Plate', made in England in effeminate Deco style, 1930. *B459*
Length: 20cm

d Forks (2)
Stainless steel, Old English pattern, one with feathered edge, made by Firth Vickers, Sheffield. c.1925. *B467*
Length: 17.5cm–20cm

Called 'Staybrite', it was probably the first of all stainless steel flatware. Stainless steel was initially a difficult material to work in traditional methods and tools. The process involved the re-melting of pure steel (i.e., low in carbon content) and alloying with nickel and chromium. Special furnaces and procedures were needed to stop the alloys being lost to the atmosphere. The resultant metal was extremely strong and rust-resistant, however, and worth the effort of development. It became obvious that this stainless steel metal had a great potential in the production of the 'one-piece' knife, a style that has been attempted many times in the past. 'Staybrite' was the first step in this direction.

In the intervening years since its introduction, the reaction of designers to the new material has been somewhat mixed. A few European companies have produced innovative, functional designs in stainless steel which are well finished and feel good in the hand, but most of the mass-produced pieces up the present day have been disappointing. The cheap, nondescript designs are often enlivened with floral relief patterns and motifs or bright coloured plastic and usually produced without a maker's mark. Large department stores are still selling a number of services by well-known designers but their stock lacks variety and vitality, and perhaps pays too much homage to an earlier age when a range of different materials were being used.

144

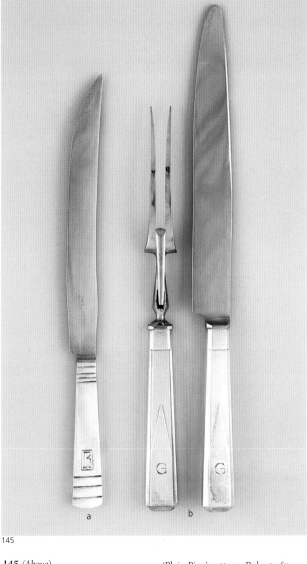

a   b

145

144 (*Above*)

Salad servers

Silver, of plain design and hammered finish, Guild of Handicraft, London, 1939. *B461*
Length of spoon: 21cm.

The Guild of Handicraft was founded in 1888 by C. R. Ashbee (1863–1942) when he was 25 years old. After some success the workshop was moved to Mile End Road where it turned into a Limited Company and opened showrooms in Central London. In 1902 the Guild moved to Chipping Camden in Gloucestershire with all its craftsmen and their families, 150 in all. However, by 1908, having trouble with marketing, the business wound up, leaving four members to start a fresh business with the same name 'The Guild of Handicraft'. In 1912 this partnership dissolved, leaving G. H. Hart to run the Guild under his own name. He died in 1973.

Cf.: Fallon, J. P., *Marks of London Goldsmiths and Silversmiths*, Jenkins, London, 1992, pp. 130–32.

145 (*Above*)

a Carving knife

Blade mark FIRTH STAINLESS, the silver flaring handle with ribbed decorative motif and engraved with the letter 'B'. Charles Boyton, London, 1936. *B464*
Length: 30cm
It is not unusual for a small silversmith firm such as Boyton's to maintain links with larger manufacturers (i.e., Firth Stainless) in order to make their goods more competitive and viable and to keep up with modern design and new technologies.

b Carving knife and fork

Stainless steel blade, and two-tined fork with pivot guard. The electroplated silver handles in 'Plain Pine' pattern. Roberts & Belk Ltd, London & Sheffield, c.1935. *B463*
Length of knife: 35cm

The silversmithing firm of Roberts & Belk was founded in Sheffield in 1908. Walter P. Bell, who had trained as an architect and worked as the firm's designer in the late 1920s and 1930s, also designed the 'Plain Pine' cutlery. This range was supplied to the Cunard liner, *Queen Mary* (see p. 153, Ill. 146).

Krekel-Aalberse, A., *Art Nouveau and Art Déco Silver*, Abrams, 1989, p. 258; Dryden, A., 'Commercial Silversmiths and the British Silver Trade during the Inter-War Years', in *Journal of the Society of Decorative Arts*, no. 17, London, 1993, p. 61.

146 (Left)

Spoons (2) and forks (2)
Nickel, dated 1937. *B465*
Length of large spoon: 22cm

Made to commemorate the
Coronation of Edward VIII,
(before Abdication). A number of
companies made commemorative
knives, which were eventually
scrapped.

The Cunard White Star liner
Queen Mary, built in
Clydebank, Scotland, was
launched in September 1934.
   A number of eminent
British artists – such as
Duncan Grant and Vanessa
Bell, Dame Laura Knight and
Cedric Morris – were
commissioned work for her
interior decoration, which
combined paintings, murals,
woodcarving and sculptural
metalwork with a vast range
of luxury fittings.
   The Birmingham firm of
Elkingtons were chosen to
provide the first-class dining
saloon with a range of 22,500
electroplate pieces. They were
praised for succeeding in
designing functional objects
pleasing to the eye and
suitable for travelling at sea.
Each piece had been carefully
designed to guarantee easy
handling and carrying and,
perhaps more importantly,
economical storage.
   About 1,300 meat and
entrée dishes were made
complete with covers and
additional devices, such as
draining racks for asparagus
or meat carving stands. The
flat top and recessed handle
of the dish covers, for
instance, would allow for
more courses/dishes to be
carried at the same time.
(See illustration on p. 68 for
exactly the same sort of
device, but 500 years earlier!)
   Utilitarian vessels were
complemented with more
elegant pieces, like finger
bowls of a special metal,
made to look like gold and
with a hand-hammered
finish, and also bowls for
grapefruit and ice buckets.
These would certainly be
used in the four private
dining rooms located just off
the main banqueting hall,
seating about 800 passengers.

147 (*Left*)

a **Forks (2) and spoons (2)**
Electroplated silver, Unity brand
of C. W. S. Ltd, Sheffield, c.1925.
B466
Length: 21.5cm

b **Knife, fork and spoon**
Electroplated silver, in 'Noreen'
pattern, Roberts & Belk Ltd,
London and Sheffield, 1936. *B468*
Length: 21cm

Also produced for Government
contracts in the late 1950s.

c **Knife, fork and spoon**
Electroplated silver, in 'Plain Pine'
pattern, designed by R. Belk of
Roberts & Belk Ltd, London and
Sheffield, for the Cunard White
Star liner *Queen Mary*, 1936. *B462*
The pieces bear the Cunard
insignia on reverse.
Length: 23cm (knife).

During the interwar period other
Sheffield cutlery manufacturers,
like Mappin & Webb and Viners,
also supplied shipping companies
and hotels.

The interiors of restaurants, hotels
and transatlantic liners of the
1930s were all decorated in the
fashionable Art Deco style.
This style dictated the need for
objects to be restrained in
decoration but highly functional.
Whilst Roberts & Belk supplied
Cunard with a design for the
second class section of the Queen
Mary, Elkington received the
contract for the provision of
22,500 cutlery pieces for the first
class.

A development of more
sophisticated machinery to satisfy
such a large demand was a
necessity. Many firms reluctantly
abandoned the Arts and Crafts
theories of hand-crafted pieces
and accepted the new methods of
mass production.

Cf.: Dryden, A., 'Commercial
Silversmiths and the British Silver
Trade during the Inter-War Years', in
Journal of the Society of Decorative Arts,
no. 17, London, 1993, pp. 59–66.

SELECT BIBLIOGRAPHY

Addy, S.O., 'The Sheffield Thwitel', *Yorkshire Archaeological Journal 8*, 1884, p.59–64.

Addy, S.O., Gales & Martin's *Director of Sheffield, 1788*' Sheffield' Pawson & Brailsford, facs. repr. of 1788 edn., 1889.

Addy, S.O., 'Mediaeval English Cutlery', Transactions of the *Hunter Archaelogical Society 3*, 1925, pp. 9–23, 1925.

Ainslie, J.A., 'Knife and Fork Handles and the Bow Collector', *The Connoisseur 131*, 1953, pp. 14–17.

Andrew, W.J., 'The Scramasax (Hunting or Sword Knife Found at Oliver's Battery, Winchester)', *Hampshire Field Club Papers and Proceedings 12*, 1934, pp. 15–16.

Ashford, R., 'Folding Fruit Knives', *Antique Collector*, August 1977, pp. 60–63.

Backhouse, J., D.H. Turner, L. Webster (ed.), *The Golden Age of Anglo-Saxon Art*, London, British Museum Publications, 1984.

Bailey, C.T.P., *Knives and Forks*, London, Medici Society, 1927.

Beard, C.R., 'Wedding Knives', *The Connoisseur 85*, 1930, pp. 91–97.

Belden, G., and M. Snodin, *Spoons*, London, *Walter Parrish International*, 1976.

Biggs, A.R., *Catalogue of the Collection of Early Spoons Formed by the Late Anna Rupert Biggs, Daughter of Charles Rupert.*, London, Christie, Manson & Woods, September 1978.

Blakemore, K., *Guide to Flatware*, London, Heywood, 1955.

Bourdon-Smith, J.H., *Catalogue of Early English Spoons*, Exhibited at J.H. Bourdon-Smith Ltd, to mark the publication of *London Silver Spoonmakers 1500–1697*. London, Timothy Arthur Kent, 1981.

Brown, P., *Pyramids of Pleasure*, York, 1990

Brown, P., *Keeping of Christmas*, York, 1992

Brown, P., *In Praise of of Hot Liquors*, York, 1995

Brown, P. & Day, I., *Pleasures of the Table*, York, 1997

Brown, P. & Schwartz M., *Come Drink the Bowl Dry*, York, 1996

Brown, W.H. (Bill), 'Eating Implements', *Antique Collecting*, 29 September 1995, pp. 21–23.

Cowgill, J., M. de Neergard and N. Griffiths, *Knives and Scabbards*, London, HMSO/Museum of London, 1987.

Cuming, H.S., 'On the Sheaths of Girdle Knives', *Journal of the British Archaeological Association 17*, 1861, pp. 113–18.

Davies, S. Kevill, 'Elizabethan Fruit Trenchers', *Antique Collecting*, 22 July 1987, pp. 56–57.

Day, I. (ed), *Eat, Drink and Be Merry*, London, 2000

Eames, P., Pageantry, Power and Plate, *Country Life 178*, 1985, p. 1756–58.

Gemeentemuseum, *The Hague, Knives and Forks in the Netherlands 1500-1800* (Introduction by J.C.G.), The Hague, 1972.

Hayward, F.J., *English Cutlery at the Victoria & Albert*, London, 1957

Himsworth, J.B., *The Story of Cutlery, from Flint to Stainless Steel*, London, Ernest Benn, 1953.

Hughes, G.B., 'Old English Wedding Knives', *Country Life 105*, 1949, pp .666–67.

Hughes, G.B., 'Old English Table Knives and Forks', *Country Life 107*, 1950, pp. 450–52.

Hughes, G.B., 'Evolution of the Silver Table Fork', *Country Life 127*, 1959, pp. 364–65.

Hughes, G.B., 'Silver Scoops for Marrow Bones', *Country Life 128*, 1960, pp. 1448 & 1450.

Karsten, W.C., 'Fruit Knife Identification', *Knife World 9*, 1983, pp.4–9, 38–39.

Karsten, W.C., *Silver Folding Fruit Knives*, Knoxville, TN: Knife World Publications, 1986.

Katz, Sylvia, *Classic Plastics*, London, 1984

Leader, R.E., *History of the Company of Cutlers in Hallamshire in the County of York*, Vols. I–II, Sheffield: Cutlers' Company, printed by Pawson & Brailsford, 1905.

London, South Kensington Museum, *Illustrated Catalogue of a Collection of Ancient Cutlery*, lent by M. Achille Jubinal to the South Kensington Museum, London, HMSO, 1874.

London, South Kensington Museum, *Masterpieces of Cutlery and the Art of Eating*, Exh. Cat., London, Victoria & Albert Museum, 1979.

Marquardt, K., *Eight Centuries of European Knives, Forks and Spoons*, Stuttgart, Arnoldsche, 1997.

Mennell, S., *All Manner of Food*, London, 1985

Moore, S., *Cutlery for the Table*, Sheffield, 1999

Moore, S.J., 'Folding Fruit Knives and Forks', *The Antique Dealer & Collectors' Guide*, September 1975, pp. 77–83.
'Cutlery', *Dictionary of Art 8*: London, Grove, (Macmillan), 1997.

Mouret, J-N, *Knives of the World*, Leicester: Magna Books, 1994.

Pickford, I., *Silver Flatware*, London, 1988

Rupert, C.G., *Apostle Spoons: Their Evolution from Earlier Types, and the Emblems used by Silversmiths*, London: Oxford University Press, 1929.

Sanford, J., 'Bridal Knives, a Rare Symbolic Bygone', *The Bazaar* (Bazaar in italics? Plus dates)

Singleton, H.R., *A Chronology of Cutlery, Sheffield*, Sheffield City Museums, 1973.

Stevenson, A., *A Review of Bow & Worcester knife and fork hafts*. Transactions of the English Ceramic Circle, 13 March 1989, pp. 194–99.

Stevenson, A., *A Review of Chelsea, Chelsea-Derby and Derby Knife and Fork Hafts*, Transactions of the English Ceramic Circle 14.1, 1990, pp. 50–58.

Trussler, J., *The Honours of the Table*, London, 1788

Wills, G., '18th Century Knife Cases', *Country Life 116*, 1954, pp. 489–90.

GLOSSARY

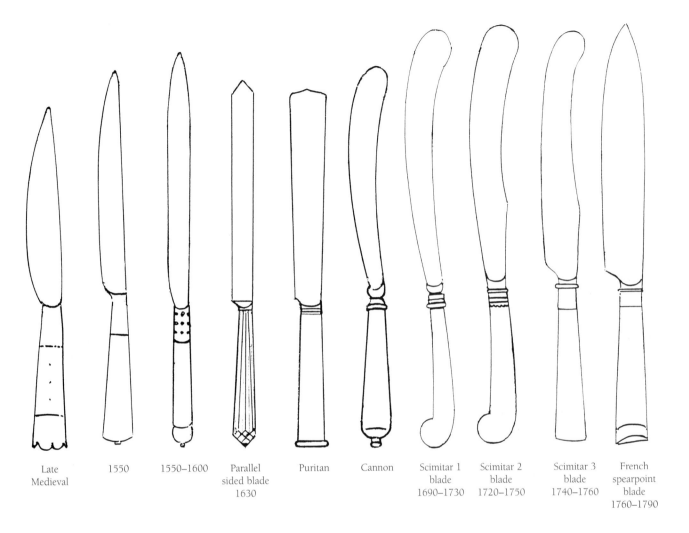

| Late Medieval | 1550 | 1550–1600 | Parallel sided blade 1630 | Puritan | Cannon | Scimitar 1 blade 1690–1730 | Scimitar 2 blade 1720–1750 | Scimitar 3 blade 1740–1760 | French spearpoint blade 1760–1790 |

Antler

Annual growth of horn of deer; the central core pith makes it weak to use in full section but good for scales. Indian Samba deer preferred for full handles.

Bolster

The support or thickening between the blade and tang.

1) Can be forged with the blade
2) Tang and bolster forged in one piece of iron and welded to a steel blade. 18th–19th century
3) Copper alloy shoulder plates applied to a scale tang by rivets or soldering. Medieval
4) White metal bolster of 'run on tin' applied after handle has been fitted. 19th century
5) Bolster as part of the construction of frame handle. 19th century
6) Egg Waterloo bolster, waisted elliptical disc between blade and tang, now made in one piece with the blade. 19th–20th century
7) Mean bolster, blade ending in small flat disc to match the section of the handle. Throughout
8) Flying bolster, a spherical bolster with the scimitar blade 'flying' away. 17th–18th century.

Cap

Separate fitting on the end of the handle usually of different material, i.e. silver.

Celluloid

Thermoplastic material used for knife handles patented by Hyatt Brothers USA in 1869. This plastic material was based on Parkesine invented by Alexander Parkes G.B., 1840. Other trade names include Ivorine and Ivoride.

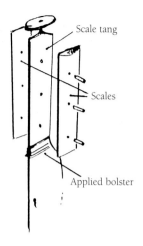

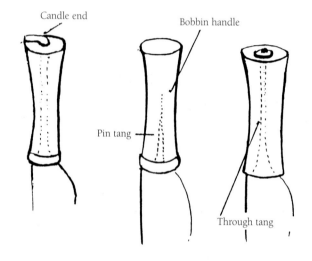

Choil
Chin of blade just below bolster.

Ferrule
Collar of metal usually between bolster and handle. Applied to the handle this collar helps to prevent splitting.

Finial
Figure or decorative device on the ends of handles.

Jigged Bone
Bone scales carved and dyed to look like stag.

Latten
A copper alloy consisting of:

Copper	72.50%
Zinc	25.22%
Iron	1.82%
Impurities	0.46%

Morse Ivory
Marine ivory; Walrus tusk.

Quillon
A short bar either side of the bolster for the purpose of a hand guard.

Tang
Part of knife to which the handle is fitted
1) Scale tang – continuation of blade to which scales (plates) are fitted on either side.
2) Knock on tang – pointed spike onto which a handle is hammered.
3) Pin tang – for fixing hollow handles onto such as silver and some hollow ceramics.
4) Through tang – this thin rod goes right through the length of the handle and is fixed at the end usually with a washer or bent over into a candle end.
5) Transverse tang – a scale tang that is at right angles to the plane of the blade.

Terminal
Protruding decorative feature applied at the end of a knife, probably as a fixing on the tang. See also Finial.

Xylonite
See Celluloid.

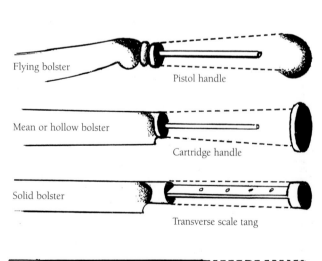

LIST OF ITEMS NOT ILLUSTRATED

B83
Knife, iron, single sided, transverse scale
tang. European, c.1550.
Length: 32.5cm

B116
Knife, with replaced ivory blade of early
shape, the silver pierced handle with gilt
metal backing, English c.1600.
Length: 28cm

B150
Fork, silver, replica of the John Manners,
Earl of Rutland fork, formed from one piece
of silver and based on a French pattern, but
with an English hallmark of 1632.
Length: 18cm

B180
Spoon, silver-gilt, rat-tail pattern with mark
of HENRY GREEN, London 1713.
Length: 20cm

B187
Spoon, silver, Hanoverian rat-tail pattern,
with mark of WILLIAM PETLEY, London,
1719.
Length: 19cm

B192
Knife and fork, iron, scimitar I blade, ebony
handles set in scalloped silver ferrules,
blade mark of PETER SPITZER, London,
c.1730.
Length: 28cm

B196
Fork, silver, with three tines, bearing the
mark of ISAAC CALLARD, London, 1737.
Length: 19cm

B204
Knife and fork, iron, scimitar II blade and
two-tine fork , both with Staffordshire
ceramic handles set in silver ferrules, blade
mark HOLMES, Sheffield, c.1750. Length:
27cm.

B205
Knife and fork, iron, scimitar II blade and
two-tine fork, both with Whieldon agate-
ware pottery handles, set in scalloped silver
ferrules. Probably Sheffield, c.1750.
Length: 28cm.

B211
Fork, silver, Hanoverian pattern, with mark
of SAMUEL TAYLOR, London, 1756.
Length: 20cm.

B214
Knife and fork, iron, scimitar II blade and
two-tine fork with solid bolsters, the faceted
ebony handles of slight pistol-shape. Blade
mark of JOSHUA CRESWICK, Sheffield,
c.1750.
Length: 22.5cm

B215
Knife and fork, iron, scimitar II blade and
two-tine fork with solid shell handles set in
scalloped silver ferrules, c.1750.
Length: 27cm

B216
Knife and fork, iron, scimitar II blade and
two-tine fork with solid bolsters and ivory
pistol handles, blade mark of HIGDEN,
Sheffield, c.1750.
Length: 27cm

B217
Knife, iron, scimitar II blade with antler
pistol handle. Probably Sheffield, c.1750.
Length: 27cm

B218
Knife, iron, scimitar II blade, with solid
bolster, scale tang with scales of stag and
steel cap. Sheffield, c.1760.
Length: 27.5cm

B219
Knife and fork, iron, scimitar II blade with
solid bolster and two-tine fork, both with
scale tang, bone scales and steel caps.
Sheffield, c.1750.
Length: 27cm

B220
Knife and fork, iron, scimitar II blade and
two-tine fork with pistol scale tang and
bone scale inlaid with decorative pins, blade
mark 'S'. Probably Sheffield, c.1750.
Length: 26.5cm

B221
Fork, silver, Hanoverian pattern, four tines,
with marks of T & V CHAWNER, London,
1766.
Length: 19cm

B222
Knife, iron, scimitar II blade, the silver
pistol handle resin filled and marked with
letters ' I P', London, c.1760.
Length: 17cm

B223
Knife and fork, iron, scimitar II blade and
two-tine fork with decorated silver pistol
handle, resin filled. Silver marks T S
THOMAS on knife, E SIEBER on fork.
London, 1760.
Length: 27cm

B224
Fork, Sheffield plate and silver, old English
pattern, made out of fused Sheffield plate,
each of the four tines tipped with solid
silver to allow for wear. Sheffield, c.1760.
Length: 20.5cm

B226
Knife and fork, iron, scimitar II blade and
two-tine fork with stag handles set in silver
ferrules and caps, blade mark OLESORTH.
Sheffield, c.1760.
Length: 29.5cm

B228
Knife and fork, iron, silver, scimitar III
blade and three-tine fork with truncated
cast silver handles, resin filled. Blade mark
GR crown IEF RIS, c.1760.
Length: 28.5cm

B231
Knife and fork, iron, scimitar III blade and
two-tine fork, both with silver ferrules and
caps and ebony handles. Blade mark of
PHILLIPS (?), London, 1760.
Length: 28.5cm

B232
Knife and fork, iron, scimitar III blade and
two-tine fork with solid bolsters and ivory
handles. Probably Sheffield, c.1760.
Length: 27cm

B234
Knife, iron, scimitar III blade with solid
bolster fitted with carved green-stained
ivory handle and silver cap. Probably
Sheffield, c.1760.
Length: 27cm

B240
Fork, silver, Hanoverian pattern with shell
and feather edge, marks of THOMAS
CHAWNER, London, 1762.
Length: 19.5cm

B242
Fork, silver, four-tine Old English pattern,
marks of PAUL CALLARD, London, 1766.
Length: 20cm

B243
Knife and fork, iron, scimitar III blade and
two-tine fork with elaborately stamped
silver handles, resin filled. Maker's mark
only, perhaps W M CAFE (?), London,
c.1760.
Length: 27.5cm

B246
Table Spoon, silver, Old English feather
edge pattern, marks of MICHAEL
KEATING, Dublin, 1776.
Length: 22.5m

B250
Spoon and fork, fused Sheffield plate, Old
English pattern, silver tips to the tines.
Unmarked, Sheffield, c.1760.
Length: 23cm

B253
Knife and fork, iron, French-style blade and
two-tine fork, both fitted with white metal
handles inlaid with shell between a white
metal bolster and ferrule integral with
handle. Blade mark CLARKE, Sheffield,
c.1760.
Length: 26.5cm

B258
Knife and fork, iron, French-style blade
with solid bolster and three-tine fork fitted
with green-stained ivory handles. Blade
mark of I PALMER, London, c.1770.
Length: 27cm

B259
Knife and fork, iron, French-style blade and
three-tine fork, both fitted with solid shell
handles and silver ferrules. Blade mark
WATSON, London (?), c.1770.
Length: 28cm

B261
Fork, silver, Old English pattern, four tines,
marks of THOS NORTHCOTE, London,
1778.
Length: 20.5cm

B266
Knife and fork, iron, French style blade and
three-tine fork with solid shell handles and
silver ferrules, c.1780.
Length: 27cm

B267
Knife and fork, iron, French style blade and
shaped two-tine fork with wrythen moulded
horn handles and silver ferrules. Blade mark
of PLANT, Sheffield, c.1780.
Length: 27cm

B271
Fork, silver, French-style fiddle and thread
pattern. Marks of GEORGE SMITH,
London, 1785.
Length: 20cm
This example has an incise duty mark.

B273
Fork, silver, fiddle thread and double drop
pattern. Maker's marks perhaps of GEORGE
SMITH & WILLIAM FEARN, London,
1795.
Length: 20cm

B280
Knife, iron, (reversion to) simplified
scimitar style with green-stained ivory
handles. Blade mark of WELLS, perhaps
Sheffield, c.1790.
Length: 28cm

B282
Knife and fork, iron, (reversion to) scimitar
III style blade and three-tine fork with solid
bolsters, the stag handles with steel caps.
Blade mark SHEER STEEL, Sheffield,
c.1790.
Length: 29cm

B284
Spoon, silver, Old English thread pattern,
marks of GEORGE SMITH & WILLIAM
FEARN, London, 1792.
Length: 23cm

B288
Carving Knife, iron, with green-stained
ivory handle and silver ferrule,
c.1750–1800.

B306
Folding Knife, steel blade of scimitar style,
the pistol –shaped handle with stag scales.
Blade mark of EATON, Sheffield, c.1753.
Length: 55.5cm (open)

B308
Knife, steel, parallel-sided blade with solid
bolster and pin tang on green stained ivory
handle. Maker's mark of MILNE, perhaps
Sheffield, c.1800.
Length: 27cm

B313
Fork, silver, Old English pattern. Marks on
upper side for PETER, ANN & W M
BATEMAN, London, 1800.
Length: 21.5cm

B314
Fork, silver, Old English bead pattern.
Marks of RICHARD CROSSLEY, London,
1801.
Length: 20cm

B315
Fork, silver, Hanoverian thread pattern.
Marks of W M SUMNER, London, 1809.
Length: 20.5cm

B316
Fork, Sheffield plate, fiddle & thread
pattern with solid silver tips to the tines,
probably Sheffield, c.1810.
Length: 20.5cm

B317
Fork, silver, fiddle pattern. Marks of
THOMAS TOWNSEND, Dublin, 1811.
Length: 21cm

B318
Knife, steel blade marked GARRARD
surmounted by crown G R. Silver handle by
W M. ELEY & W M. FEARN, London,
1816.
Length: 27.5cm

B319
Fork, silver, Hanoverian military thread
pattern, by PAUL STORR, London, 1813.
Length: 19cm

B320
Knife, steel blade marked SIMMONS. Silver
handle by JAMES STANIFORTH, Sheffield,
1808.
Length: 28cm

B321
Dessert knife and fork, silver, King's pattern. Marks of MARK BOCK, London, 1814.
Length: 22cm.

B323
Fork, silver, fiddle & shell pattern. Marks of J McKAY, Edinburgh, 1824.
Length: 20cm.

B326
Knife, close plate iron blade marked JONES PATENTEE, with papier mâché handle. Birmingham, c.1820.
Length: 20cm.

B328
Fork, silver, King's pattern, by W M. CHAWNER, London, 1830.
Length: 20cm.

B330
Dessert knife and fork, paktong (nickel alloy) blade and four-tine fork with carved ivory handles. Probably Sheffield, c.1825.
Length: 20.5cm.

B332
Knife and fork, silver and steel, slotted and folding, with steel blade marked PALMER. The handles with shell scales. London, 1824.
Length: 20.5cm.

B333
Knife, iron, scimitar blade with silver handle in the form of a nautilus shell. Marks of ATKIN & OXLEY, Sheffield, 1836.
Length: 22cm.

B335
Cake knife and fork, close plated steel blade and fork tines with stamped silver handles by CHARLES NEEDHAM. Blade and fork engraved by THOMAS SANSOM & SON, Sheffield, 1837.
Length: 28cm.

B337
Bachelor set (6), steel and silver, fiddle and thread pattern by MARY CHAWNER, London, 1836.
Length: 28.5cm.

B343
Fork, silver, Hanoverian military thread pattern, marks of ELIZABETH EATON, London, 1849.
Length: 21cm.

B344
Knife, steel blade marked RB & Co with silver handle designed to match fiddle & thread pattern, marks of THOMAS CORDING, London, 1840.
Length: 27.5cm.

B347
Forks (5), all close plated, of different styles.
A: Close plate on iron
B: Close plate on Britannia metal
C: Close plate on brass
D: Close plate on steel
E: Close plate on nickel
All probably Sheffield, c.1840 (pre-electroplate).
Length: 23cm.

B348
Place-set, part (4), steel blades and fork tines, the handles of Staffordshire bone china. Patterns taken from silver models, c.1850.
Length: 18.5cm-37.5cm.

B369
Cake knife, engraved electroplated nickel silver blade and ferrule, the Celluloid handle in imitation of ivory, Sheffield, c.1857.
Length: 24.5cm.

B371
Fish knife and fork, electro-silver plated blade and fork tines engraved and saw-cut by hand, with ivory handles. JOSEPH RODGERS, Sheffield, c.1860.
Length: 24.5cm.

B372
Fish knife and fork, electro-silver plated blade and four-tine fork both engraved and saw-cut by hand, with ivory handles. ELKINGTON, Birmingham, c.1865.
Length: 24cm.

B373
Knife, steel blade marked HUNT & ROSKELL. Silver thread and shell handle by FRANCIS HIGGINS, London, 1865.
Length: 27.5cm.

B375
Knife, steel blade (parallel sided) marked MORTIMER & HUNT. The silver handle in Albert pattern by HUNT & ROSKELL, London, 1869.
Length: 27.5cm.

B380
Serving spoon, electro-silver plate, embossed with 'Berry' type fruit. Maker's mark W & D, possibly WILSON & DAVIS, Sheffield, 1872.
Length: 22.5cm.

B382
Knife, close plated on steel, the electro-silver plated handle , of unusual design, JOSEPH RODGERS, Sheffield, c.1860.
Length: 24.5cm.

B383
Knife, steel blade marked HUNT & ROSKELL, the silver handle by GEORGE ADAMS. Probably a sample. London, 1873.
Length: 26.5cm.

B387
Carving fork, the steel tines close plated with silver, the handle of non-ferrous metal also close plated with silver, with patented finger guard and dated 1875.
Length: 28.5cm.

B388
Serving spoon, electro-silver plate, embossed with 'Berry' type fruit. Registered design mark for 1876.
Length: 22.5cm.

B396
Knife and fork, engraved silver blade and three-tine fork with Japanese Shibayema ivory handles inlaid with semi-precious stones, in red velvet covered gift box, by Elkington & Co., Birmingham, 1880.
Length: 24.5cm.

B402
Spoon and fork, electro-silver plate, with fretted scrolling handles. JOSEPH RODGERS, Sheffield, c.1850.
Length: 20.5–23cm

B405
Serving spoon, electro-silver plate, with traces of gilt on bowl, embossed with two cranes in Japanese style. Registered design mark for 1884.
Length: 23.5cm.

B406
Poultry carvers, steel blade and tines, the handles of carved bone, by LONG & CO, Sheffield, c.1880.
Length: 28cm.

B409
Knife and fork, steel blade and tines with minute bolster. The handles of stag horn with steel end caps. 'Encore' brand by THOMAS TURNER, Sheffield, c.1890.
Length: 25cm.

B411
Knife and fork, steel blade and tines, with minute bolster. The handles of buffalo horn tip with brass caps, Unity brand of CWS Ltd, Sheffield, c.1890.
Length: 24cm

B413
Servers and carvers (6 from a larger set), all with decorative silver plated ferrules and Ivorine (celluloid) handles. 'Encore' brand by THOMAS TURNER, Sheffield, c.1900.
Length: 17.5–32.5cm

B414
Dessert knife and fork, silver blade, tines and ferrules, with rectangular section hardstone handles, by HARRISON BROS & HOWSON, Sheffield, 1900.
Length: 21cm

B424
Carving knife and fork, steel blade and fork tines, with silver ferrules and caps in the form of a hare's head mounted on ivory handles, by HARRISON BROS & HOWSON, Sheffield, 1907.
Length: 34cm

B442
Knife, stainless steel parallel sided blade, with pin tang and block tin bolster fitted with Ivorine (celluloid) handle. Mark FIRTH BREARLEY, Sheffield, c.1920.
Length: 22.5cm

B443
Knife, stainless steel parallel sided blade (made in 'old style' construction), scale tang, block tin bolster and handle of bone scales. Marks of JOHN McCLORY & SONS, Sheffield, c.1920.
Length: 23cm

B444
Knife, stainless steel blade, with pin tang, silver ferrule and ivory handle. Marks of W R HUMPRHEYS, Sheffield, c.1920.
Length: 25.5cm

B445
Knife, stainless steel blade, pin tang and integral 'Waterloo' bolster fitted with celluloid handle. Marks of A C BLOXHAM, Sheffield with RUSNORSTAIN Trade mark, c.1920.
Length: 21.5cm

B446
Knife, stainless steel blade of new shape (finger point) with brown celluloid handle. The blade mark with retailer's name CHAMBERS, Colchester. Perhaps the 'prime knife' of the mid-20th century. Probably Sheffield, c.1950.
Length: 23.5cm

B457
Place setting (6), electroplated silver on nickel knife with stainless steel blade, fork, spoon, fish knife and fork and teaspoon. Stamped letter B on handles, fashioned in the 'Nile' pattern and made by Walker & Hall for the Berkeley Hotel, London.

B472
Cased travelling campaign set with dismantling cutlery (6), steel and silver, comprising: knife, fork, spoon (with replacement dessert knife blade), scissors and ivory spatula. The hinged case of flat slightly flaring rectangular shape is covered in black fishskin and has a silver panel engraved with a crest representing a stork standing on a torse. Perhaps French, c.1765.
Height: 16.5cm; width: 9.5cm. Depth: 3cm

B474
Tea spoons in standing box, comprising: 13 silver-gilt tea spoons (6 Dog Nose and 7 plain Old English) and a silver mote spoon, housed in a spoon box of black fishskin. English, c.18th century.
Height: 20cm; width: 11cm.

B475
Tea spoons in standing box, comprising 12 silver tea spoons (Old English pattern with rat-tail) and 2 silver mote spoons, housed in a spoon box of black fishskin. English, 18th century.
Height: 19.5cm; width: 12cm

B476
Table knives and table forks in standing box (12 + 12), scimitar III steel blades marked 'EXTRA' and steel two-tine forks, ebony handles and silver ferrules, all housed in black fishskin standing box. Sheffield, c.1760.
Height: 32cm; width: 20cm

B479
Table knives and table forks (9 + 11), French shape steel blades and two-tine forks fitted with wrythen shape horn handles, housed in black leather covered standing box. Marked PLANT, Sheffield, c.1790.
Height: 22.5cm; width: 19cm

B480
Table knives and forks (9 + 12), dessert knives and forks (12 + 12) and spoons (12) in standing box, steel blades and steel three-tine table and dessert forks, all with ivory handles of oval section with silver ferrules and caps (cap missing on 1 dessert fork). Blade mark of SHEAR STEEL WARRANTED on all knives, c.1790. The silver spoons of various dates, London, 18th century, housed in a large black fishskin bow fronted box.
Height: 38cm; width: 28cm

B481
Table knives (12), forks (12) and pair of carvers (2), spoons (6) and serving spoon in standing box, steel blades and steel two-tine forks (the same for carvers), all with stamped silver handles. Sheffield, late 18th century. The silver spoons with London hallmark, c.1769 and the silver serving spoon by SAMUEL NEVILLE, Dublin, 1800. All housed in a mahogany serpentine fronted box.
Height: 37cm; width: 22.5cm

B483
Dessert knives (12) and forks (12) in cutlery box, close plate blades and tines fit with carved ivory handles housed in tray within a rectangular flat box with hinged lid and brass handle. Sheffield, c.1820–40.
Height: 6.5cm; width: 25cm

B484
Dessert knives (12) and forks (12), close plate blades and tines fit with mother of pearl handles, housed in 4 trays within a mahogany casket box. Sheffield, c.1820.
Height: 11cm; width: 20.5cm

INDEX

Numerals in **bold** show the page of captions to illustrations other than those on the catalogue pages, which are not indexed. Items in *italic* are catalogue numbers rather than page numbers. Page numbers preceded by G are in the Glossary.